**Free Video** 

**Free Video**

## *Essential Test Tips* Video from Trivium Test Prep

Dear Customer,

Thank you for purchasing from Trivium Test Prep! We're honored to help you prepare for your MTEL exam.

To show our appreciation, we're offering a **FREE *MTEL Essential Test Tips* Video by Trivium Test Prep.*** Our video includes 35 test preparation strategies that will make you successful on the MTEL. All we ask is that you email us your feedback and describe your experience with our product. Amazing, awful, or just so-so: we want to hear what you have to say!

To receive your **FREE *MTEL Essential Test Tips* Video**, please email us at 5star@triviumtestprep.com. Include "Free 5 Star" in the subject line and the following information in your email:

1. The title of the product you purchased.
2. Your rating from 1 – 5 (with 5 being the best).
3. Your feedback about the product, including how our materials helped you meet your goals and ways in which we can improve our products.
4. Your full name and shipping address so we can send your **FREE *MTEL Essential Test Tips* Video**.

If you have any questions or concerns please feel free to contact us directly at 5star@triviumtestprep.com.

Thank you!

– Trivium Test Prep Team

*To get access to the free video please email us at 5star@triviumtestprep.com, and please follow the instructions above.

# MTEL Early Childhood Education Study Guide 2019–2020

## MTEL Early Childhood Test Prep and Practice Questions for the Massachusetts Tests for Educator Licensure

# Table of Contents

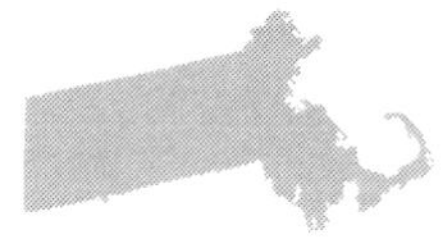

# Online Resources

To help you fully prepare for your MTEL Early Childhood exam, Cirrus includes online resources with the purchase of this study guide.

## Practice Test

In addition to the practice test included in this book, we also offer an online exam. Since many exams today are computer based, getting to practice your test-taking skills on the computer is a great way to prepare.

## Flash Cards

A convenient supplement to this study guide, Cirrus's flash cards enable you to review important terms easily on your computer or smartphone.

## From Stress to Success

Watch From Stress to Success, a brief but insightful YouTube video that offers the tips, tricks, and secrets experts use to score higher on the exam.

## Reviews

Leave a review, send us helpful feedback, or sign up for Cirrus promotions—including free books!

Access these materials at:

**www.cirrustestprep.com/mtel-early-childhood-online-resources**

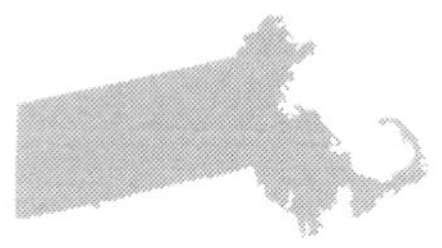

# Introduction

Congratulations on choosing to take the Massachusetts Tests for Educator Licensure (MTEL) Early Childhood (02) exam! By purchasing this book, you've taken the first step toward becoming an early childhood educator.

This guide will provide you with a detailed overview of the MTEL, so you know exactly what to expect on test day. We'll take you through all the concepts covered on the test and give you the opportunity to test your knowledge with practice questions. Even if it's been a while since you last took a major test, don't worry; we'll make sure you're more than ready!

## What is the MTEL?

MTEL tests are a part of teaching licensure in Massachusetts. Along with the MTEL communication and literacy skills test, passing an MTEL subject test is a part of a prospective teacher's application for licensure. These tests are criterion referenced and standardized to measure your skills and knowledge of early childhood concepts and processes. For more information about credentialing in Massachusetts, refer to the MTEL website at https://www.mtel.nesinc.com/.

## What's on the MTEL?

The content in this guide will prepare you for the MTEL Early Childhood (02) exam. This test assesses whether you possess the knowledge and skills necessary to become an early childhood educator. You will be asked to answer 100 multiple-choice questions and two open-response questions.

What's on the MTEL?

| Concepts | Approximate Number of Questions | Percentage of Exam |
|---|---|---|
| **Subarea I: Knowledge of Child Development**<br>▸ child development from prenatal through early elementary years<br>▸ child development and learning in students with disabling conditions or exceptionalities | 30 – 32 multiple choice | 25% |
| **Subarea II: Knowledge of Children's Literature and the Writing Process**<br>▸ genres, elements, and techniques of children's literature<br>▸ principles and concepts of writing | 18 – 20 multiple choice | 15% |
| **Subarea III: Core Knowledge in the Content Areas**<br>▸ principles and concepts of mathematics<br>▸ principles and concepts of history and social science<br>▸ principles and concepts of science, technology, and engineering | 49 – 51 multiple choice | 40% |
| **Subarea IV: Integration of Knowledge and Understanding**<br>analysis of concepts in child development related to language arts, mathematics, history, social science, and science | 2 open response | 20% |

## How is the MTEL Scored?

On the MTEL, the number of correctly answered questions is used to create your scaled score. The multiple-choice questions consist of 80 percent of your overall score, while the open-response questions compose the other 20 percent. Scores are scaled to a number in the range of 100 – 300, a passing score being 240. The score shows your performance on the test as a whole and is scaled to allow comparison across various versions of the test.

There is no penalty for guessing on the MTEL, so be sure to eliminate answer choices and answer every question. If you still do not know the answer, guess; you may get it right! Keep in mind that some multiple-choice questions are experimental questions for the purpose of the MTEL test makers and will not count toward your overall score. However, since those questions are not indicated on the test, you must respond to every question.

Scores are reported three to four weeks after testing on your online account. Your score report indicates whether you passed and your general performance in each subarea of the test. For more information about scoring, refer to http://www.mtel.nesinc.com/.

## How is the MTEL Administered?

The MTEL is administered continuously year-round at testing centers located throughout Massachusetts and across the nation. To register for a test and find a testing site near you, go to http://www.mtel.nesinc.com/. At this site, you can create an MTEL account, check testing appointment times, and find instructions for registering. The MTEL is administered as a computerized test, and the website offers computer-based testing tutorials so that you can become acclimated to that format.

On the day of your test, be sure to bring your admission ticket (which is provided when you register) and photo ID. The testing facility will provide an area outside of the testing room to store your personal belongings. You are allowed no personal effects in the testing area. Cell phones and other electronic, photographic, recording, or listening devices are not permitted in the testing center at all, and bringing those items may be cause for dismissal, forfeiture of your testing fees, and cancellation of your scores. For details on what is and is not permitted at your testing center, refer to the MTEL website.

## About Cirrus Test Prep

Cirrus Test Prep study guides are designed by current and former educators and are tailored to meet your needs as an incoming educator. Our guides offer all of the resources necessary to help you pass teacher certification tests across the nation.

Cirrus clouds are graceful, wispy clouds characterized by their high altitude. Just like cirrus clouds, Cirrus Test Prep's goal is to help educators "aim high" when it comes to obtaining their teacher certification and entering the classroom.

## About This Guide

This guide will help you master the most important test topics and also develop critical test-taking skills. We have built features into our books to prepare you for your tests and increase your score. Along with a detailed summary of the test's format, content, and scoring, we offer an in-depth overview of the content knowledge required to pass the test. Our sidebars provide interesting information, highlight key concepts, and review content so that you can solidify your understanding of the exam's concepts. Test your knowledge with sample questions and detailed answer explanations in the text that help you think through the problems on the exam and two full-length practice tests that reflect the content and format of the MTEL. We're pleased you've chosen Cirrus to be a part of your professional journey!

# Child Development

## Child Growth and Development

Many theories on cognitive and social development drive instructional practices in the early childhood education profession. Furthermore, many theorists have contributed to current practices and their impact on student learning. **Cognitive development** refers to the way in which people think and develop an understanding of the world around them through genetics and other learned influences. The areas of cognitive development include information processing, reasoning, language development, intelligence, and memory.

**Social development** refers to learning values, knowledge, and skills that allow children to relate to others appropriately and effectively and contribute to family, the community, and school in positive ways. Social development is directly influenced by those who care for and teach the child; it is indirectly influenced through friendships, relationships with other family members, and the culture that surrounds them. As children's social development progresses, they begin to respond to influences around them and start building relationships with others.

> DID YOU KNOW?
>
> The "founding father" of behaviorism, psychologist B.F. Skinner, was also a pioneer in educational technology. In 1954, he invented a prototype for what he called the *teaching machine*. The machine used a system of hole punches and tapes to give students immediate feedback after answering a question, much like today's educational technology platforms.

Many theories about child cognitive and social development fall into one of two broad categories: behaviorism and constructivism. **Behaviorism** concerns observable stimulus-response behaviors and suggests that all behaviors are learned through interactions with the environment through classical or operant conditioning. Therefore, our mind is a *tabula rasa*, or blank slate, at birth. In contrast, **constructivism** presents the idea that learning is an active process and knowledge is constructed based on personal experiences. The learner is not a "blank slate" as suggested by behaviorism; instead the learner uses past experiences and cultural factors to gain knowledge in new situations.

## Theories of Child Development

Cognitive development in children has been studied in many ways throughout the years. In 1936, the prominent theorist **Jean Piaget** proposed his **theory of cognitive development**. Piaget's theory came from several decades of observing children in their natural environments. He posited that a child's knowledge developed from schemas, or units of knowledge that use past experiences to understand new experiences.

According to Piaget, schemas constantly change due to two complimentary processes: assimilation and accommodation. *Assimilation* is taking in new information and relating it to an existing schema, or what the child already knows. *Accommodation* occurs when schema changes to accommodate new knowledge. Piaget states that there is an ongoing attempt to balance accommodation and assimilation to gain equilibration.

The core of Piaget's theory is the idea that cognitive development happens in four stages of increasing sophistication and abstract levels of thought. The stages always happen in the same order and build upon learning that occurred in the previous stage.

The first stage is the **sensorimotor stage**, which takes place in infancy. During this stage, infants demonstrate intelligence through motor activities and without using symbols. They have limited knowledge of the world around them; however, their world knowledge is developing through physical interactions and experiences. At around seven months of age, children develop object permanence, or memory. The increase in physical development, or mobility, in this stage allows for the progression of new intellectual abilities. Symbolic language abilities begin to develop at the end of this stage.

The second stage, the **pre-operational stage**, takes place from toddlerhood to early childhood. This stage is characterized by the demonstration of intelligence through symbols. Furthermore, language abilities mature at this stage, and memory and imagination are developing rapidly. Thinking, however, is nonlogical, nonreversible, and egocentric.

The **concrete operational stage** is the third stage and takes place from the elementary years to early adolescence. In this stage, children begin to use actions that are logical and rational when thinking and solving problems. They begin to understand permanence and conservation, or the concept that weight, volume, and numbers may remain the same even though appearance may change. In this stage, operational, or reversible thinking, develops and egocentric thinking is reduced.

The final stage is the **formal operational stage** that occurs from adolescence through adulthood. During this stage, children become able to independently navigate through problems and situations. They should be able to adapt to different situations by applying learned knowledge. A major cognitive transition occurs in this stage in that adolescents are better able to think in more advanced, efficient, and complex ways.

The theorist **Lev Vygotsky** introduced the **social development theory** and the zone of proximal development. This theory is characterized by the idea that social development plays a critical role in cognitive development and that there is a **zone of proximal development (ZPD)** which cognitive development depends upon. The ZPD is achieved when children are engaged in social behavior with adults or peers. According to Vygotsky, cognitive development is better achieved through interactions or help from peers or an adult than what can be accomplished alone.

The ZPD is the distance between a child's actual developmental level, as demonstrated by independent problem-solving, and the potential developmental level as demonstrated under adult or peer guidance. Children will typically follow an adult's or a more capable peer's example and eventually be able to complete certain tasks alone.

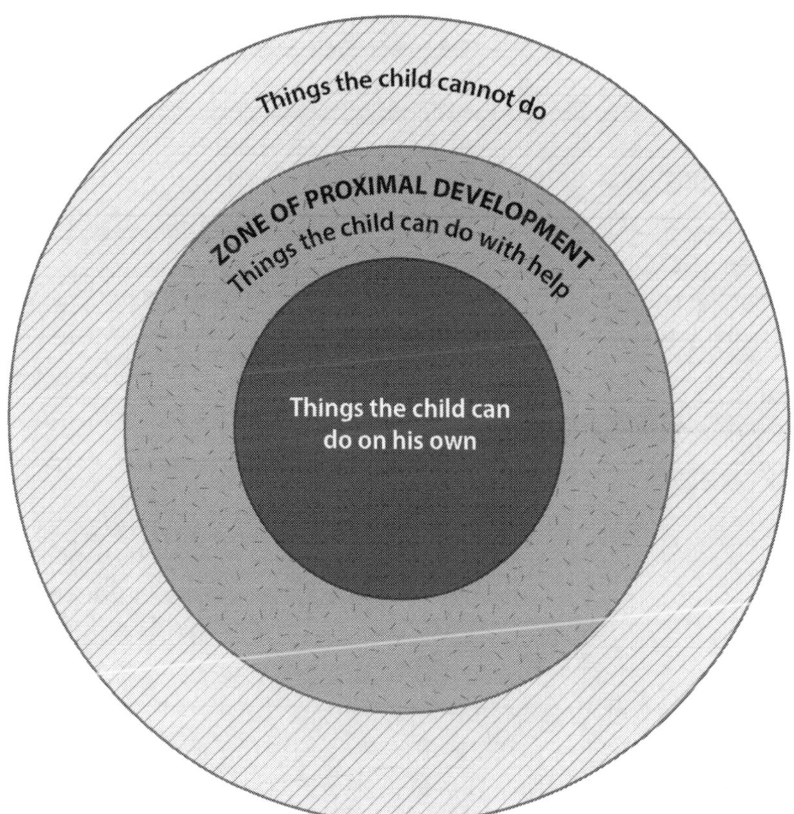


**Figure 1.1. The Zone of Proximal Development**

Vygotsky's ZPD has been modified and changed over the years and forms the foundation for the concept of scaffolding. **Scaffolding** is when a teacher or more capable peer provides guidance and support to the child in his or her ZPD, as appropriate, and gradually scales back the support when it is no longer necessary.

A third theorist contributing to the field of early childhood development is **Howard Gardner**. Dr. Gardner is a professor of education at Harvard whose **theory of multiple intelligences** was published in 1983. This theory suggests that the traditional method of testing intelligence, IQ testing, is limited and that there are nine different types of intelligence to characterize the ways in which children and adults develop skills and solve problems. One's potential is correlated to his or her learning preferences. Dr. Gardner's suggested intelligences are as follows:

- verbal-linguistic intelligence
- logical-mathematical intelligence
- spatial-visual intelligence
- bodily-kinesthetic intelligence
- musical intelligence
- interpersonal intelligence
- intrapersonal intelligence
- naturalist intelligence
- existential intelligence

Dr. Gardner states that, although today's schools and culture focus heavily on linguistic and logical-mathematical intelligence, we should equally focus on other intelligences. The theory of multiple intelligences encourages educators to reflect on how schools operate and implement changes to ensure teachers are trained to deliver instruction in a variety of ways to meet the intelligence needs of all children. Implementing this theory can develop children's strengths and build confidence as well as provide teachers with a set of teaching and learning tools that reach beyond the typical lecture, textbook, and worksheet methods.

QUICK REVIEW

Which developmental domains would be addressed within each of Gardner's multiple intelligences?

**Jerome Bruner** is yet another significant theorist in the field of early childhood education. According to Bruner, there are **three modes of representation** in which learners interpret the world: enactive, iconic, and symbolic. He explains that these modes are followed in sequence, but in contrast to other theorists, they are not age dependent. The modes of representation are dependent upon how familiar the learner is with the subject matter. Thus, Brunner presents the idea that what is being taught must be appropriate and ready for the learner instead of the learner being ready for the subject matter. In other words, any subject can be taught to any individual at any age, but the material must be modified to the appropriate form and stage for the learner.

Bruner's enactive stage is characterized by the idea that knowledge is stored through motor responses. This stage not only applies to children but adults as well. Some tasks completed as adults would be difficult to describe in the iconic (picture) mode or the symbolic (word) form. Next, the iconic stage is characterized by the idea that knowledge is stored through visual images. Finally, in the symbolic stage, knowledge is stored through words, mathematical symbols, or other symbol systems.

Another important theorist is **Albert Bandura** and his **social learning theory**, which presents the idea that people learn best by observing, imitating, and modeling behaviors, attitudes, and emotional reactions. In contrast to some theorists, Bandura's social learning theory includes a social element—the idea that people can learn new information and behaviors simply by observing other people.

Three core concepts encompass this theory. The first is that people can learn by observation through three basic models: a live model, a verbal instructional model, and a symbolic model. A live model is an individual demonstrating or acting out a behavior. The verbal instructional model provides descriptions and explanations of a behavior. The symbolic model is when real or fictional characters portray behaviors in books, movies, television, or online media.

The second core concept is the idea that a person's mental state and motivation can determine whether a behavior is learned or not. Bandura presents the idea that not only external environmental reinforcement contributes to learning, but so does intrinsic reinforcement, or internal reward.

The final concept of Bandura's theory is the idea that even though a behavior is learned, there may not be a change in behavior. In contrast to behaviorist learning, which states that there is a behavioral change once something new is learned, observational learning states that new information can be learned without behavioral changes.

Bandura's theory is said to combine the cognitive and behavioral learning theories with four requirements for learning: attention, retention, reproduction, and motivation. The first requirement is attention. To learn new information, one must be paying attention; any distractors will negatively affect observational learning. The next is retention, or the ability to store and retrieve information at a later time. The third requirement is reproduction, which is performing the observed and learned behavior. The last requirement is motivation. One must be motivated to reproduce the observed behavior, either by external or intrinsic motivators.

**Erik Erikson** is an additional theorist who contributed to the field of child development with his **theory of psychosocial development**, which outlines eight stages from infancy through adulthood. Each stage is characterized by a psychosocial crisis that will have a positive or negative effect on personality development. This theory suggests that a healthy personality is developed by the successful completion of each stage; an inability to successfully complete a stage may lead to the inability to complete upcoming stages. This may result in an unhealthy personality and sense of self. However, this can be successfully resolved in the future.

Erikson's first stage, **trust versus mistrust**, takes place during a child's first eighteen months of life. This stage is characterized by an infant's uncertainty about the world around him or her. These uncertain feelings can be resolved by a primary caregiver who provides stability and consistent, predictable, and reliable care that will help develop a sense of trust and secure feelings in the infant, even when threatened. However, if an infant has received care that is inconsistent, unpredictable, or unreliable, he or she can develop a sense of mistrust and carry the feeling into other relationships, which may lead to anxiety and insecurities.

Erikson's second stage is **autonomy versus shame and doubt**. This stage is characterized by a child's physical development and occurs between the ages of eighteen months and three years. During this stage, children begin to assert their independence and autonomy and discover their many skills and abilities. Erikson believes that parents and caregivers should exhibit patience and allow children to explore their independence by providing support and encouragement. If children are supported and encouraged, they will become confident and secure with their abilities. However, if they are criticized, controlled, or not allowed to exhibit independence, they may have feelings of inadequacy, shame, and doubt, and become dependent upon others.

The third stage is **initiative versus guilt**, which occurs between the ages of three and five and is characterized by children continuing to assert their independence more frequently while interacting with other children. During this stage, children develop interpersonal skills through play by planning and initiating activities or making up games with other children. If these skills are encouraged, a child will feel secure in taking initiative. However, if a child is not allowed to develop these skills, he or she can develop a sense of guilt—like they are a nuisance—and lack self-initiative.

**Industry versus inferiority** is the fourth stage of the psychosocial development theory. During this stage—between the ages of five and twelve—teachers play an important role since children are now in school. Additionally, friends begin to play a significant role in a child's self-esteem during this time as they seek the approval of their peers. If children are encouraged by parents, teachers, and peers, they begin to develop a strong sense of confidence. In contrast, if children are not encouraged, they can begin to feel inferior and doubt their abilities.

Four final stages characterize psychosocial development during the transitions from childhood to adolescence and adulthood through the senior citizen years. Since these stages do not pertain to early childhood, however, they will not be discussed.

**Abraham Maslow** is another theorist with significant contributions to the field of early childhood development. Maslow is best known for the **hierarchy of needs**, a motivational theory that consists of five needs: physiological, safety, love, esteem, and self-actualization. He presented the idea that basic human needs are arranged hierarchically. In order for one to be able to attain the highest level—self-actualization—one must reasonably meet the growth needs in each stage.

These needs are presented in a hierarchical order and shown in a pyramid, with physiological needs at the bottom of the pyramid and self-actualization at the top. Physiological needs, placed at the bottom of the pyramid, include basic needs such as air, food, drink, shelter, warmth, sex, and sleep. Following physiological needs are safety needs, which include order, law, stability, protection from elements, security, and freedom from fear. Next is love and a feeling of belonging, or friendships, intimacy, trust, receiving and giving affection, and feelings of acceptance or feeling like a part of a group. Maslow divided esteem needs—which appear after love—into two categories: esteem for oneself and the need for respect from others. Children and adolescents have a greater need for respect and reputation as these arrive before real self-esteem, or dignity, can develop. The final level is self-actualization, or a feeling of personal growth, self-fulfillment, or reaching maximum personal potential.

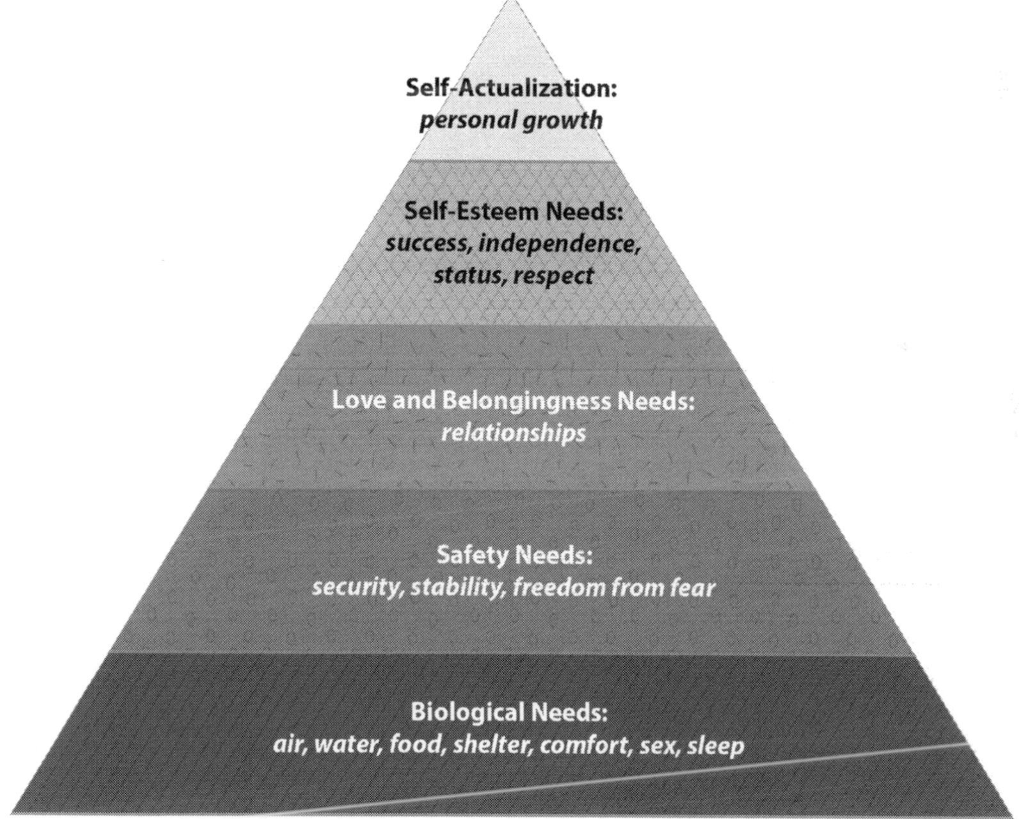


**Figure 1.2. Maslow's Hierarchy of Needs**

Maslow describes that everyone has the capability and desire to move up the hierarchy. However, sometimes progress can be disrupted by the inability to meet lower-level needs. One's life experiences can influence progression up the hierarchy and some may even move back and forth between levels, which means everyone will progress in different ways.

Finally, **Benjamin Bloom** made major contributions to classifying educational objectives and the theory of mastery learning or **domains of learning**. He is best known for developing **Bloom's taxonomy**, which is a hierarchy of skills that build upon each other from simple to complex and concrete to abstract. Bloom created the original taxonomy in 1956. It was revised in 2001 to include more action words to describe the cognitive processes through which learners work through knowledge.

The original taxonomy categories included knowledge, or simple recall of information; comprehension, or the ability to understand and use information; application, or being able to use abstract thinking in concrete situations; analysis, or the ability to break down an idea or concept into parts and recognize the relationships between ideas or concepts; synthesis, or putting together elements or parts to make a whole; and evaluation, or the ability to judge material and the method of its purpose.

In 2001, a group of professionals across the fields of education and psychology revised Bloom's original taxonomy to include action words to label the categories and subcategories and describe the process in which learners work through knowledge. The first category is remembering, or the ability to recognize and recall. Next is understanding—interpreting, exemplifying, classifying, summarizing, inferring, comparing, and explaining. The third category is applying, or being able to execute or implement. The fourth is the ability to analyze or differentiate, organize, or attribute. The fifth category is evaluating, or checking or critiquing. The final category is creating—generating, planning, and producing.

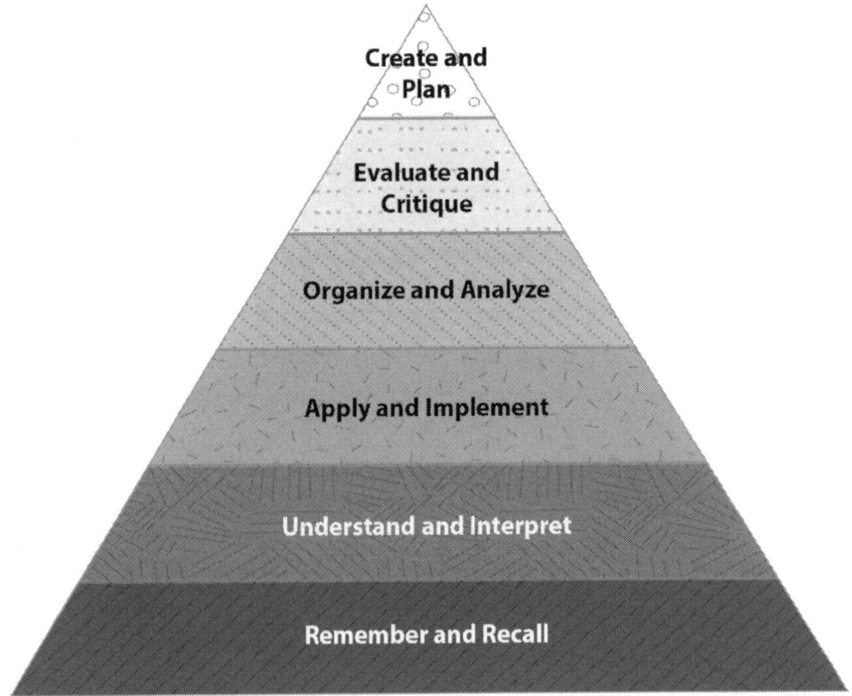


**Figure 1.3. Bloom's Taxonomy**

Incorporating Bloom's taxonomy into current practices includes many benefits. One of these is establishing objectives or learning goals so that teachers and children or students understand the purpose of instruction. A second benefit is that Bloom's taxonomy provides teachers with a framework with which to organize objectives. From these objectives teachers can plan and implement appropriate instruction, design and implement purposeful and valid assessments, and ensure that instruction and assessments are objective driven.

## SAMPLE QUESTIONS

1) **Which theorist is recognized for developing a hierarchy of skills, ranging from simple to complex, that many schools use today when developing learning objectives?**

   A. Benjamin Bloom

   B. Abraham Maslow

   C. Lev Vygotsky

   D. Jean Piaget

2) **Which of the following characterizes Gardner's idea of verbal-linguistic intelligence?**

   A. the ability to think abstractly, explore patterns and relationships, reason, and calculate

   B. the ability to learn through songs, rhymes, and musical instruments

   C. the ability to learn through relationships with others by working collaboratively

   D. the ability to learn through written and spoken words

## DEVELOPMENTAL STAGES AND MILESTONES

Another area of child growth and development in which early educators must be knowledgeable is developmental domains. The early childhood years are marked by rapid growth and development with five main areas that develop concurrently: social-emotional, cognitive, language, physical, and moral. Within each domain are typical stages and milestones that children should reach within a certain time frame. However, keep in mind that each child develops at his or her own pace, and some children may meet the stages and milestones earlier while some will meet them later. Conversely, early educators must also be aware of **atypical development**, or when behaviors fall outside of the expected range of development.

The **social-emotional** domain is described as feelings and emotions, self-concept, self-esteem, autonomy, and

### QUICK REVIEW

Many early childhood educators are tasked with screening young children for atypical development using standardized assessment instruments, developmental milestone charts, and other observational methods. What is your school, state, or district's policy on screening young children? At what age or grade level does screening take place?

behaviors and skills used to build and maintain positive relationships. Typical social-emotional development is the ability to manage one's own feelings, understand the feelings and needs of others, and positively interact with others.

Atypical social-emotional development may emerge in many different ways. Some indicators of atypical social-emotional development are difficulty to comfort or calm when upset; an inability to calm oneself down; the inability to self-soothe; little or no self-regulation; difficulty adapting to changing situations; avoiding eye contact with others; showing a similar level of affection to caregivers and strangers; hurting oneself or others; and acting withdrawn. Social-emotional development that is misaligned with developmental milestones can be an indication of serious developmental difficulties and should be addressed immediately.

**Cognitive development** is described as the way in which children process thoughts, maintain attention, remember, understand, and plan, predict, regulate, and evaluate tasks and situations. Typical cognitive development shows a child's progression in observing and interacting with the world around them. It includes engagement in goal-directed, intentional behaviors; progression in how children process, store, and use information; and an increase in imaginative play.

Atypical development may take the forms of difficulty with problem-solving skills, deficits in acquiring new or basic information, such as colors and shapes; difficulty in learning advanced concepts, such as counting, reading, and writing; difficulty generalizing information from one situation to the next; difficulty adapting to new situations; and delays in early concepts, such as object permanence or recognizing the function of objects.

**Language development** describes the way in which children understand, process, and produce language. This involves communication behaviors, such as listening and talking; literacy skills, such as reading, writing, comprehension, and expression; and nonverbal communication skills.

Although children develop language and speech at varying rates, typical development follows a predictable progression. Children are said to have typical language development when they have an increasing vocabulary; are able to answer questions about a story read independently or aloud; can easily communicate with adults and peers; can follow multiple-step directions; have developing phonological skills, such as knowledge of letters and sounds, can understand rhyming, or putting sounds together to form words; and have an increasing ability to remember and read sight words.

Children displaying atypical language development may have difficulty with different aspects of language, in varying situations, and during numerous stages of language development. Some children may have a challenging time with phonological development, or the speech-sound system; trouble understanding and producing language; a limited working memory; a hard time remembering sight words; experience frustration trying to comprehend a story while reading or while being read to; difficulty understanding questions; limited vocabulary; only use short, simple sentences; make frequent grammatical errors; have limited social play skills; and have a tough time carrying on conversations or choose to avoid them altogether.

> QUICK REVIEW
>
> What are some particular language development issues that early childhood educators will need to keep in mind when working with English language learners?

**Physical development** includes fine motor skills (the use of small muscles) and gross motor skills (the use of large muscles) as well as the development of the five senses: hearing, seeing, touching, tasting, and smelling. Typical motor development follows a predictable sequence that starts from the inner body, develops to the outer body, and moves from top to bottom. For example, children will gain control of their arms before their fingers and control their head first before their legs and arms. Children with typical gross motor development have balanced muscle tone and are able to sit, stand, walk, run, jump, skip, and throw an object along with performing other activities within certain time frames. Children with typical fine motor development are able to grasp and pick up objects, hold a pencil or crayon, turn off a light, or play with toys.

Children with atypical gross motor development may have difficulty walking, running, jumping, or hopping; throwing, rolling, or catching a ball; irregular muscle tone (either low tone or high muscle tone); challenges with motor coordination; delays in the vestibular system, which provides one's sense of balance, or proprioceptive system, which is the awareness of where one's body is in space. Atypical fine motor development may involve difficulty grasping objects; an inability to eat with utensils; difficulty dressing or undressing oneself; or challenges cutting with scissors, drawing, or writing.

Finally, **moral development** is described as the sense of right versus wrong and the understanding of how to make the right choices. Moral development is influenced by experiences at home and within the daily environment, as well as the development of physical, cognitive, emotional, and social skills. Early social and emotional experiences and interactions with primary caregivers, as well as other children and adults, are indicators of moral development.

Typical moral development is when children understand the difference between right and wrong and behave accordingly; understand the importance of family values; understand that others have viewpoints; learn how to be considerate; show empathy; and understand the necessity of rules and the consequences for breaking them.

Atypical moral development may take the form of an inability to show empathy; disregarding rules and consequences; inability to understand and accept the viewpoints of others; difficulty forming relationships; inappropriately expressing and managing emotions; and difficulty controlling inhibitions.

Early childhood educators should use these five developmental domains, the milestones and stages within, and information on typical and atypical development when considering each child's overall development. Additionally, when planning lessons and activities, each developmental domain should be addressed.

Table 1.1. Developmental Milestones

| Developmental Milestone | Definition | Typical Development | Atypical Development |
|---|---|---|---|
| Social-Emotional | feelings, emotions, self-concept, self-esteem, autonomy, relationship-building skills | ability to manage feelings, understand the feelings of others, and engage in positive interactions | difficult to comfort when upset; inability to self-soothe; difficulty self-regulating; difficulty adapting to new situations; acting withdrawn; avoids eye contact |
| Cognitive | how children process thoughts; maintain attention; remember, understand, plan, predict, regulate, and evaluate tasks and situations | shows progress in observation and interactions with world around them; engages in goal-directed behavior; displays progress in how to store, process, and use information; increasing imaginative play | difficulty solving problems; difficulty acquiring new or basic information; difficulty learning advanced concepts; difficulty generalizing information |
| Language | how children understand, process, and produce language | increasing vocabulary, answers questions about a story, communicates easily, follows multi-step directions, developing phonological skills, understands rhyming, increasing ability to read sight words, puts sounds together to read words | difficulty developing speech-sound system; difficulty understanding or producing new language; limited vocabulary; limited working memory; difficulty with comprehension; struggles to remember sight words; uses short, simple sentences; limited social-play skills |

| Developmental Milestone | Definition | Typical Development | Atypical Development |
|---|---|---|---|
| Physical | development of fine motor (small muscles) and gross motor (large muscles) skills<br>also includes development of the five senses | balanced muscle tone; ability to sit, stand, run, jump, skip, and throw; ability to grasp and pick up object; holds a pencil or crayon; turns off a light; plays with toys | difficulty running, jumping, throwing, or catching; difficulty with muscle tone (too high or too low); difficulty with motor coordination; delays in vestibular and proprioceptive systems; difficulty grasping objects; inability to eat with utensils; difficulty dressing or undressing; difficulty cutting, writing, or drawing |
| Moral | sense of right versus wrong and understanding how to make the right choices | understands difference between right and wrong; understands importance of family values; understands others' viewpoints; is considerate; shows empathy; understands rules and consequences | inability to show empathy; disregards rules and consequences; inability to understand other's viewpoints; inappropriately expresses and manages emotions; difficulty forming relationships; difficulty controlling inhibitions |

## SAMPLE QUESTIONS

3) **A teacher in a toddler classroom notices a student with hypertonic muscle tone. What might this be an indicator of?**

A. atypical gross motor development

B. typical gross motor development

C. atypical fine motor development

D. typical fine motor development

4) **Which of the following describes typical language development for a first grader?**

A. ability to name most familiar objects

B. ability to focus on one activity for 5 – 10 minutes

C. understanding and following multi-step directions

D. interest in writing poetry

## Factors Affecting Child Development

As a young child grows, many factors can positively or negatively influence his or her progression in all developmental domains. An early childhood educator must be informed of the factors that may affect the children in their classroom and how they are developing.

One important factor that may affect young children's development is **genetics**, or inherited characteristics. Heredity plays a key role in growth and development. Children typically inherit at least some of their parents' characteristics of temperament; cognitive functions, such as intelligence, aptitudes, mental disorders or ailments; and physical attributes, such as height, weight, hair and eye color, and body structure.

**Nutrition** also plays a critical role in growth and development as growth is directly impacted by nutrition. A child's nutritional health has been linked to their parents' income and education and can have lifelong lasting effects. Children who are malnourished tend to be underweight, shorter than average, and slower to grow. Additionally, inadequate nutrition can impair cognitive and motor development. Furthermore, if children come to school lacking proper nutrition, they struggle to focus and complete activities as they are preoccupied with feeling hungry. Nutritional deficits are often irreversible.

Another important component of child development is a child's overall **health**. Overall health includes physical health, mental health, and social-emotional health. Social and economic factors, such as family income, education, nutrition, quality of housing, household and community safety, and access to resources can dramatically affect a child's overall health. Healthy child development contributes to school readiness and appropriate coping and social skills, which ultimately reduce academic, social, and behavioral difficulties.

Conversely, inadequate health experiences can lead to poor health outcomes throughout life, which may include cognitive limitations, behavioral problems, poor physical and mental health, cardiovascular disease and stroke, hypertension, diabetes, obesity, and mental health disorders. However, intervening early by providing resources and education to families can interrupt an unhealthy life cycle and lead to improved child health and development that spans a lifetime.

Another important factor affecting child development is **public policy**. Under President Barack Obama, the Preschool for All bill was passed. The legislation establishes partnerships between federal and state governments to improve funding to provide high-quality preschool for four-year-olds from low- and moderate-income households. Obama's administration dramatically increased investments to early childhood programs through childcare subsidies, programs for infants and toddlers with disabilities, high-quality preschool, Head Start, and evidence-based home visiting programs.

> **QUICK REVIEW**
>
> What were some changes implemented by the Obama administration that positively impacted early childhood education?

However, national policies and practices still fall behind the incredible body of research and science regarding the benefits of access to high-quality early childhood education. Critical steps must be taken to ensure all families have access to this high-quality care. The first is providing appropriate funding in any state or setting. The second step is ensuring that all families can choose and afford high-quality, early childhood programs most appropriate for them. Finally, national policies must ensure that all early childhood professionals are diverse and effective leaders who are adequately compensated.

The **environment** in which children are raised also plays a key role in their development and shapes behavior, thinking, relationships with others, growth, and how emotions are processed. Environmental influences include social and economic factors, characteristics of the family and household, urbanization, nutrition, pollutants, and the physical environment, such as climate, altitude, and temperature. A nurturing environment promotes positive development with fewer developmental obstacles. Children learn to appropriately process, regulate, and verbalize their emotions; cope with stress; and build and maintain relationships with adults and peers. Furthermore, children from nurturing environments prove to be more successful in school.

Consequently, several environmental factors can adversely affect a child's growth and development. An impoverished environment can lead to stunted growth and inadequate weight gain, poor academic performance, difficulty focusing and controlling impulses, physical health problems, and mental health disorders. Impoverished environments are also associated with child abuse and an increased incidence in physical injuries. Within a challenging home environment where children are exposed to parental stress, inappropriate discipline methods, discord, and parental mental health issues, children can have difficulty processing emotions and controlling their own behaviors.

Another critical factor that may affect child development is **substance abuse**. Unfortunately, too many children are exposed to family members or caregivers who abuse alcohol or misuse legal drugs, or who use, manufacture, or distribute illegal drugs. Children exposed to substance abuse have a higher risk of behavior and medical problems, experience developmental and educational delays or mental health disorders, and may eventually abuse drugs or alcohol themselves. Additionally, parents who abuse drugs and alcohol often struggle to provide a safe and nurturing environment and prioritize their children's basic physical, physiological, and emotional needs.

**Physical abuse** is yet another factor that can affect children's overall development and, unless properly addressed, can last a lifetime. The primary effects begin during or immediately after physical abuse has taken place with pain, medical issues, and sometimes even death. The lasting effects of physical abuse may include brain damage leading to cognitive delays, vision loss, hearing loss, and the development of severe emotional, behavioral, or learning problems. Furthermore, the effects of physical abuse can manifest into high-risk, unhealthy, and dangerous behaviors. Individuals may engage in excessive promiscuity, smoking, and alcohol and drug abuse to cope with the physical and emotional pain.

The emotional effects can manifest into numerous psychological problems. Children who have been abused struggle significantly with their home lives, at school, and when developing relationships with peers. They are more likely to suffer from low self-esteem, fear, anxiety, and act aggressively toward peers, and other family members, especially siblings.

Physical abuse can also have damaging effects on children's social development. These children may struggle with trusting others, building and maintaining relationships, communicating appropriately, and might turn to aggression to solve problems. If not resolved, these issues can negatively influence their adult lives as well. Thus, it is critical for early childhood professionals to recognize the signs and symptoms of abuse and report any suspected abuse immediately.

**Emotional distress** is another facet of a child's life that can affect growth and development. Several factors can cause emotional distress: poverty, repeated abuse, loss of a loved one, parental substance abuse or mental illness, exposure to violence, a natural disaster, a serious injury, or a frightening experience like a car accident or getting robbed. If a child has experienced one of these situations but is protected by supportive adult relationships, their stress levels can return to normal.

However, if a child experiences prolonged exposure to stressful situations without supporting and caring adults, stress can become toxic and disrupt normal brain development. And, the more adverse the situation, the greater the likelihood is that a child will experience developmental delays and other issues. Providing children with stable, caring, and responsive relationships as early as possible is key in preventing or reversing the damage caused by toxic stress.

Finally, **economic factors** can affect children's development across all domains. The term *socioeconomic status* (SES) includes a person or family's income, educational achievement, occupational achievement, and social class and status. SES is proven to be a reliable indicator of outcomes throughout a person's life. SES impacts where a child lives, quality and quantity of food, and learning experiences the child has inside and outside of the home. Children who come from families with low-to-moderate SES typically have fewer opportunities and privileges than their higher SES counterparts do, which can lead to difficulties in psychological and physical health, education, and family well-being. However, there are many programs, including charter schools and after-school programs, that seek to change these trends through education and intervention.

## SAMPLE QUESTIONS

5) **A child in Ms. Jones's class has become withdrawn and often comes to school wearing long sleeves and long pants, even when the weather is warm. What is this child probably being affected by?**

   A. poor nutrition

   B. physical abuse

   C. emotional distress

   D. substance abuse

6) **Which of the following is a genetic condition that impacts a child's cognitive development?**

   A. Down syndrome

   B. autism spectrum disorder

   C. poverty

   D. low birth weight

## FAMILY SYSTEMS

Our current culture represents a diverse society of family systems that directly impact how early childhood professionals communicate with families, form partnerships, and involve families in their child/children's development and learning. Family structure has changed dramatically, and early childhood educators should be familiar with all its variations. The first and most traditional is the **conjugal** or **nuclear family**, which consists of two parents and children. Children raised within this system have been found to have more opportunities because both adults may earn an income. They also receive more stability and support from the two-parent structure.

A second family structure is the **single-parent family**, which consists of one parent raising one or multiple children. Typically, the single-parent family consists of the mother and her child or children; however, there are single fathers, too. Because there is only one income and guardian in this family system, children may have limited opportunities.

Another type of family unit is the **extended family**, which consists of two or more adults who are related in some way and living in the same home. Many relatives live and work together to raise children and manage the household. An extended family may include cousins, aunts, uncles, or grandparents.

### DID YOU KNOW?

Approximately 38 percent of US children live in single-parent households. What modifications might a teacher need to make for this in his or her classroom?

The **blended family** is another common family system. A blended family is formed when two individuals with children from previous relationships choose to bring the two separate families together in the same household. For step families, this structure includes a new husband and wife and their children from previous relationships or marriages.

A family in which grandparents are raising their grandchildren—a **grandparent family**—is yet another family system. In this structure, the child's parents are typically not involved due to parental death, addiction, abandonment, or being deemed unfit.

Finally, early childhood professionals may experience the **polygamist family structure**. The polygamist family structure includes polygyny, where a man is married to multiple wives, or polyandry, where a woman is married to multiple husbands. Polyamory describes a situation including multiple partners of varied genders.

Because of the multiple family systems that may exist within an early childhood classroom or program, it is critical to implement a variety of strategies to involve families in their child's development and learning. Developing strong relationships with families is a key component of developmentally appropriate practice and leads to improved social, behavioral, and academic outcomes for children. Furthermore, families who communicate regularly and in a variety of ways with their child's program feel more involved and knowledgeable about their child's education. And, teachers who establish partnerships with families feel more satisfied in their roles. Developing family partnerships can greatly improve program quality.

Several strategies are available to ensure that all families are involved in classroom activities and their child's overall program. When implementing family activities, it is important to consider each family's time constraints, access to technology, home language, and communication preferences. Within the early childhood program, one way to involve families is with a family center, or a dedicated place where families can gather, talk informally with their child's teacher, and have access to a computer and the internet. This space can also be used to conduct family-teacher conferences.

Another strategy is a monthly or weekly newsletter. The newsletter should be available in multiple languages as appropriate and in multiple formats, such as electronic and paper copies. Program events, curriculum information, community resources, and researched information on child development are some examples of content that may be included in such a newsletter.

Incorporating program events is another way to involve families. Program events offer activities all family members can attend and participate in. Additionally, the program can encourage families to become involved in planning such events. Some events may include an open house to showcase the program, classrooms, and children's work; a family movie night; a family science night where families can come and participate in different simple science activities together; fall fun night with fall-themed activities for families to work on together; family fitness night, where health and nutrition information are presented and fitness activities are available; and family field trips.

A program may also develop a website to communicate information about classroom activities, share photos of children, and provide daily information as well as links to additional community resources and events. An individual classroom can incorporate family involvement strategies on such a site as well. Some examples may include the following:

- inviting families for breakfast, lunch, or snack
- a parent questionnaire for families to complete when beginning a program
- a limited-access class website
- text message reminders
- daily notes home
- frequent phone calls
- conversations at drop-off and pickup
- group email
- classroom newsletter provided in multiple languages and formats
- family-teacher conferences to discuss child progress and information sharing
- take-home activity kits that children and families complete together at home
- home visits

Regardless of the activity, regular and direct communication will ensure that families receive information that is relevant, accurate, and timely.

Because the family systems experienced in early childhood programs are so diverse, it is also important for programs and early childhood teachers to encourage and provide information on community involvement and resources. A characteristic of a high-quality program is linking families to resources within the community that can extend learning beyond the classroom. This information should be provided in multiple formats to ensure all families have access. Community activities may include health, nutrition, and fitness resources; educational resources, fairs, and activities; community events; public library information and activities; cultural events like plays, concerts, or museum events; sporting events; and organizations and resources within the community that support children and families.

DID YOU KNOW?

Students whose parents are involved in their education adapt well to school, have better social skills, and have higher grades, scores, and attendance rates, regardless of income or background.

A great indicator of a high-quality early childhood program is the way in which it develops relationships, involves families, and links families to community resources. How families perceive the school environment and staff determines their level of involvement in their child's school experiences. Creating an environment of trust, respect, open communication, and one where families feel welcome is critical to successful family involvement.

SAMPLE QUESTION

7) **Which of the following is NOT a strategy used to involve families in the early childhood program?**

A. a weekly or monthly newsletter

B. program events, such as family fitness night

C. scheduling activities on a weeknight

D. connecting families with community resources

## Models of Early Childhood Curriculum

Several different models of early childhood curriculum are available for programs to implement depending on the program's philosophy. Early childhood professionals should be knowledgeable of all curriculum models available, as each program adopts the one that best fits the needs of the children, families, and communities they serve.

One time-tested model is the **Montessori method**. This method was developed by Maria Montessori with the idea that children are naturally eager to learn and able to initiate their own learning in an environment that is supportive and purposefully planned. Montessori focuses on the development of the whole child—social, emotional, physical, and cognitive. For a program to be considered authentically Montessori, several components must be in place, including properly trained Montessori teachers, multiage groupings that encourage peer learning, extended periods of uninterrupted work time, and an appropriate choice of activities. Additionally, a variety of specially designed Montessori learning materials must be available and specifically arranged so that children are able to see and choose their own work materials.

Teachers who understand that children develop naturally are key to the Montessori method. Teachers invest time in observing children and introduce them to new lessons, activities, and materials that are developmentally appropriate, yet challenging, and based on the individual needs, interests, and abilities of each child. The teacher serves as a guide to support the development of each child through purposeful activities, instead of providing children with information. Children choose work that interests them, ensuring they are engaged, intrinsically motivated, and able to develop a sense of responsibility to themselves and others.

In addition, children are allowed to work on an activity for as long as they are interested. When finished, they are expected to clean up, return the activity to its proper location, and choose another. During this time, teachers are observing, supporting, and guiding individual children or teaching small group lessons.

The Montessori method offers many benefits, including recognizing the uniqueness of each child and allowing him or her to progress through the curriculum at his or her own pace; supporting children's development of self-regulation through thoughtful classroom design, materials, and daily routines; creating a close-knit, caring community by offering multiage classrooms that create a sense of family; guiding children to be active in their own learning by allowing them freedom to choose their own learning experiences within parameters; and providing learning materials that support self-assessment and self-correction.

Early childhood educators should also be knowledgeable of the **HighScope** curriculum model. The HighScope approach encourages active learning in which children have direct, hands-on, carefully planned experiences with people, objects, events, and ideas in reading, math, and science. Similar to the Montessori method, individual children's interests, needs, and choices encompass this philosophy. Children develop their own knowledge through experiences with their environment and people around them. Teachers and adults support children's learning choices through diverse learning materials and physical, emotional, and cognitive support.

HighScope embraces the idea of scaffolding, first introduced by developmental psychologist Jerome Brunner, where adults support and expand children's learning. Scaffolding is based on Lev Vygotsky's idea of the zone of proximal development—the fine line between what children can learn independently and what they can learn with support from an adult. Teachers thoughtfully observe and support children in their current knowledge so they know exactly when to enter this "zone" with children and extend their thinking to the next level.

Early childhood professionals should also be familiar with the **Reggio Emilia approach**.This philosophy focuses primarily on preschool and primary education through student-centered, self-directed experiential learning that is guided by children's natural development and relationships within the environment. The curriculum is "emergent in nature," self-guided, and based upon the ideas of respect, responsibility, and community. However, this emergent curriculum does not just allow children to do as they please. The Reggio Emilia approach is unique in that children have rights and are upheld as beautiful, powerful, competent, creative, and full of potential. Additionally, children are seen as active participants in the acquisition of their own knowledge instead of simply receivers of instruction, so learning becomes individualized.

Activities are project based so children have the opportunity to explore, observe, hypothesize, question, and discuss their learning with others, as well as work with their peers to solve real-life problems. The project topics are based upon the teacher's observations of children's play and selected according to their academic curiosity. All topics are provided by the children; they are not chosen by the teacher. The teacher then questions children about the topic and from gained information, introduces activities, materials, questions, and opportunities to generate exploration. A project is considered successful if it generates interest; sparks children's curiosity, creative thinking, and problem-solving skills; and has multiple ways to explore and draw conclusions. Through the project approach, children participate in authentic activities and make connections between previous and new learning.

The role of the teacher is to purposely plan for mistakes or plan a project with no clear end result so that children use their own viewpoints, interests, needs, and abilities to complete the activity. Furthermore, teachers follow each child's lead, trusting the child's interests and responding appropriately to their ideas. Families are expected to be productive participants in their child's education, creating a community and sense of collaboration that is developmentally appropriate for both children and adults.

Another type of curriculum is **integrated curriculum**. This curriculum type is holistic and focuses on the interrelatedness of all subject areas without the restrictions that subject boundaries can impose. Children acquire and use basic skills across content areas. Learning occurs through projects or themes that reflect the interests, needs, abilities, and skills of the children. Characteristics of this approach include experiences that develop attitudes, skills, and knowledge to facilitate connections across the curriculum; activities that cater to a wide range of abilities; both teacher-initiated/directed and child-initiated/directed activities; large group, small group, and individual activities; opportunities for children to think creatively and critically; and teacher, peer, and self-assessment. Integrated curriculum also recognizes the importance of partnering with families and having extensive knowledge of how children learn and develop.

Finally, early childhood educators must have an understanding of **The Creative Curriculum**. This curriculum model offers a balance between teacher-directed and child-initiated learning. However, similar to the previously discussed models, The Creative Curriculum emphasizes an appreciation of children's general growth and development while responding to each child's learning style and planning experiences to build on their strengths, needs, and interests.

DID YOU KNOW?

HighScope and The Creative Curriculum are both proprietary, meaning schools need to purchase specific products to use these curricula. The Montessori and Reggio Emelia methods can be used by any school.

The Creative Curriculum focuses on concepts and skills in literacy, math, science, social studies, the arts, and technology through ten interest areas set up in the physical environment. The interest areas include blocks, dramatic play, toys and games, art, library, discovery, sand and water, music and movement, cooking, computers, and outdoor play space. Multiple interest areas are available so that children have a variety of opportunities to explore academic content and gain new skills.

The Creative Curriculum provides teachers with guidance on how to arrange the physical environment and maintain interest areas; establish a daily routine that balances time for child choice and small and large group opportunities; foster a classroom community of positive relationships; and guide children in social problem-solving and the development of relationships with peers. The teacher's role is a continuous cycle of observing, guiding children's learning, and assessing progress. Additionally, teachers motivate children and support their learning through a variety of strategies and purposefully planned activities to build upon knowledge and skills.

**Table 1.2. Early Childhood Curriculum Models**

| Curriculum Model | Characteristics | Teacher's Role |
|---|---|---|
| Montessori method | focuses on development of whole child; multiage groupings; extended, uninterrupted work time; choice of activities; child progresses through curriculum at own pace; specific arrangement of materials; creates a close-knit, caring environment | observe children and introduce them to new activities, lessons, and materials as children are ready; serve as a guide instead of a provider of info; work with individuals or small groups of children instead of one large group |
| HighScope | active learning through direct hands-on experiences; driven by children's interests, needs, and abilities; knowledge developed through experiences with people and environment; incorporates scaffolding | support learning choices through diverse materials and physical, cognitive, and emotional support; observe and support children in current knowledge; extend children's thinking to next level |
| Reggio Emilia | self-centered, self-directed learning guided by natural development and relationships with the environment; respects rights of children; children actively acquire own knowledge; activities are project based and solve | observe children and plan projects based on their curiosity; introduce a variety of activities and materials; facilitate exploration; plan projects with mistakes or with no clear end result; |
| Reggio Emilia (continued) | real-life problems; project topics provided by children's interests; projects offer multiple ways to explore and draw conclusions; children use own viewpoints, interests, needs, and abilities to complete projects | follow each child's lead; trust children's interests; respond appropriately to their ideas |

Table 1.2. Early Childhood Curriculum Models (continued)

| Curriculum Model | Characteristics | Teacher's Role |
|---|---|---|
| The Creative Curriculum | balance between teacher-directed and child-initiated, and small and large group activities; responds to each child's learning style; incorporates ten interest areas to provide a variety of activities to explore and gain new skills | carefully arrange environment; establish a balanced routine; foster positive relationships; continuously observe children, guide learning, and assess progress; motivate children and support learning with purposely planned activities |

SAMPLE QUESTIONS

8) **Mr. Martinez, a preschool teacher, would like to implement a curriculum that focuses on project-based activities so his students are self-guided and have opportunities to work with others to solve real-life problems. Which of the following would be the best choice for Mr. Martinez?**

A. Montessori method

B. Reggio Emilia approach

C. The Creative Curriculum

D. HighScope

9) **A school in which students of different grades are grouped in the same classroom is most likely using which type of curriculum method?**

A. HighScope

B. The Creative Curriculum

C. Montessori

D. integrated curriculum

## Developmentally Appropriate Practices

The concept of Developmentally Appropriate Practice drives everyday instruction, classroom management, and child guidance in the early childhood program and classroom. **Developmentally Appropriate Practice (DAP)** is based on current research about how children learn and develop as well as effective practices in early education. In DAP, teachers meet children at their current developmental level individually and as a group, guiding each child toward challenging yet attainable learning goals. There are three core considerations of DAP: knowledge about child development and learning, knowledge of what is individually appropriate, and knowledge of cultural importance.

When implementing DAP, an early childhood educator should incorporate a **Universal Design for Learning (UDL)**. A UDL provides all children with the opportunity to access, participate, and make progress in the general curriculum by modifying how information is presented, selecting available materials and activities, and choosing how they demonstrate and engage in learning. In a UDL, the traditional curriculum should provide multiple, varied, and flexible options to accommodate the needs of all children. In return, children become experts who are in control of their own learning. They can assess their own learning needs, monitor progress, and regulate and maintain their own interest, effort, and persistence.

## LEARNING OBJECTIVES

**Learning objectives** are statements that describe the expected goal of a lesson or activity, the demonstrable knowledge children will acquire, and through what means children will demonstrate their knowledge. It is critical that both children and teachers clearly understand the learning objectives of an activity. Furthermore, activities should be directly aligned with the objective so that the assessment method effectively measures performance.

Learning objectives are based upon the revised version of Bloom's taxonomy, with six levels of learning that can be used to structure objectives, lessons, and activities. These levels include remembering, understanding, applying, analyzing, evaluating, and creating. The levels are organized in terms of complexity from low-level to high-level thinking and skills. According to Bloom, mastering the higher-level skills is dependent upon attaining lower-level skills.

Furthermore, in order to increase rigor in the classroom, learning objectives can be developed using Norman Webb's depth of knowledge (DOK) levels, which categorize tasks by the complexity of thinking needed to complete them. In contrast to Bloom's levels of learning, the depth of knowledge levels are not defined by the verb but instead by the cognitive effort used to complete the task. The levels are divided into four categories.

Table 1.3. Webb's Depth of Knowledge Levels

| Level | Category | Description |
|---|---|---|
| Level one | recall and reproduction | recalling facts, rote application, or remembering a response |
| | | low cognitive effort |
| Level two | skills and concepts | tasks include more than one cognitive step, such as organizing, comparing, predicting, or estimating |
| | | requires more cognitive effort in making decisions about how to approach a task |

Table 1.3. Webb's Depth of Knowledge Levels (continued)

| Level | Category | Description |
|---|---|---|
| Level three | strategic thinking | must use planning and evidence |
| | | thinking is more abstract and requires reasoning |
| | | tasks include solving nonroutine problems, analyzing characters, or developing an experiment |
| Level four | extended thinking | requires the most complex cognitive effort |
| | | information is synthesized over a period of time |
| | | students use knowledge from one domain to solve a problem in another |
| | | tasks may include developing a survey and analyzing the results or analyzing a variety of texts |

Even the youngest preschoolers can think strategically since DOK levels are not developmental or sequential. This means that students are not required to master content in level one before moving to level two, or what may be a level three task for a kindergartener may be a level one task for a student in middle school. The goal of the DOK levels is to create a rich environment in which all students are learning at a high level.

A well-constructed learning objective is specific, concise, observable, and measureable, and contains three parts:

1. *Performance* or *behavior*, each of which describes what the children should be able to do as a result of the lesson or activity. This part of the objective should contain one action verb that is observable and describes the behavior children should display.
2. *Conditions*, which describe how children will complete the task. These usually include time, place, resources, and circumstances.
3. *Criteria*, which describe how children's performance on the task will be evaluated. These should explain the expected proficiency level and how the children are expected to perform in terms of quality, quantity, and time. Learning objectives are an integral part of the early childhood classroom. They ensure that activities and lessons are developmentally appropriate, purposeful and goal oriented, and provide for assessment that will drive further instruction.

QUICK REVIEW

Can you write a learning objective that would accompany a phonics lesson in a kindergarten classroom?

Learning objectives should be incorporated into both short- and long-term planning. **Short-term planning** describes what children are expected to learn during a short period of time. They are more specific than long-term plans and include the lessons, activities, and experiences organized to cover about a week. With short-term plans, teachers can address the individual needs and interests of children. This may begin with setting goals for an individual or group of children. Next, teachers must plan the activity or lesson that is to be implemented and take into account the equipment or materials needed. Also, it is critical for teachers to consider modifications or adaptations that need to be made for specific children. Finally, teachers should choose the assessment tool they will use to determine if the goal was met. An example of short-term planning in a preschool classroom might be an activity that allows children to interact socially by encouraging them to take turns while they pretend they are running a store.

**Long-term planning** can be carried out for up to a year and describes the framework a child or group of children is expected to learn throughout the time he or she is in a particular classroom or setting. When planning long-term, early educators incorporate the early learning standards or outcomes children are expected to meet by a particular time and consider experiences and opportunities that will guide children in meeting goals. In addition, teachers should include when and how informal and formal assessments will be implemented. A long-term plan is simply a guide and should be revised as appropriate to meet the needs, interests, knowledge, and abilities of individual children as well as the group.

### SAMPLE QUESTIONS

**10) Which of the following is NOT a characteristic of short-term planning?**

A. It describes what children are expected to learn during the time they are in a program.

B. It describes what children are expected to learn during a short period of time.

C. It usually covers about a week.

D. It describes specific lessons and activities that will be implemented.

**11) A second-grade student is asked to describe how two stories read in class are different from each other in terms of the setting. Which DOK level would this task employ?**

A. level one

B. level two

C. level three

D. level four

## LESSON PLANNING

Another critical component of developmentally appropriate instruction is developing, implementing, and assessing lesson plans. **Lesson plans** are a detailed description of instruction on how a lesson will be delivered. They ensure the teacher is prepared and on track. They can be developed daily, or more long-term, but typically cover several days and include activities and lessons across all developmental domains.

The philosophy of the program or school will determine the structure; however, there are components that should be included in a lesson plan to ensure successful implementation and assessment. The first component is the **objective**, the knowledge or skills students are expected to gain from the lesson. Next are the materials needed to carry out the entire lesson and accompanying activities. A teacher should also include the procedures for direct instruction or how the lesson will be presented. During direct instruction, lesson plans should include notes about how teaching will be modeled and how children will be involved. Another component is **guided practice**, or through what means children will apply and practice the new skills independently, cooperatively with other students, or with support from the teacher. In addition, a teacher will want to consider accommodations or modifications that may be needed for individuals or small groups. Finally, the **method of assessment**, or how the teacher determines if the children met the learning objective, is included in a lesson plan.

Implementing lesson plans should follow a predictable cycle and start with a "hook," or introduction, that gains the interest of the children. Next is a brief overview of the lesson topic, activities, assessment method, and expectations. This overview should be developmentally appropriate. The next step in the cycle is delivering instruction. During this step it is important to encourage active participation from students and model how to complete activities. After instruction is delivered, time must be allowed for guided practice. During this step, children have the opportunity to practice skills either independently, cooperatively, or in a small group setting with the teacher. In an early childhood classroom, a teacher may assess children's progress during guided instruction. However, beginning in kindergarten or first grade, assessment may be done at the end of the lesson cycle. The final step in the lesson cycle is closure, where the teacher will quickly review the instruction and activities and may ask a few questions.

After a lesson plan is implemented, it is equally important to conduct a lesson plan assessment. This is a personal reflection on what went well in the lesson as well as what needs to be modified and how for next time. The information gained can be a valuable resource when planning for upcoming lessons. Furthermore, it can be used to track student progress—who did well, who struggled, and how to differentiate instruction.

QUICK REVIEW

Implementing a lesson plan:

1. introduction (hook)
2. overview
3. delivering instruction
4. guided practice
5. closure

Another important piece of DAP is identifying and selecting developmentally appropriate and/or age-appropriate learning materials.

When choosing materials, it is important to consider the goals or objectives children are expected to meet and select materials that are engaging and guide children to meet those goals. Learning materials should respect cultural diversity; provide opportunities for problem solving; support cooperative play; support language development in English as well as the child's home language; provide multiple learning opportunities; encourage critical thinking and reasoning, questioning, and experimenting; and develop social skills.

When selecting learning materials, it is essential for the teacher to choose those that will support and guide learning through meaningful play. Learning through **play** describes how children make sense of the world around them through real-life and imaginary activities. In other words, children are active participants and involved in their own learning and are able to practice and enhance their emerging skills.

Many researchers and educators have proven that play enhances learning and develops skills in inquiry, expression, experimentation, and cooperative skills. Furthermore, children learn and develop self-confidence, cognitive skills, physical abilities, new vocabulary, social skills, and literacy skills. Play presents itself in many forms:

- physical play: climbing, running, and jumping
- social play: playing together and influencing each other's behavior
- parallel play: playing near each other but not influencing each other's behavior
- object play: playing with objects such as blocks, dolls, cars, and manipulatives
- language play: talking to self, peers, or caregivers
- pretend play: pretending something is different from what it really is

## SAMPLE QUESTIONS

**12) Which of the following describes a developmentally appropriate lesson plan for a first-grade class to learn about natural resources?**

A. an activity where students are assigned two countries and asked to compare the natural resources of each by conducting online research

B. an activity where the teacher shows a video on tin mining and then asks students to create an outline of what they learned

C. an activity where students visit a nearby factory that produces electronics and learn about the process of production

D. an activity where the teacher gives students pictures of natural resources and asks them to classify each one as living or nonliving

13) **A preschool teacher wants her class to develop print awareness. As students are role playing at a center, she hands the student playing the role of customer a menu to use to order from the waiter. What can be said about this teacher's instructional strategy?**

    A. She is using direct instruction.

    B. She is scaffolding students as they learn through play.

    C. She is encouraging dramatic play over parallel play.

    D. She is attempting to modify the activity based on the universal design for learning.

## Classroom Management

**Classroom management** is another important component of DAP and describes the techniques teachers use to keep children organized, focused, engaged, and academically productive throughout the day. Additionally, effective classroom management ensures that disruptive behavior does not compromise lessons and activities and promotes prosocial behavior. Within an **inclusive classroom**, or classroom where children with varying needs and abilities learn together, teachers must incorporate classroom management strategies that meet the needs of all children.

Effective classroom management and organization include several key components. First, a teacher must implement, model, and practice clear rules and expectations that promote prosocial behavior. **Rules** should be few—about four or five—and include short, positive phrases. If children are allowed to participate in rule development, they will be more motivated to follow the rules.

Second, a teacher must explicitly teach and model acceptable behaviors and provide opportunities to practice self-regulation skills. Next, teachers should plan and implement engaging lessons and activities that meet the interests, needs, and abilities of the children and are a balance between active and passive.

A teacher must also create consistent, predictable **routines**, or specific behaviors and activities, taught to children to ensure smooth class operation as well as a schedule that plans for **transitions** from one activity to the next. The **schedule**, which is the process for carrying out daily routines, including a list of events and times, should be predictable yet flexible. Finally, teachers should create a plan for managing inappropriate, disruptive behavior. It is advisable to think of creative strategies to use when a child needs to take a break or calm down.

In addition to classroom management strategies, early childhood professionals must organize furniture, equipment, materials, and other resources in developmentally appropriate ways. There are many ways to organize a classroom, but teachers should always offer defined areas for quiet and active play. Furniture must be arranged in a way that allows children to get around easily but reduces runways (where children can run). The furniture arrangement must also clearly define activity areas and create boundaries. Finally, each child needs a space to store personal items.

Furthermore, it is necessary to keep activities and materials that are in use organized and avoid having too many materials available at one time—this can overstimulate children. Materials and equipment not in use should be stored in a location that is easy to access for adults, but inaccessible to children.

Classroom management also includes incorporating a positive and effective behavioral management system in the classroom. A **behavior management system** describes the actions and procedures in place to increase the probability that children will engage in behaviors conducive to learning. It teaches socially appropriate behaviors for both school and home. A successful system should be proactive and designed to prevent inappropriate behavior, reinforce positive behavior, directly address problem behavior as it happens, and work in partnership with families to deal with behavior at school and at home.

Incorporating a variety of flexible grouping strategies is also a key component of developmentally appropriate classroom management. **Flexible grouping** describes the concept of grouping and regrouping children from differing ages, backgrounds, and abilities to meet instructional needs during small group activities, cooperative activities, and seating purposes in the classroom or other environments. Early educators must first observe children and make decisions on grouping and regrouping according to dynamics, advantages, goals, activities, and the individual needs of children. The incorporation of a variety of informal, flexible grouping strategies throughout the day is proven to help children be more productive since they are able to work with and learn from each other in a variety of ways and situations.

> STUDY TIP
>
> Within a flexible grouping strategy, students may sometimes be placed in homogeneous groups (groups of students with a similar skill level) or heterogeneous groups (groups of students with varying levels of proficiency with a given task). Which type of instructional scenarios would benefit from each grouping system?

Several options are available for flexible grouping and may include grouping by interest, learning style, readiness for a certain activity or concept, teacher choice, student choice, background knowledge, interest, social skills, or random grouping. The following include some creative ideas for random grouping:

- putting students' names on popsicle sticks and randomly grouping
- placing stickers on index cards and then having each child choose an index card and find other children with a matching sticker
- birthdays within the seasons—winter, spring, summer, fall

Whichever method is chosen, flexible grouping has proven successful because it prevents labeling children by ability, facilitates cooperative learning, builds communication skills, and supports the idea that no single group meets all of a child's needs.

## SAMPLE QUESTIONS

**14) Flexible grouping is described as**

A. grouping students by ability.

B. keeping students in the same group during all activities.

C. grouping and regrouping students from different backgrounds, ages, and abilities.

D. grouping students by age—all older children together and all younger children together.

**15) Ms. Gregory is a first-year kindergarten teacher and would like to implement a set of rules in her classroom. Developmentally appropriate rules should**

A. include ten to twelve rules to make sure everything is covered.

B. include four or five short, positive phrases.

C. be written before the children start school.

D. be explained on the first day of school, but time shouldn't be wasted discussing them extensively.

## Child Guidance

Guiding children's behavior in developmentally appropriate ways is a key role of an early childhood educator. There are several focus areas a teacher must consider when planning strategies to guide children's behavior in the early childhood classroom. Strategies must be implemented for building relationships; guiding behavior and responding to challenging behaviors; problem-solving for conflict-resolution, self-regulatory behavior, and social interactions; teaching character development; and promoting positive social-emotional development.

Building positive, nurturing, and trusting relationships with students is a fundamental component of high-quality teaching. All children thrive on supportive, caring relationships that are loving and nurturing. A positive relationship between a teacher and a child will lead to cooperation and motivation, increase positive academic outcomes, and decrease challenging behavior. Relationship building begins with investing time and attention in children. Teachers must get to know their students' interests, background, preferences, and culture through observations; spend time with students; engage in conversations; and speak directly to families. Teachers can share personal information with children as well, such as interests, hobbies, likes and dislikes, family information, and favorite food, movies, and other activities.

Another strategy used to form relationships is to allow multiple opportunities for positive interactions throughout the day. Positive interactions include giving praise and encouragement, giving high fives, listening to children, playing a game or completing an activity together, acknowledging effort, and sending positive notes home.

Unfortunately, there will be occasions when some children have a difficult time forming relationships with adults. It is easy to build relationships with children who are responsive, follow directions, and seem to enjoy being in the class. However, it can be difficult to build relationships with children who are uncooperative, unmotivated, and disruptive. In these situations, additional time and effort may be needed to build the relationship. The most effective way to achieve a high-quality relationship with a student is to embed multiple opportunities for positive interactions throughout the day.

Early childhood teachers must also have plans in place for positively guiding behavior and responding to challenging behaviors in developmentally appropriate ways. A teacher's strategies for guiding children's behavior should be proactive, driven by positive interactions, and incorporate strategies throughout the day, not just when inappropriate behavior occurs.

Positive behavior guidance strategies begin with setting limits and clearly explaining them. Other strategies include teaching and modeling appropriate behavior and social skills; redirection by diverting and distracting a child away from an inappropriate behavior or activity; providing choices when appropriate; allowing natural consequences, if appropriate; incorporating logical consequences; and supporting and reinforcing new, positive behavior. Teachers must also be reflective and consider how their actions and reactions to a situation affect children's behavior and make changes as necessary.

Sometimes challenging behavior occurs even though a teacher has a successful behavior management system in place that positively guides behavior. Several strategies are available to respond to challenging behavior; however, these strategies should always be used in combination with positive and preventative guidance strategies. The following are examples of such strategies:

- limiting attention: keeping conversations and interactions to a minimum while ensuring the child is safe
- redirection: redirecting to a different activity or location
- teaching/practicing appropriate behavior: planning opportunities to teach the appropriate behavior when inappropriate behavior is NOT occurring. For example, if a child consistently throws blocks, the teacher should plan a time to sit with the child while playing blocks and instruct how to build a tower, bridge, house, and so forth.
- diffusing and discussing: providing a child who is upset time and a quiet space to calm down, then listening to the child, discussing what happened, defining replacement behaviors for next time, and reinforcing appropriate behavior in the future
- incorporating reinforcers: finding an individualized reinforcer and using it frequently when appropriate behavior occurs
- incorporating a behavior plan: making a specific plan for when a behavior occurs, documenting it, and making sure all adults who interact with the child know how to implement it

Teaching children appropriate ways to resolve conflict, engage in acceptable social interactions, and self-regulate behavior is another component of developmentally appropriate child guidance. **Self-regulatory** behavior is the ability to manage and control one's emotions and behavior in socially acceptable ways depending on the situation. Children should be explicitly taught how to self-regulate and resolve their own conflicts so that they are able to independently explain to peers why they are upset, find a resolution, and follow through. In order for children to resolve their own conflicts, they must first be able to calm themselves down; speak to peers in an assertive, yet kind and honest way; listen and accept another's point of view; and come up with agreed upon solutions. When children are able to resolve their own conflicts, the classroom is more peaceful, teachers can focus on instruction, and children learn a firm foundation for conflict resolution.

Developmentally appropriate child guidance also includes teaching children **character development**, or children's understanding of social rules and how their behavior and actions affect others. Positive character development is directly correlated to positive, trusting, nurturing relationships between caregivers and children. This concept can be taught during multiple activities and routines throughout the day with intention and purpose. Children should have opportunities to see how their behavior, words, and actions directly affect others. They should also have opportunities to foster relationships, work cooperatively, practice sharing and taking turns, and solving problems when they arise. The most important strategy a teacher can use is modeling appropriate moral behavior. In addition, teachers can incorporate literature that focuses on prosocial behavior and presents opportunities for children to discuss the rights and wrongs of a character's behavior.

A final component of DAP when considering child guidance is the promotion of positive self-concept and self-esteem, prosocial skills, and social-emotional development. **Self-concept** describes peoples' beliefs about their abilities and who they are. Promoting a positive self-concept begins with a nurturing, trusting, supportive, and caring relationship with adults. Early childhood educators must recognize, appreciate, and develop a genuine concern for the unique interests, abilities, strengths, and needs of individual children, as well as help children recognize and appreciate their own unique abilities. Additionally, teachers must show children they believe in their abilities by providing encouragement and opportunities for success. Finally, children should be taught how to accept and learn from their mistakes and weaknesses. When children are able to do this, they know they are competent.

QUICK REVIEW

How, specifically, might a teacher provide scaffolding during center-based learning activities to help children develop prosocial skills?

In addition to promoting a positive self-concept, early educators also incorporate strategies for teaching **prosocial skills**, or skills that are voluntary and intend to benefit others, such as sharing, helping, and cooperating. In order for students to successfully develop prosocial skills, they must be able to recognize when someone needs help, determine if they are willing to help or not, and choose and act upon an appropriate behavior for the situation. Teachers can promote prosocial skills by allowing children to work cooperatively; make their own choices and experience the consequences; learn how to initiate play with others; and navigate conflicts.

SAMPLE QUESTIONS

16) **Mr. Garcia is having a difficult time developing a relationship with Angelica, a new preschool student. She is often disruptive and refuses to complete any activities. An appropriate next step for Mr. Garcia to build a relationship with Angelica might be to**

A. sit down with Angelica during activities throughout the day and engage in conversations to get to know her.

B. ignore her behavior; she's probably just trying to get attention.

C. call the parents and tell them what is going on.

D. send her to another classroom so she can have a break after each time she disrupts a lesson or activity.

17) **Curtis is a second grader who engages in screaming, crying, and tantrums every time he does not get to sit where he wants during lunch. Which of the following is Curtis probably struggling with?**

A. prosocial skills

B. positive self-concept

C. character development

D. self-regulatory behavior

## Developmentally Appropriate Curricula

A developmentally appropriate curriculum is based on the interests, needs, and abilities of individual children as well as the group. The early childhood teacher should provide a balance of teacher-directed and child-initiated activities that are guided by objectives and goals and provide for engaging learning experiences that promote growth across all developmental domains. Developmentally appropriate opportunities should be provided for physical education, fine arts, reading and vocabulary, mathematics, science, and social studies.

### PHYSICAL DEVELOPMENT

The developmentally appropriate physical development curriculum should support motor and physical skills as well as teach children to live an active, healthy lifestyle. Activities should be varied to promote motor skill development and provide each student the opportunity to participate.

DID YOU KNOW?

Though all children vary, the average weight of an American five-year-old is around 40 pounds.

Additionally, children should be provided opportunities to develop cognitive skills related to motor development as well as social and cooperative skills. For example, while learning to physically write the letters of the alphabet, a child will also learn to recognize and name them.

Basic skills should be taught first and lead to the development of more advanced skills. For instance, young children ages three to third grade are still developing complex motor skills, so an activity like jumping rope would be appropriate. Finally, appropriate assessments should be implemented to determine child progress.

SAMPLE QUESTION

**18) Which of the following is NOT an example of developmentally appropriate activities for kindergarteners?**

A. passing a ball back and forth

B. jumping rope

C. basketball

D. freeze tag

## Fine Arts

The early childhood fine arts curriculum, sometimes referred to as creative arts, engages children in activities through art, dance, dramatic play, theater, and music across all developmental domains. Fine arts activities should be open ended and focus on the process of the work, not on the end product. A developmentally appropriate fine arts curriculum offers activities that promote fine and gross motor skills; social-emotional skills, such as self-regulation and self-control; and opportunities for collaboration, negotiation, and problem-solving. Additionally, activities should be stimulating and engaging, but not frustrating, and based upon the skills and interests of the group as well as individual children.

SAMPLE QUESTION

**19) A developmentally appropriate activity to promote preschool children's gross motor skills through fine arts would be**

A. a painting activity so children can practice grasping a paint brush.

B. to allow children to choose roles to act out "Goldilocks and the Three Bears."

C. gluing feathers onto a piece of paper.

D. skipping to music with a partner.

## Literacy and Language Development

A developmentally appropriate literacy and language curriculum provides opportunities for children to actively engage in meaningful language and early print activities that support reading and writing development. Reading is a developmental process that requires children to master a combination of foundational skills that are dependent upon one another. Opportunities for children to build emergent reading skills in alphabetic knowledge, phonemic awareness, phonics, word recognition, fluency, vocabulary, and comprehension should be taught in a developmental sequence.

QUICK REVIEW

Why would phonological and phonemic awareness be needed before phonics instruction can begin?

Children typically develop appreciation and awareness of print first, followed by phonological and phonemic awareness, and, finally, phonics and word recognition. Children must master these skills before they are able to read fluently and comprehend what they are reading. Effective instruction includes meaningful and developmentally appropriate learning experiences that actively engage children. This instruction includes a cycle that involves explicitly teaching skills and concepts, modeling, guided practice, and independent or cooperative practice.

SAMPLE QUESTION

**20) Mr. Johnson is working with his kindergarten class on the sound of the letter *P* at the beginning of words. He has just finished reading the nursery rhyme "Peter Piper Picked a Peck of Pickled Peppers" and would like to plan an extension activity. Which of the following might be a developmentally appropriate activity?**

A. asking students to sort picture cards by those that start with the letter *P*

B. having students practice writing the letter *P* on a dry erase board

C. having students copy the words to the nursery rhyme in their journal

D. asking students to circle all of the *P* letters in the nursery rhyme

## MATHEMATICS

A developmentally appropriate mathematics curriculum actively introduces concepts, language, and methods and allows for active participation through a variety of hands-on activities and experiences. Early childhood math experiences should include the concepts of numbers and operations, geometry, algebraic reasoning, and measurement in developmentally appropriate ways.

Because math concepts are often abstract, young children should be provided with concrete objects, such as manipulatives, to solve problems. Moreover, teachers must guide children to recognize connections between math concepts. Teachers should also encourage students to explain their thinking, which will deepen their understanding as they acquire new skills and concepts.

SAMPLE QUESTION

21) **All of the following describe developmentally appropriate math activities for kindergarteners EXCEPT**

A. worksheets on which children can practice addition and subtraction problems.

B. encouraging children to explain their thinking when solving problems.

C. hands-on activities that encourage active participation.

D. concrete objects, such as manipulatives.

## Science

The early childhood science curriculum should provide experiences through play and active exploration for children to observe, investigate, ask questions, and solve problems. A developmentally appropriate curriculum provides hands-on activities that engage children physically and mentally to investigate and manipulate things in their environment in order to gain an understanding of the world around them.

Science exploration should begin with a child-based inquiry. A teacher can then provide support and guidance through a variety of materials and settings that encourage children to ask questions, investigate, and develop their own ideas and conclusions. In this way, children will gain a deeper understanding of science concepts.

DID YOU KNOW?

Many educators once believed that most scientific concepts were too abstract for young children to understand, so early childhood programs included only limited science instruction. In recent years, new research and the nationwide push for science, technology, engineering, art/design, and mathematics (STEAM) education have led to increased science education in early childhood classrooms.

SAMPLE QUESTION

22) **Mrs. Grace's preschool class has shown interest in mixing colors while painting to make a new color. She would like to plan a color-mixing activity. A developmentally appropriate activity might be**

A. to have children watch a video about color mixing and then discuss with the class.

B. to demonstrate how to mix colors with paint but not allow children to try since it will be messy.

C. to provide a variety of activity choices that allow students to combine colors, such as mixing different colors of play dough, finger paints, and watercolors.

D. to divide children into small groups and have one child from each group mix different colors of play dough while everyone else observes.

### SOCIAL STUDIES

The social studies curriculum in the early childhood setting should focus on history as well as physical and human geography. Physical geography is simply the study of the natural environment. Human geography describes the relationship between humans and their environment. Developmentally appropriate social studies activities should teach children about the world around them, their place in the world, and the social and cultural world. Activities or projects should facilitate children's connections between themselves and their environment in order to develop a sense of belonging and encourage active participation in society.

#### SAMPLE QUESTION

**23) Social studies activities in a preschool classroom should**

A. include activities or projects that facilitate students' connection between themselves and their environment.

B. encourage children to draw maps of the city and state in which they live.

C. teach children the fifty states and their capitals.

D. teach children about different climates throughout the United States.

## Assessment and Evaluation

### ASSESSMENT

Assessment is an essential element of any high-quality, developmentally appropriate curriculum and describes the process of gathering information about a child through formal or informal assessment methods, analyzing the information, and planning instruction based on the results. Assessment is so critical because it provides information to teachers, families, and administrators on individual child progress, effectiveness of instructional practices, and future planning for individual or groups of children. Two forms of effective assessment methods are available to early educators: formal and informal assessments.

**Formal assessments** are data driven, assess overall achievement, and compare performance with other children of the same age or grade or against predetermined criteria. Some examples of formal assessments are standardized tests developed by school districts or states and criterion-referenced tests. Standardized tests, or **norm-referenced tests**, are required to be administered the exact same way to all individuals in terms of questions, instructions, and scoring; results are compared against those of children of the same age. **Criterion-referenced tests** measure performance against predetermined criteria that children are expected to know and do at a particular stage of development.

- **Informal assessments** are not data driven; they measure performance and are used primarily to drive instruction. Several informal assessment methods are available and provide invaluable information to the educator:

- A **diagnostic-assessment** is a pre-assessment that teachers administer prior to beginning instruction in order to gain information on individual children's strengths, abilities, knowledge, and skills. The information is then used to guide lesson and activity planning and identify students who may have difficulties.
- **Curriculum-based** assessments measure how students are performing in the local curriculum. They typically test and retest target outcomes using probes developed from the curriculum.
- **Observations** describe when a teacher simply observes a child within his or her environment and documents behaviors and skills. One observation method is anecdotal records, or short written descriptions of observed behaviors or skills. These descriptions should be factual and objective.
- **Checklists** are lists of skills or developmental milestones that children are expected to meet at certain times. When they meet the criteria, it is checked off the list. It is a good idea to document the date and how the criteria were met.
- **Time-sampling** is an observation tool that records the number of occasions a child engages in a behavior or skill during different time intervals. An early childhood teacher observes a child over an extended period of time, such as an entire morning or afternoon. During that time, behavior is recorded at regular intervals for a predetermined length of time.
- **Portfolios** are a record of data on an individual child over a period of time and clearly document child progress. Portfolios may include authentic work, observations, checklists, and parent and educator ratings.
- **Educator rankings** are a series of statements on a child's development for which a teacher provides a ranking.
- **Parent rankings** include parents in the assessment process and encourage them to observe their child and note developmental milestones.

QUICK REVIEW

An early childhood educator wants to perform a functional behavioral assessment to determine the roots of a student's behavior. Which methods of evaluation would be best and why?

Early childhood educators must have procedures in place to establish, maintain, and use information gained from formal and informal assessments. In order for assessments to support learning and development, they must be aligned with state standards, the curriculum in place, and correspond to the dates on which children are learning specific concepts. It is important to establish assessment methods and administration dates at the beginning of a school year or when a child first begins a new program. Formal and informal assessment methods should be used to determine a child's skills, abilities, knowledge, and any difficulties, as well as help set goals for future instruction. Additionally, the information can be shared with families to help create a plan to establish goals at both home and school.

SAMPLE QUESTION

**24) Teacher observations are an example of which type of assessment?**

A. norm-referenced test

B. informal assessment

C. criterion-referenced test

D. diagnostic assessment

## EVALUATION

After assessments have been completed, an early childhood educator must evaluate the data to make instructional decisions, particularly for monitoring struggling students and planning student conferences or home visits. First, the teacher must look at assessments as a whole to make sure the information comes from a variety of resources. Next, they should examine the data and look for patterns within groups of children as well as children who do not fit within a particular group or pattern. Finally, instructors should reflect on the data to establish goals and plan instruction based on their knowledge of the group and individual children.

After evaluating instruction, it is critical to identify those children who are struggling and plan and implement intervention strategies. Some intervention strategies may include mentoring and practicing basic skills; reteaching a concept to small groups or to individual children; modeling strategies and providing extended guided practice; and allowing additional time for students to practice and extend new skills. Educators must then implement **progress monitoring** strategies to continue to assess group and individual child performance, improvement rate, response to instruction, and the effectiveness of instruction. Progress monitoring should be continuous and incorporate several informal assessment methods in order to achieve accurate information and revise and set new goals.

Following assessment and evaluation, early childhood teachers should plan to meet with families through parent-teacher conferences or home visits to discuss progress, work together to set goals, and build relationships. A home visit is one way for families and teachers to come together. The goal of a home visit is typically to get to know the student and his or her family. When planning a home visit, there are a few important procedures early childhood educators must follow:

- They should plan to visit each child's home. If this is not possible, they should plan to visit a variety of children's homes, not just those who are in trouble or struggling.

- Educators should offer alternative times, dates, and locations for meeting. When teachers are flexible, most families will participate.
- Teachers should always go with a partner, either another instructor, an administrator, or support staff.

During the visit, it is imperative for early childhood educators to do the following:

- They should introduce themselves and get to know the family and their experiences.
- They should plan to discuss the goals the families have for their child as well as their own goals for the child and create a partnership so that everyone takes into consideration the best interest of the child.
- They should communicate what they need from the family and, in turn, ask what the family needs from the child's teachers.
- They should not take any notes or write anything down, but instead simply have a conversation with the family so that the family does not feel like they are being evaluated.

Home visits typically last from 30 to 45 minutes. Academics are often the intended focus, but home visits can also be planned just to get to know the family. Most teachers report that building relationships is the most beneficial outcome of home visits.

Parent-teacher conferences are another opportunity for families and teachers to come together to discuss the best interest of the child. These conferences can take place at the school, an alternate location, or at the child's home. In contrast to home visits, the goal of parent-teacher conferences is to have a conversation with parents about their child's progress in school. During a conference, it is important to discuss the following information:

- what their child is learning and how
- assessment information, including examples of work, observation notes, rubrics, and so forth, and a discussion of strengths and progress
- the child's relationships with other children and teachers
- behavior information
- strategies incorporated at school to support the child
- strategies incorporated at home to support the child
- what the parent notices at home about the child
- reinforcing to parents that what they do at home is equally as important as what happens in school
- reinforcing that their child's success in school is equally important to both parties

DID YOU KNOW?

It is good practice to send invitations to parents about parent-teacher conferences. Information may include time, date, location, and a reminder that parents are a critical part of their child's learning.

After the conference, it is important for educators to follow up with parents on how the child is progressing at school and how they think the child is progressing at home. Finally, teachers should let parents know that they are available and willing to communicate as needed.

## SAMPLE QUESTION

**25) A successful home visit should include**

A. taking notes the entire visit so you have documentation.

B. only discussing areas in which the child is struggling.

C. getting to know the family and their goals for the child.

D. only discussing concerns regarding behavior.

# Answer Key

**1)** **A.** **Correct.** Benjamin Bloom developed Bloom's taxonomy, a hierarchy of skills ranging from simple to complex and concrete to abstract that build upon each other. Many schools use the revised version today.

B. Incorrect. Abraham Maslow contributed the hierarchy of needs.

C. Incorrect. Lev Vygotsky contributed the zone of proximal development.

D. Incorrect. Piaget contributed the four stages of cognitive development.

**2)** A. Incorrect. This describes logical-mathematical intelligence.

B. Incorrect. This describes musical intelligence.

C. Incorrect. This describes interpersonal intelligence.

**D.** **Correct.** This describes verbal-linguistic intelligence.

**3)** **A.** **Correct.** Hypertonic, or high muscle tone, is an indicator of atypical gross motor development.

**4)** A. Incorrect. A child should be able to name most familiar objects by first grade.

B. Incorrect. First graders should be able to focus on one activity for several minutes. Furthermore, this ability is characteristic of typical social-emotional development, not language development.

**C.** **Correct.** A first grader who understands and follows multi-step directions is displaying typical development in receptive language.

D. Incorrect. Interest in poetry is not necessarily reflective of typical language development as not all first graders may share that interest.

**5)** A. Incorrect. An inability to focus and complete activities may be signs of poor nutrition.

**B.** **Correct.** Becoming withdrawn and wearing clothing to cover injuries may be signs of physical abuse.

C. Incorrect. Emotional distress may be caused by abuse, neglect, loss of a loved one, poverty, or a parent's substance abuse or mental illness.

D. Incorrect. Substance abuse is the misuse of alcohol and/or legal drugs, or the use, manufacture, or distribution of illegal substances.

**6)** **A.** **Correct.** Down syndrome is a genetic condition that impacts cognitive development.

B. Incorrect. Autism spectrum disorder (ASD) may or may not be genetic and is classified as a developmental disability.

C. Incorrect. While poverty may be correlated to cognitive development, it is not a genetic condition.

D. Incorrect. Low birth weight is often the result of environmental factors, not genetics. It may or may not impact a child's cognitive development.

**7) C. Correct.** Scheduling events only on weeknights does not consider time constraints for families. Some families may not be able to attend in the evening, so it is important to schedule events at different times during the day and on different days of the week.

**8)** A. Incorrect. The Montessori method is not project based; instead, it focuses on how the individual child is progressing through the curriculum.

**B. Correct.** Reggio Emilia focuses on a project-based approach where children are self-guided and work collaboratively with others to solve real-life problems.

C. Incorrect. The Creative Curriculum is a balance between teacher-directed and child-initiated activities.

D. Incorrect. HighScope emphasizes the individual development of children through the concept of scaffolding.

**9)** A. Incorrect. HighScope does not necessarily promote multiage grouping.

B. Incorrect. The Creative Curriculum explores a balance of teacher- and student-directed activities; it does not necessarily advocate multiage grouping.

**C. Correct.** In the Montessori method, students are typically in multiage groups.

D. Incorrect. Integrated curriculum merely refers to meeting multiple objectives across different subjects or developmental domains with a single activity.

**10) A. Correct.** This describes long-term planning.

**11)** A. Incorrect. Level one addresses simple recall. In this case, the student might only be asked to recall an event from the story.

**B. Correct.** Level two often involves making comparisons between two things, such as the setting of a story.

C. Incorrect. Level three involves more strategic thinking. DOK level three might apply if the student had been asked to analyze the possible motivations for the characters' actions in the stories, for instance.

D. Incorrect. Level four involves more synthesis over time. If students were asked to poll the class on which story they liked better and why, and to present the results to the class in some form, this would be an example of DOK level four.

**12)** A. Incorrect. Many first graders will not have the reading skills to take on this project.

B. Incorrect. This activity is too advanced for a first-grade class.

C. Incorrect. This activity is experiential learning but not necessarily related to natural resources.

**D. Correct.** This activity is developmentally appropriate and engaging.

**13)** A. Incorrect. The students are engaged in play-based learning, not direct instruction.

**B. Correct.** The teacher is providing scaffolding to aid students to meet class objectives as they play.

C. Incorrect. The students were not engaged in parallel play since they were already playing with one another.

D. Incorrect. The teacher is scaffolding student learning, but she is not modifying the activity to meet the needs of any particular student.

**14)** A. Incorrect. This describes ability grouping.

B. Incorrect. Keeping children in the same group for all activities does not describe flexible grouping.

**C. Correct.** Grouping students in multiple ways throughout the day describes flexible grouping.

D. Incorrect. Grouping students by age only is not a characteristic of flexible grouping.

**15)** A. Incorrect. Only a few rules should be included.

**B. Correct.** Developmentally appropriate rules are few and described with short, positive phrases.

C. Incorrect. If children are involved in generating the rules, they will be more likely to follow them.

D. Incorrect. Rules should be explicitly taught and modeled by the teacher frequently.

**16) A. Correct.** The best method to develop a relationship with Angelica would be to engage in multiple positive interactions throughout the day.

B. Incorrect. Ignoring Angelica's behavior would not work to build the relationship.

C. Incorrect. Talking to Angelica's parents would not directly work to build the relationship.

D. Incorrect. Sending her to another classroom might damage the relationship even further by communicating to Angelica that Mr. Garcia does not want her in his class.

**17)** A. Incorrect. Prosocial skills describe those that help others, such as sharing, volunteering, or cooperating.

B. Incorrect. Positive self-concept describes how one feels about his or her own abilities and skills.

C. Incorrect. Character development describes the understanding of social rules and how behavior affects others.

**D. Correct.** Curtis is struggling to control his emotions and behavior in socially acceptable ways.

**18) C. Correct.** Playing a game of basketball requires children to perform motor skills in addition to thinking about what they are doing and why, which would be developmentally inappropriate. The other answer choices all focus on complex motor skill development, such as running, throwing, and jumping, that would be appropriate for kindergarten students.

**19)** A. Incorrect. A painting activity would promote fine motor skills.

B. Incorrect. A collaborative role-play activity would promote negotiation and problem-solving skills.

C. Incorrect. Gluing feathers to paper would promote fine motor skills.

**D. Correct.** Skipping to music would promote gross motor development.

**20) A. Correct.** This sorting activity would provide children with extra practice recognizing pictures that start with the sound of the letter *P*.

B. Incorrect. Students would only practice their handwriting by writing the letter *P*.

C. Incorrect. Copying all the words to an entire nursery rhyme is not developmentally appropriate for kindergarten.

D. Incorrect. This activity will help children recognize the letter *P*, but it will not help them practice the sound it makes at the beginning of words.

**21) A. Correct.** Worksheets are not developmentally appropriate for children of this age.

**22)** A. Incorrect. Watching a video is not a hands-on activity.

B. Incorrect. A demonstration does not allow children to explore and solve their own problems.

**C. Correct.** Here, children choose the activity that interests them; the experience is both engaging and hands-on.

D. Incorrect. All children should have the opportunity to explore, not just one student in the group.

**23) A. Correct.** Developmentally appropriate activities should focus on children's connection between themselves and their environment.

**24)** A. Incorrect. Norm-referenced tests are standardized tests that compare results of children of the same age.

**B. Correct.** Teacher observations are a form of informal assessment and are used to plan further instruction.

C. Incorrect. Criterion-referenced tests measure performance against predetermined criteria.

D. Incorrect. Diagnostic assessments are administered before instruction begins to gain information on children's current knowledge.

**25)** A. Incorrect. It is advised not to take notes during home visits so that families do not not feel like they are being evaluated.

B. Incorrect. The purpose of a home visit is to get to know the family and discuss their goals for the child, not to only discuss areas in which the child is struggling.

**C. Correct.** The goal of a home visit is to get to know the family and their goals for the child.

D. Incorrect. The purpose of a home visit is to get to know the family and discuss their goals for the child; it is not to discuss behavior only.

# Meeting the Diverse Needs of Students

## English Language Learners

Early-childhood classrooms are diverse places that include children from many cultural backgrounds. Students may speak English fluently, speak English only at school and another language at home, or have little experience with English at all. This makes early-childhood classrooms very linguistically and culturally diverse places. Because of this, early-childhood teachers must strive not only to create environments that are accepting and embracing of diversity but also to build cultural competency among students and the school community at large. **Cultural competence** is the awareness of one's own cultural identity and the ability to understand, appreciate, and respect different cultural norms.

Promoting cultural competency requires opening the classroom to different cultures. Students of different cultures and their families have much to share with the class and the school community. An Indian American family might show a kindergarten class traditional Indian clothing, music, and dance as part of a unit on different places around the world. A Chinese American family might share a special holiday and its traditions, such as the Lunar New Year, with the class. The more that students are exposed to different cultural elements in contexts where they can ask questions and feel safe to explore, the more likely they will be to embrace their differences as a fundamental part of well-rounded citizenship.

Teachers should also be respectful when they interact with families from different backgrounds who might have differing expectations of their children's educational experiences. When teachers model tolerance, understanding, and interest in broad cultural perspectives, students are likely to follow. Even in more homogeneous school environments where one dominant culture prevails, teachers must still make an effort to introduce students to cultural diversity any way that they can. As the United States continues to become more diverse, all students need to practice developing cultural competency from a young age, even if they are born into somewhat non-diverse communities.

In addition to coming from different cultural backgrounds, some students may have **limited English proficiency,** which is a limited ability to read, speak, write, or understand English based on English not being one's primary language. Students who enter an early-childhood classroom with limited English proficiency will need extra support. They will need **differentiation,** or different techniques and adaptations to instruct students with varying needs. Teachers may have to provide visual cues and directions alongside explicit instruction in vocabulary and oral-language skills.

These students, like all young students, will need multiple opportunities to practice listening and speaking. They will also need multiple opportunities to show what they know independently of their language skills. The **Universal Design for Learning,** a learning framework popular in many schools today, emphasizes giving students:

- **multiple means of representation**, or multiple ways of gaining new knowledge
- **multiple means of expression**, or multiple ways to show what they know
- **multiple means of engagement**, or multiple ways to motivate and engage students in their learning

Students who have limited English proficiency, for example, might learn certain science concepts better visually, such as through graphics and videos, if they find the vocabulary in the science textbook challenging. They might also need accommodations or modifications during assessments to ensure that they can fully demonstrate their knowledge.

For example, an elementary school student who has just arrived in the United States speaking very little English might receive a math assessment containing extra math problems with only numerals. Meanwhile, the rest of the class would receive an assignment divided between numerals-only problems and word problems. This lets the student demonstrate knowledge of mathematical concepts independently of their English language skills. This type of differentiation can go a long way to build student confidence and student interest in the classroom environment. It also prevents students from becoming disengaged in school while they build the skills to communicate in English.

Since early childhood is when students best learn new languages, many schools have programs designed to develop **dual language learners**, which is defined as those who are learning two languages simultaneously. This may take the form of a language-immersion program where young English-speaking children are placed in an environment where another language is spoken for part or most of the day. These programs are generally made up of students with a monolingual English background and students with some proficiency in a second language, with the goal for students to develop both languages through classroom instruction and social interaction with their peers.

Dual language programs can also take another form where students who speak only English at home are placed in a completely immersive environment to quickly become proficient in a second language. These programs have become very popular in many large cities as the need for a workforce that is fluent in more than one language continues to grow.

Young children whose home languages are not English will be dual language learners in most typical, majority English education programs. These young children, who are still developing skills in their home languages as part of the natural arc of child development, will also be developing skills in a second language. Teachers working with dual language learners must promote English language skills while supporting the ongoing development of the children's home languages. This **bilingualism**, or the ability to speak two languages fluently, is a huge benefit to the child that should be nurtured. Children who develop two or more languages simultaneously have been found to have advantages in socio-emotional development, early language and literacy, and overall cognitive development.

These students should also be encouraged to pursue **biliteracy**, or the ability to proficiently read and write in two languages. While language-immersion programs will likely offer this component explicitly, all early-childhood teachers can encourage students and families to read and write in both English and their home languages as appropriate so as to develop these proficiencies. Some districts and schools offer classroom curriculum resources in languages other than English to encourage this, and many educational publishers and technology companies offer resources in commonly spoken second languages, such as Spanish. Above all, when there are students who are learning English, teachers should not push them to discard their heritage languages or to stop developing them.

Children who are learning two languages may engage in **code switching**, or alternating between two languages or dialects. It occurs most often in children when they begin a sentence in one language but complete it in another. This is a somewhat remarkable thing, and it shows that these children are maintaining grammatical rules in both languages. Code switching is natural, normal, and expected, and it is no cause for concern. Rather than chiding students for code switching, teachers should use these opportunities to expand students' vocabulary and knowledge in both languages, dependent, of course, on the teacher's proficiency in the children's native languages. Constantly correcting students for code switching undermines their overall development and does not validate their need to communicate.

Students in the primary grades who have already developed fluency in their home languages but who have limited English proficiency are not considered dual language learners but rather **English language learners (ELLs)**, which is defined as students who need specialized instruction in English and other academic subject areas due to a lack of English proficiency. Instruction for these students will also vary considerably based on the program. However, most research suggests that best practices include helping students obtain English proficiency quickly while providing appropriate support and differentiation so that students can continue learning across content areas. It is important for teachers, especially of young students who may feel nervous in a new environment at first, to make English language learners feel comfortable in the classroom. Teachers can do that by using strategies such as using visuals and predictable routines and by not forcing students to speak until they are ready.

Some students will go through a **silent period** where they may not speak much, and this is normal in learning a new language. Some students may also be reluctant to practice newly acquired English language skills for fear of making mistakes, so teachers should make sure the classroom is a safe space where all attempts to use the new language are validated and praised.

Partnering with families, a key part of any successful early-childhood classroom, can be more challenging with English language learners if their parents also have limited English proficiency. However, teachers should never discount the value of creating trusting relationships with all families, irrespective of their home languages. Having classroom newsletters, websites, and other communications translated into other languages and having a translator available for parent conferences can increase communication with families and help overcome language barriers to parent involvement. Since research indicates a strong positive correlation between a solid home-school connection and student engagement in school, every effort should be made to reach out to families through all available means. Some schools in large urban areas have school administrative staff (such as social workers, parent engagement representatives, and school culture officials) for this express purpose, and some even offer English as a second language classes for parents as part of a community school model.

## SAMPLE QUESTIONS

1) **A first-grade teacher is monitoring the lunchroom when she sees a student, Juan, with a package of food labeled in the student's home language. What might be an appropriate response?**

   A. asking Juan to write an English translation of the packaging

   B. saying to Juan, "That looks yummy! What are you eating?"

   C. asking Juan to show his food to the native English speakers at the table

   D. asking the other students at the lunch table to describe the interesting packaging in English

2) **A third-grade teacher is working on a social studies unit about comparing different communities and ways of life. He wants to help his class develop cultural competency as part of this unit, and he also wants to make a connection between home and school. Which activity would be most useful to meet these goals?**

   A. organizing a cultural festival where families showcase different parts of their cultural heritages

   B. asking students to do research on their cultural heritages and present their information to the class

   C. encouraging students to check out nonfiction books on different parts of the world

   D. having students create labels for different parts of the school in languages other than English

## STUDENTS WITH SPECIAL NEEDS

The **Individuals with Disabilities Education Act (IDEA)** is the main piece of federal legislation that governs special-education services. Part B of IDEA covers students from the age of three to twenty-two, and it provides guidelines to schools to help address the needs of special-education students. IDEA establishes the framework for identification, parental rights, placement decisions, modifications and accommodations, and behavior supports. It also covers transitioning to adulthood and the process for handling disputes between parents and schools. Part C provides state-run early-intervention services for children from birth to age three.

IDEA mandates that all students be educated in the **least restrictive environment (LRE)**, meaning that students with special needs should be educated with their peers to the fullest extent they are able. This provision creates a more inclusive environment where all students fully participate, and it also means that the early-childhood classroom will likely contain students with a variety of special needs who will need differentiated instruction.

IDEA defines thirteen types of disabilities for which students are eligible to receive special services.

- **Specific learning disabilities (SLD)** is a broad category that includes processing disorders that affect a student's ability to read, write, speak, or do math (such as dyslexia, dysgraphia, and dyscalculia).
- **Speech or language impairments** include communication disorders that cause children to having trouble forming or comprehending words.
- **Other health impairments** include any condition that limits children's strength or alertness (such as ADHD, Tourette's syndrome, and illnesses such as diabetes).
- **Autism spectrum disorder (ASD)** is a development disorder whose key traits include poor communication skills, repetitive behaviors, resistance to change in environment or routine, and sensitivity to sensory stimuli.
- **Intellectual disabilities** cause students to have below-average intellectual functions and adaptive functioning, meaning that their capacity to function independently is diminished (such as Down syndrome and fetal alcohol syndrome).
- **Emotional disturbances** include several mental health conditions such as bipolar disorder, obsessive-compulsive disorder, and oppositional-defiance disorder.
- Children with **multiple disabilities** have more than one condition that cannot be accommodated in a program designed for only one of those conditions.
- **Deafness** is "a hearing impairment that is so severe that the child is impaired in processing linguistic information through hearing, with or without amplification."

- **Hearing impairments** affect children's hearing but do not fall under the definition of deafness.
- **Visual impairments** include blindness and partial sight.
- **Deaf-blindness** is defined as having visual and hearing impairments.
- **Orthopedic impairments** (physical disabilities) limits children's physical functioning (such as epilepsy, muscular dystrophy, and cerebral palsy).
- A **traumatic brain injury** is caused by an accident or outside force. This category does not include congenital or degenerative brain injuries.

Because IDEA provides for special services for any student with a health impairment that limits his or her functioning, it is important to recognize that students with special needs may have many complex conditions that affect their learning, so teachers must focus on inclusion and accommodation rather than limitations.

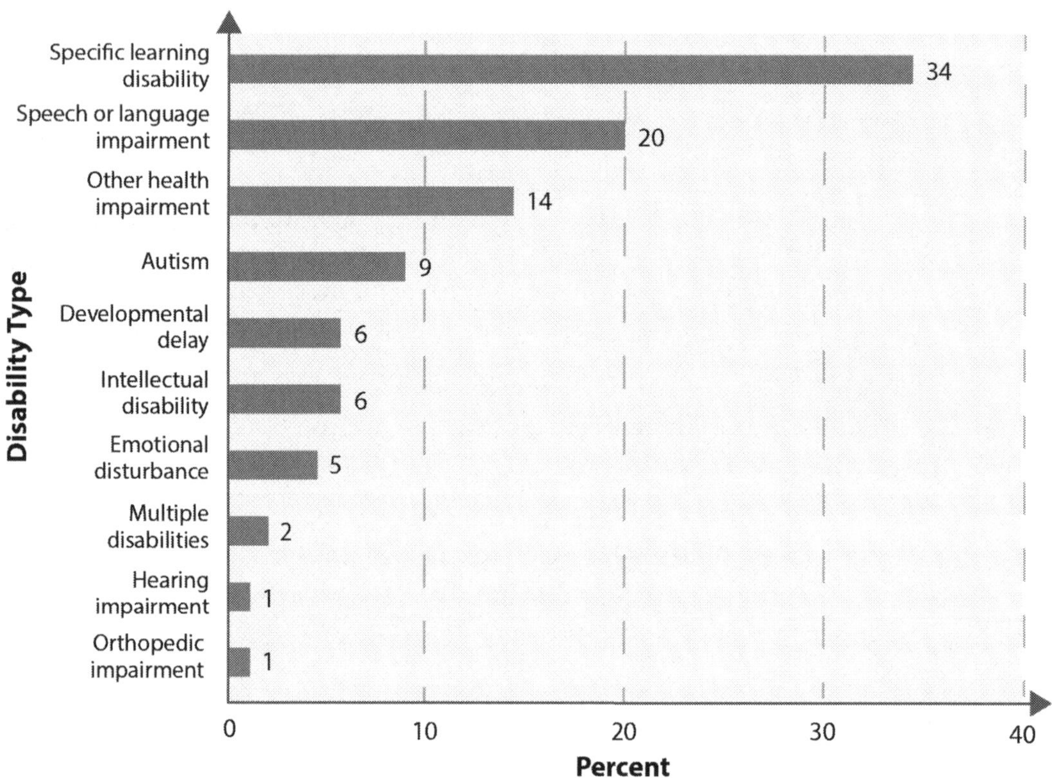


**Figure 2.1. Percentage of Students with Disabilities**

IDEA provides for early identification and intervention concerning children with special needs through federal grants to states. Students under age three who have been identified as needing special services because of a developmental delay or health condition that might lead to an educational delay will be provided with an **individualized family services plan (IFSP)**. This plan will outline the services that the child will receive from doctors, social workers, and other early interventionists. These services must take place in a natural setting where the child will feel comfortable, and this setting is often the child's home.

The plan is typically highly collaborative, and it involves a team of practitioners and parents. Teachers of very young children in an early-childhood setting may be called on to participate in progress monitoring and development of students being served by an IFSP. The goals of the plan are reviewed every six months and updated annually. Typically, IFSPs differ in eligibility in that they tend not to cover specific learning disabilities. But all states have their own criteria for eligibility, and states have varying definitions for what constitutes a developmental delay. Young children who receive services through an IFSP may or may not continue to need and receive special services once they turn three. The IFSP team will normally meet then to decide whether a child needs services under an individualized education program (IEP).

An **individualized education program (IEP)** is similar to an IFSP, but it is for students between the ages of three and twenty-one. The IEP determines what the child's particular learning needs and goals are and how the school will accommodate and provide for the growth of the student. It also lays out how progress will be tracked and measured.

Teachers at the early-childhood grade levels should also be highly aware of the collaborative nature of the IFSP and IEP. They will be collaborating with any number of specialists: speech therapists, physicians, diagnosticians, social workers, and district and school personnel, just to name a few. Of course, they will also be collaborating, first and foremost, with the parents of each student with an IFSP or IEP. Parents of students with special needs often experience a range of emotions, particularly if they feel that their children's unique needs are not being addressed adequately. It is paramount to act proactively, communicate, and document each child's progress toward their goals.

Students with special needs with an IEP may need a combination of **modifications**, or changes in what they learn, alongside **accommodations**, or changes in how they are taught. Modifications change the learning goal or objective itself, while accommodations simply change how an individual student goes about meeting a goal or objective.

Modifications and accommodations can happen as part of both instruction and assessment. For example, a third-grade student with the diagnosed specific learning disability of dyslexia might be allowed to use a spell-checker for a writing assignment. That is an accommodation. However, if he or she is given the task of writing only three sentences while other students are asked to write five sentences, that is a modification. Similarly, a kindergarten student with a speech or language impairment might be tested on their letter sounds in a different way from their peers. That is an example of an assessment modification. If the same student is not assessed on letter sounds entirely, that is an example of an accommodation.

One very helpful type of accommodation for many students is assistive technology. **Assistive technology** can include a calculator that helps a student with dyscalculia solve math problems and seat cushions that help students with physical disabilities sit more comfortably at their desks. This technology, both low- and high-tech, can help students with a variety of special needs participate more fully in classroom activities and meet IEP objectives.

STUDY TIPS

Accommodation = help

Modification = change

Accommodations help a learner meet the learning goal. Modifications change the learning goal.

Students with certain disabilities may benefit greatly from systems and devices that can be used for **augmentative and alternative communication**, which are techniques to aid those with communication-related disorders. Students might use various low-tech aids, such as a picture board to communicate through pointing or gesturing. They may also use more high-tech devices, such as speech-generating devices or applications. These devices or programs can help students communicate in the classroom, which can be critical to helping students meet IEP goals for social learning.

When instructing students with special needs, teachers should be mindful of evidence-based best practices. Students with intellectual and learning disabilities are often served best with systematic and explicit instruction. Instruction that is **systematic** follows a sequence of mastering each component before moving to the next. For example, systematic math instruction would involve learning to count before learning to add. **Explicit instruction** is very clear and direct. An explicit math lesson might involve the teacher modeling and explaining as she works through each step of a problem. Explicit instruction also frequently employs the "I do, We do, You do" model where the teacher first models, then the student and teacher do the task together, and then the student does the task independently.

Another popular and research-validated strategy for addressing the needs of the inclusive classroom with students of varying learning needs is **peer tutoring**. This strategy pairs students to reinforce key concepts. There are several peer tutoring models with **ClassWide Peer Tutoring (CWPT)**, where students are divided into tutoring groups with differing skill levels, being the most popular. Variations include **Peer-Assisted Learning Strategies (PALS)**, where ability grouping is less emphasized. Peer tutoring has been found to be quite effective in getting more students one-on-one assistance and giving struggling readers more opportunities for practice and immediate feedback. It has also been found to promote self-confidence and to help students develop positive social relationships with their peers.

## SAMPLE QUESTIONS

3) **Which of these is an accommodation that might be used for a first-grade student who is blind?**

   A. having the student focus more on oral reading and less on writing

   B. excusing the student from participating in visual art projects

   C. providing the student with more time at the sensory table

   D. giving the student reading material in braille

**4) Randy, a third grader, has been diagnosed with the specific learning disability of dyscalculia. This disability makes it very hard for Randy to recall math facts. What accommodation might his math teacher use for certain assignments?**

A. She might give Randy more time to complete these assignments.

B. She might put Randy with a peer tutor for more help.

C. She might allow Randy to use pre-printed math fact tables.

D. She might give Randy shorter assignments with fewer problems.

## GIFTED AND TALENTED STUDENTS

The early-childhood classroom will likely also have students who are **gifted and talented**, or those who have abilities significantly above the norm for their age. These students, estimated at around 6 percent of the public-school population in the United States, need special instruction to fully develop their talents. These talents may lie in a variety of domains: the arts, sciences, social skills and leadership, or overall cognitive abilities. Unlike students with other special needs for whom services are federally mandated, most decisions surrounding identification and services for gifted and talented students happen on the state level or sometimes even on a district or school level. Programs for these students vary considerably from place to place, but the most common are:

- specialized schools designated for gifted and talented students
- specialized magnet schools for the arts, sciences, or other pursuits that attract children with talents in these areas
- district- or school-wide gifted-and-talented programs that generally involve special instruction in pull-out programs
- grade advancement beyond the students' ages
- class grouping strategies

Gifted and talented students also receive modifications and accommodations within the regular classroom such as:

- purposeful and meaningful assignment extensions and enrichment activities
- differentiated curriculum
- curriculum compacting

Research shows that whatever structure a gifted program takes, even if it is the classroom teacher consistently differentiating instruction, it is vital that there be some program in place for these students. Ensuring that all members of the class are being adequately challenged and given multiple opportunities to learn new things each day can certainly be tough when balancing the needs of many learners. Studies have shown that teachers tend to focus more on students performing below grade-level expectations because of pressures related to benchmark or statewide-standardized testing. However, encouraging gifted students' pursuits in youth has been very strongly correlated to their achievement over the lifetime.

**Curriculum compacting** is one of the simplest and most effective ways to provide meaningful educational experiences for gifted students. Using this method, students who have already mastered certain skills can move on to new material without wasting time reviewing material that they find rudimentary. In a kindergarten class, for example, a gifted student who is already a fluent reader may become bored with the memorization of high-frequency sight words. This student can then be given an extension or enrichment activity more appropriate to their current skill level, such as writing and illustrating a short "book" using ten high-frequency sight words. A third-grade student who has shown mathematical giftedness might, instead of continuing to work on third-grade objectives that she has already mastered, begin working with the fourth-grade math textbook. The key is eliminating parts of the curriculum that the student has mastered and replacing those elements with engaging, challenging activities and assignments that are more appropriate for the student's current developmental level.

DID YOU KNOW?

Some research suggests that gifted students develop asynchronously. One domain, such as their cognitive or language development, may be quite advanced, while other domains, such as socio-emotional or physical development, may lag behind. This means that gifted and talented students need just as much differentiation across all domains of early learning as any other students.

Another component of successful gifted and talented instruction, which can be used in conjunction with curriculum compacting, is **grouping**. This simply means that students with similar giftedness are placed in a group and complete certain classroom activities together. This can also help with practical concerns as teachers differentiate instruction. Grouping could be used as part of learning-center rotations in a kindergarten classroom, for example, and this lets the teacher provide more calibrated instruction at the appropriate level for each group. In the elementary grades, grouping can give teachers a chance to modify cooperative learning assignments for the needs of gifted and talented learners.

Early-childhood educators also need to avoid common pitfalls in instructing gifted and talented students. These students, like all students with diverse needs, should be included in whole group activities and instruction as much as possible without excessively isolating them. They should also not be expected to work on the exact same material as other students, only faster or more accurately. The curriculum must be thoughtfully differentiated so that they are still challenged and they are not participating in assignments that they find boring or rudimentary.

QUICK REVIEW

What is your school's, district's, or state's policy on identifying gifted and talented students?

Gifted and talented instruction needs to be thoughtful and purposeful. While it can be challenging to devise a new set of objectives for gifted students beyond the existing multiple sets of objectives for the class and the grade at large, enrichment activities for gifted and talented students should have a purpose and goal in mind. Having a student simply read independently (assuming that the student's interests lie elsewhere) while the remainder of the class practices the weekly spelling words will likely not drive engagement or promote a feeling of belonging. And while gifted students can and should use their talents to help their peers who might be struggling with a particular skill, they should not become full-time peer tutors at the expense of their own learning.

Early-childhood educators need to be proactive and supportive in the identification of gifted and talented students. While the process for identifying gifted students will vary widely by state, district, and program, most involve teacher input in the form of checklists, recommendations, or portfolio collection. Teachers should be prepared to help other personnel to identify these students through honest and candid feedback when requested.

## SAMPLE QUESTIONS

5) **Mark, a second grader, is an academically gifted student in Ms. Hayes's math class. Mark knows his addition and subtraction, but during practice time, he becomes extremely disruptive to those around him. What is Ms. Hayes's best course of action?**

   A. moving Mark forward a grade

   B. applying ability grouping

   C. using curriculum compacting

   D. creating a behavioral-modification plan

6) **Myra is a third grader who is very artistically gifted. Her art teacher, Mr. Wong, wants to nourish this gift and encourage Myra to grow in her artistic ability. Which instructional strategy would best meet his goal?**

   A. Mr. Wong should instruct Myra to research famous artists.

   B. Mr. Wong should ask Myra to draw several pictures for each picture that the other students draw.

   C. Mr. Wong should give Myra instruction and practice in new media and techniques.

   D. Mr. Wong should encourage Myra to teach other students her drawing techniques.

# Answer Key

**1)** A. Incorrect. This is not developmentally appropriate for a first grader, particularly one who might have limited English proficiency.

**B.** **Correct.** This shows interest in Juan's culture and encourages him to engage in conversation, further developing his oral language skills.

C. Incorrect. While this might help Juan develop some oral language skills, choice B is a better option as it is an open-ended question that sparks conversation.

D. Incorrect. This might spark some conversation, but choice B is still the best option as it encourages Juan to practice speaking, and it shows interest in his food.

**2)** **A.** **Correct.** Organizing a cultural festival develops cultural competency as students learn about and develop an appreciation for cultural differences, and bringing families into the classroom helps make the home–school connection.

B. Incorrect. A cultural research activity might help develop cultural competence when students present to the class, but it does not necessarily make a connection between home and school.

C. Incorrect. A reading assignment will not help create a home–school connection, and it also does not directly promote cultural competence.

D. Incorrect. Multilingual labelling might help develop cultural competence as students appreciate other languages. However, it does not help create a home–school connection.

**3)** A. Incorrect. Shifting focus to a different skill would be a modification, not an accommodation. It represents a change in what the student is learning.

B. Incorrect. Excusing the student from participation in an activity altogether is a modification and not an accommodation.

C. Incorrect. If the student is learning the same things at the sensory table that other students are learning, but in a different way, this might be an accommodation. However, sensory tables are more developmentally appropriate in preschool classrooms than first-grade classrooms.

**D.** **Correct.** The student is still learning the same material, only in a different way.

**4)** A. Incorrect. This does not address Randy's disability directly.

B. Incorrect. Peer tutoring likely will not help Randy with recalling math facts, though it might help with other math skills.

**C.** **Correct.** This will allow Randy to complete the assignment with the aid of the fact table when he gets stuck on recalling a certain fact.

D. Incorrect. This is an assignment modification, not an accommodation.

**5)** A. Incorrect. This is likely not Ms. Hayes's choice to make, and we do not know whether Mark's academic giftedness warrants skipping the entirety of second grade.

B. Incorrect. Grouping would only help if the group worked on something other than addition and subtraction since Mark already knows those well.

**C. Correct.** Curriculum compacting would allow Mark to move on to new material while the rest of the class continues to learn about addition and subtraction.

D. Incorrect. Mark is likely acting out because he is bored, so using curriculum compacting is a more helpful solution than a behavioral-modification plan.

**6)** A. Incorrect. A research project is an enrichment activity that does not align with the teacher's goal to encourage Myra to grow in her artistic ability.

B. Incorrect. If Myra has already mastered the material, asking Myra to do more work at the same degree of difficulty as the other students is not productive, and it does not aid in her development.

**C. Correct.** Teaching Myra new skills will help her develop her artistic ability in new ways.

D. Incorrect. Having Myra teach other students will not directly help her to develop her own artistic ability.

# 3 Children's Literature and the Writing Process

## Emergent Literacy

### Language Acquisition

Language acquisition is the process through which humans develop the ability to understand and create words and sentences to communicate. Many experts believe that children have an innate ability to acquire **oral language** from their environment. Even before babies can speak, they cry and coo in reaction to environmental stimuli or to communicate their needs. They recognize basic variants in the speech patterns of those around them, such as articulation; they can also identify contrasts when exposed to new languages. This awareness, cooing, and crying quickly turn into **babbling**, the first stage of language acquisition. This stage generally lasts from six months to around twelve months. In this stage, infants make a variety of sounds but may begin to focus on sounds for which they receive positive reinforcement. For example, babbles such as *baba* and *yaya* tend to garner praise and excitement from parents, so these may be repeated until the coveted *mama* or *dada* is produced.

> DID YOU KNOW?
>
> Ninety-five percent of all babbling by babies throughout the world is composed of only twelve consonants: p, b, t, d, k, g, m, n, s, h, w, j.

At around one year old, but varying from child to child, children start using first words, generally nouns. During this single-word stage, or **holophrastic stage**, these solitary words are generally used to express entire ideas. For example, "Toy!" may mean "Give me the toy." After a few months, this shifts to two-word utterances such as "Mommy go" or "David bad." The **two-word stage** may last through early toddlerhood but generally gives rise to the **telegraphic phase** of oral language development at around age two and a half. In this stage, speech patterns become more advanced, though sometimes prepositions, articles, and other short words are missing. Telegraphic speech includes phrases such as "See plane go!" and "There go teacher." This stage persists until children are mostly fluent in the home language, generally at age three or four.

Like language, a child's journey to writing happens in phases and is heavily influenced by encouragement from parents, teachers, and caretakers. Writing development generally involves three areas:

1. conceptual knowledge (understanding the purpose of writing)
2. procedural knowledge (understanding how to form letters and words)
3. generative knowledge (using words to communicate a meaning)

Even children as young as two begin to draw pictures they use to communicate ideas—their first written representations. This develops into scribbling, which takes on a form more similar to letters. Wavy scribbling or mock handwriting may soon appear as children are exposed to print-rich home environments and classrooms. This emerges into forms that look like individual letters and then forms with actual letters that have some likeness to individual words strung together.

In the **transitional writing stage**, children begin writing letters with spaces in between, although real words are generally not yet being formed. Even in the transitional writing stage, however, many children can make successful attempts at copying letters and words from environmental sources. Writing a child's name or the name of a common classroom object on a card for a child to copy is a way to encourage transitional writing. Be mindful, however, that writing is still emergent, and children may invert letters or fail to make accurate copies of letters.

Table 3.1. Stages of Emergent Writing

| Stage | Example |
|---|---|
| Drawing |  |
| Scribbling |  |
| Wavy scribbles | 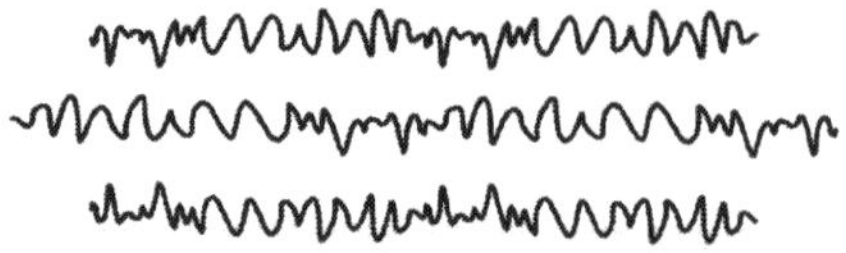 |
| Letter-like forms |  |

| Stage | Example |
|---|---|
| Letter strings | MPLITOHS |
| Transitional writing | JIO MPITE |
| Invented and phonetic spelling | MY NAM IS HANA |
| Word and phrase writing | DOG<br>PIG |
| Conventional spelling and sentences | HANNAH |

As children gain knowledge of sounds, they begin a phase of invented **spelling**. They start communicating words and ideas more clearly, though many words may be represented by only a beginning and ending sound. It is vital to understand this stage as a natural part of the process of emergent writing and allow children to express ideas and practice writing without an overemphasis on spelling errors. As children gain more knowledge of sounds and words, they will begin writing whole words, first with simple single-letter sound constructions such as *dog*, *hat*, and *fun*. This progresses to the correct spelling of more words and eventually the stringing together of words to make phrases and even short sentences.

Supporting a young child's oral language development is crucial in the classroom. Teachers can help build vocabulary through conversation, songs, and reading aloud to students. Songs and developmentally appropriate books can help reinforce new vocabulary through cadence and repetition. Teachers narrating their own actions ("Now, I am getting the lunch ready") and introducing students to new vocabulary ("This is a drum") through pictures or objects paired with language can help young students as they look to adults for exposure to new words and phrases.

Above all, early childhood educators must ensure their classrooms are rich in conversation and questions. The more adults speak to and ask open-ended questions of young students, the greater students' opportunities to grow in oral language skills.

Print-rich classrooms, full of labeled objects and centers, will help students grasp conceptual knowledge as they see writing used to convey meaning behind objects in their surroundings as well as generative knowledge if students are asked to help in the labeling of such objects. Having a writing center full of different writing implements and other artistic media will encourage students' procedural knowledge as they practice writing letters and words and build fine motor skills. Teachers modeling their own use of writing and providing many opportunities for writing practice throughout the day will aid in students' understanding of the communicative purpose of writing.

It is also vital to encourage frequent writing practice, even outside of explicit instruction. Students at a dramatic play center, for example, might be encouraged to use a notepad to write down a customer's order or a chalkboard to model a teacher giving a lesson. Above all, teachers should ensure that they are scaffolding children's learning to accommodate multiple stages of development happening in a single classroom.

### SAMPLE QUESTION

1) **During free-choice center time, a kindergarten teacher notices that one of her students has gone to the writing center, taken a piece of lined paper, and written several misspelled phrases. What should the teacher do?**

   A. explain the correct spelling of each word

   B. praise the student for the attempt and choosing to practice writing

   C. provide hand-over-hand guidance for the student to erase and rewrite the words

   D. target the student for more explicit spelling instruction

## Print Awareness

Print awareness involves a basic understanding of the nature of reading: that we read from left to right and top to bottom, and that we are reading words on a page. Very young children without solid print awareness may believe that meaning is gleaned from pictures on a page rather than words. Some younger children may understand that books convey meaning but may not quite know how. Teachers may see these children modeling reading a book upside down.

Key to print awareness are many **concepts of print**. These are the many underlying principles that must be mastered before learning to read. They include things such as knowledge and identification of a word, letter, and sentence; knowledge of the many uses of print; and knowledge of the overarching structure of a book or story (title, beginning, middle, end).

Many students have some print awareness through **environmental print**, or the words printed throughout their everyday environment. Environmental print includes product names, street signs, business names, menus at restaurants, and any other print that students encounter in the normal course of their lives. Teachers can use popular environmental print such as the names and logos of popular children's products, stores, and restaurants to encourage pre-readers to "read" these names. Teachers should also consider using environmental print in the classroom in each of the home languages of their students. For example, a teacher may label the door in English, Spanish, Thai, and Vietnamese. This builds confidence and familiarity and reinforces the idea that these words in languages other than English also have meaning.

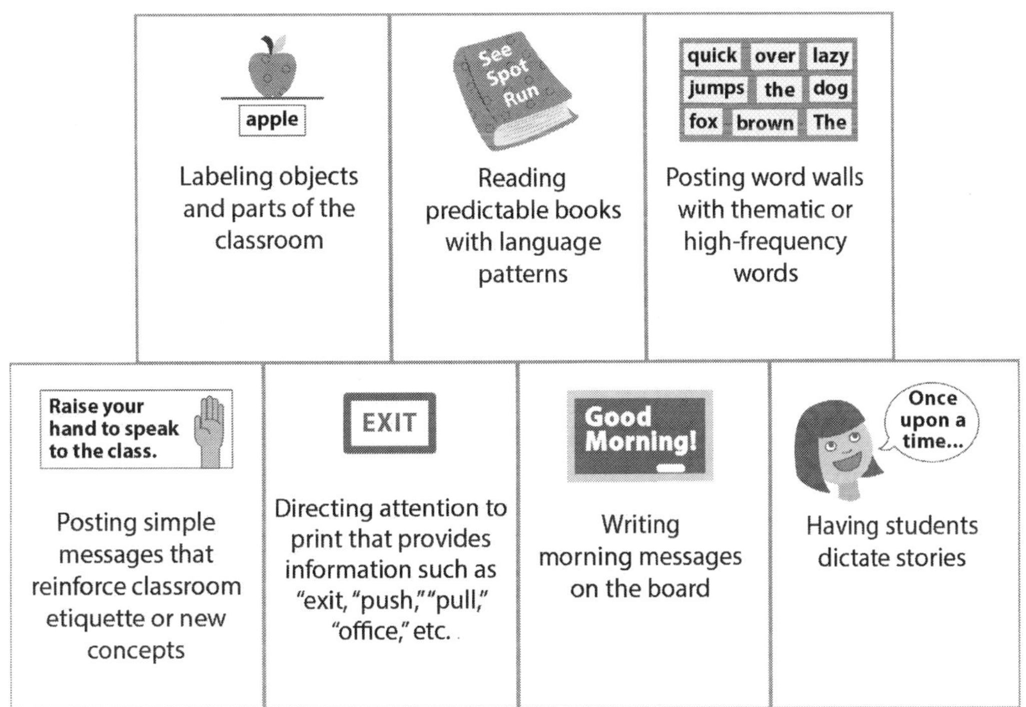


**Figure 3.1. Concepts of Print Classroom Strategies**

When working with young students, teachers should have students point to words on a page and also point to words (versus pictures) themselves during storybook reading since this will reinforce concepts of print and help students develop print awareness. This will help even very young students begin to understand that while both the pictures and words on the page contribute to the overall meaning, the part being read is the words, not the pictures.

## SAMPLE QUESTION

2) **Which of the following will help gauge a student's print awareness?**

A. asking a student to recount story events

B. asking a student to point to a sentence

C. asking a student to write the letter P

D. asking a student what sound P makes

## Phonological Development

**Phonological awareness** is the general ability to understand that within the structure of oral language, there are subparts. These parts include individual words; **syllables**, or units (typically containing a single vowel sound) within words; **onsets**, or the beginning consonant sounds of words (*sw*-im); and **rimes**, or the letters that follow (sw-*im*). Having phonological awareness is a crucial early stage in learning to read and write, and it can be fostered in the initial levels through singing songs and repeating rhyming words and phrases. Any activities or speech that seek to break language into component parts or that help establish an understanding of syllables, onsets, and rimes—"Would *Son*-ya come to circle time?" "Do you want a *c*-at or a *h*-at for your birthday?"—are good choices for helping students begin to recognize the parts within language.

HELPFUL HINT

Remember that onsets are the first part of the word, or the first "button" readers see—the ON button. Rimes are the parts of the word that rhyme such as c-*at*, h-*at*, b-*at*, and so on.

The **alphabetic principle** presumes an understanding that words are made up of written letters that represent spoken sounds. In order to proceed with more advanced reading concepts, children must first have a firm grasp of letter sounds. There is no firm rule on the pace at which the letter sounds should be mastered in their entirety, although most experts agree that those with the greatest frequency and those that will allow children to begin sounding out short words quickly should generally be introduced first. It is also sometimes easiest for children to master simple sounds—/t/ and /s/, for example—over more challenging or confusing sounds such as /b/, /d/, and /i/. Regardless of the way a curriculum breaks up practice with the alphabetic principle (a letter of the week or a teaching of the letters and sounds in rapid succession, etc.), teachers should recognize that repetition is key and students must be given multiple exposures to each letter and sound.

DID YOU KNOW?

The alphabet song was copyrighted in 1835 but is actually an adaptation of a Mozart melody.

**Phonemes** are distinct units of sound and are the basic units of language. There are twenty-six letters in the alphabet, and there is some agreement among researchers that there are at least forty-four phonemes in English—some letters represent different phonemes and some phonemes are made up of more than one letter. There are eighteen consonant phonemes such as /r/ and /t/, fifteen vowel phonemes such as /Ā/ and /oi/, six r-controlled vowels such as /Ä/, and five digraphs such as /ch/ and /sh/.

Table 3.2. Phoneme Chart

| Phoneme | Example | Phoneme | Example | Phoneme | Example |
|---|---|---|---|---|---|
| **Consonants** | | **Vowels** | | **R-Controlled Vowels** | |
| /b/ | bat | /a/ | lap | /ã/ | hair |
| /d/ | dog | /ā/ | late | /ä/ | art |
| /f/ | fish | /e/ | bet | /û/ | dirt |
| /g/ | goat | /ē/ | see | /ô/ | draw |
| /h/ | hat | /i/ | hit | /ēə/ | rear |
| /j/ | jump | /ī/ | ride | /üə/ | sure |
| /k/ | kick | /o/ | hop | **Diagrams/Digraphs** | |
| /l/ | laugh | /ō/ | rope | /zh/ | measure |
| /m/ | milk | /oo/ | look | /ch/ | chick |
| /n/ | no | /u/ | cut | /sh/ | shout |
| /p/ | pot | /ū/ | cute | /th/ | think |
| /r/ | rat | /y//ü/ | you | /ng | bring |
| /s/ | sit | /oi/ | oil | | |
| /t/ | toss | /ow/ | how | | |
| /v/ | vote | /ə/ (schwa) | syringe | | |
| /w/ | walk | | | | |
| /y/ | yak | | | | |
| /z/ | zoo | | | | |

**Phonemic awareness** refers to the knowledge of and ability to use these phonemes. This awareness generally does not come naturally, and students will need explicit instruction to master these skills. It is often best to differentiate instruction and work with students in smaller groups when working on phonemic awareness because proficiency levels may vary substantially.

Various activities can aid students in developing phonemic awareness. **Phoneme blending** involves students putting given sounds together to make words. To work on phoneme blending, teachers can say sounds and ask students what word is made: "I like /ch/ /ee/ /z/. What do I like? That's right, I like cheese." Teachers can also ask students to simply repeat or chorally repeat the sounds in words during circle time or storybook reading: "The car went vvvvv-rrrrr-oooo-m!"

HELPFUL HINT

Phoneme blending involves students blending sounds together like putting them in a blender to make a word. Phoneme segmentation involves students unblending, or segmenting, each sound like the segments of a worm.

**Phoneme segmentation** is generally the inverse of phoneme blending and involves students sounding out a word. Phoneme segmentation is important both for reading and spelling a word. More advanced phonemic awareness activities include **phoneme deletion**, in which a phoneme is removed to make a new word (e.g., ramp – /p/ = ram) and **phoneme substitution**, where one phoneme is changed to make a new word (e.g., fla/t/ to fla/p/).

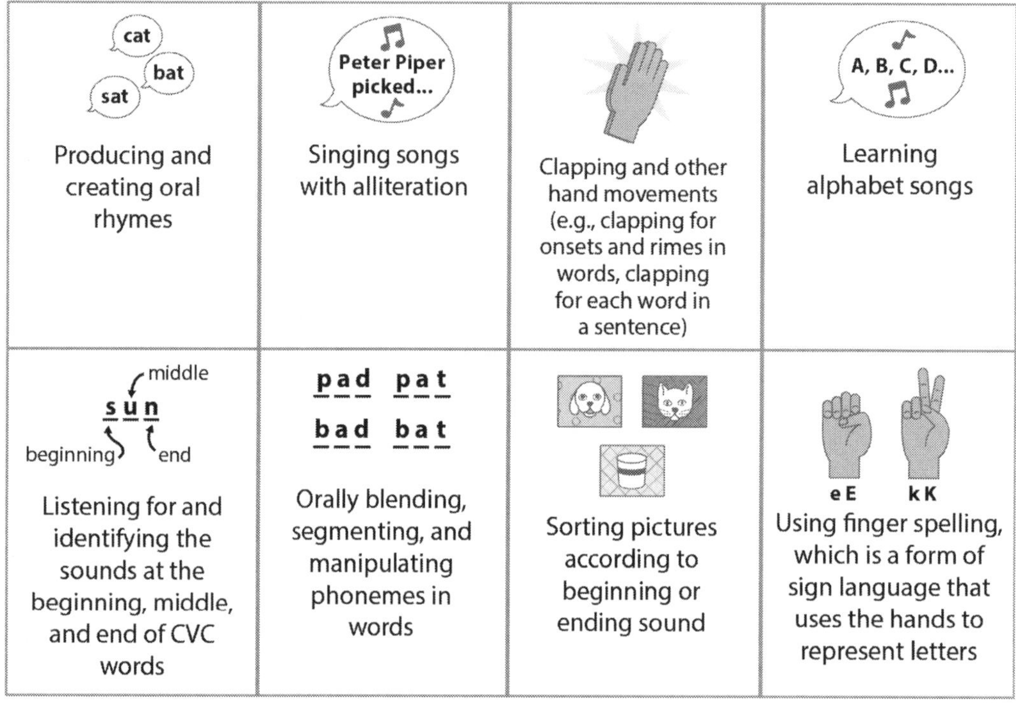


**Figure 3.2. Phonological Awareness Classroom Strategies**

Early childhood teachers should work on phonemic awareness with students in a variety of contexts. Having students manipulate language orally—"What word could I make if I took away the first letter of cow?"—and encouraging students in high-interest literacy activities in centers with alphabet boards, letter cards, alphabet sorters, and other manipulatives will provide multiple opportunities for students. Educators should also remember students will have varying backgrounds, skill levels, English language proficiencies, and possibly speech and language delays and hearing loss. Some students may need modifications for certain activities; this should be considered in the planning of inclusive activities.

## SAMPLE QUESTIONS

3) **Which activity would be most appropriate for students to practice onsets and the alphabetic principle?**

   A. sorting small animals into tubs based on the initial letter sound of the animal's name

   B. asking students to help clap out the syllables in a student's name

   C. asking students to point to a sentence on a page

   D. having students remove a sound from a word and say the new word

4) **Mark, a kindergartener, has mastered his letter sounds. He is sitting at the oral reading table with Ms. Hayes, who has him practice reading a short sentence. He gets stuck on the word *glad* and looks up at her. Which strategy might Ms. Hayes have Mark use?**

A. phoneme substitution

B. phoneme blending

C. phoneme segmentation

D. thinking of a rhyming word

# Foundational Reading Skills

## PHONICS

**Phonics** is an age-old strategy for helping students read by connecting written language to spoken language or by correlating certain sounds with certain letters or groups of letters. Seminal to phonics instruction is a subset of the alphabetic principle—**letter-sound correspondence**. This correspondence is simply the knowledge of a phoneme associated with a given letter. Letter-sound correspondence is a foundational skill for effective phonics instruction, as most phonics strategies will require students to draw rapidly on this memory bank of letter sounds. As previously mentioned, most strategies for introducing students to the letter sounds draw on **high-frequency letter-sound correspondence**, where the most frequent and useful letter sounds are taught first. This will allow students to begin reading as soon as possible without having to wait for mastery of each letter sound.

Phonics instruction draws on the strategy of **decoding**, or the ability to pronounce the sounds of written words orally and glean meaning. Because of its focus on the specific sound structures of words, phonics instruction tends to involve more explicit, direct instruction and is not without critics, who believe it overemphasizes the mechanics of reading while sacrificing the enjoyment. However, most classrooms today employ a combination approach that balances inquiry-based student learning, allowing for the open exploration of high-interest literacy games and activities, with more direct instruction when necessary. Teachers may have any number of mandated or suggested organizational structures for teaching decoding, such as centers balanced with a teacher-directed table or a mandatory computer-based phonics drill segment, but it is highly likely that whatever curriculum a program or school uses, it will contain some phonics component. This approach is proven to work for most students and is adaptable to a variety of student skill levels and special learning needs.

Some words are decodable, meaning they follow basic principles of phonics. These words can typically be sounded out effectively if basic structural deviations, like long vowel sounds with a word ending in –e, and various digraphs, where two letters make a single sound such as /th/ and /ay/, are mastered.

However, there are some words that deviate from basic sound structures and cannot be sounded out. These words must be presented to students with great frequency so they can simply be memorized. These words must become **sight words**, or words that require no decoding because they are instantly recognized and read automatically. It is recommended that some high-frequency decodable words, such as *and* and *get*, also be memorized by sight so as to increase reading rate and fluency. There are many lists of such words. The most popular is the Dolch Word List, which contains 315 words that are purported to be the most frequently used in English. Early childhood teachers might post some of these high-frequency words around the classroom for maximum exposure or encourage students to play games with sight word flashcards. Repetition will lead to mastery of these words and will help students read more quickly, fluently, and easily.

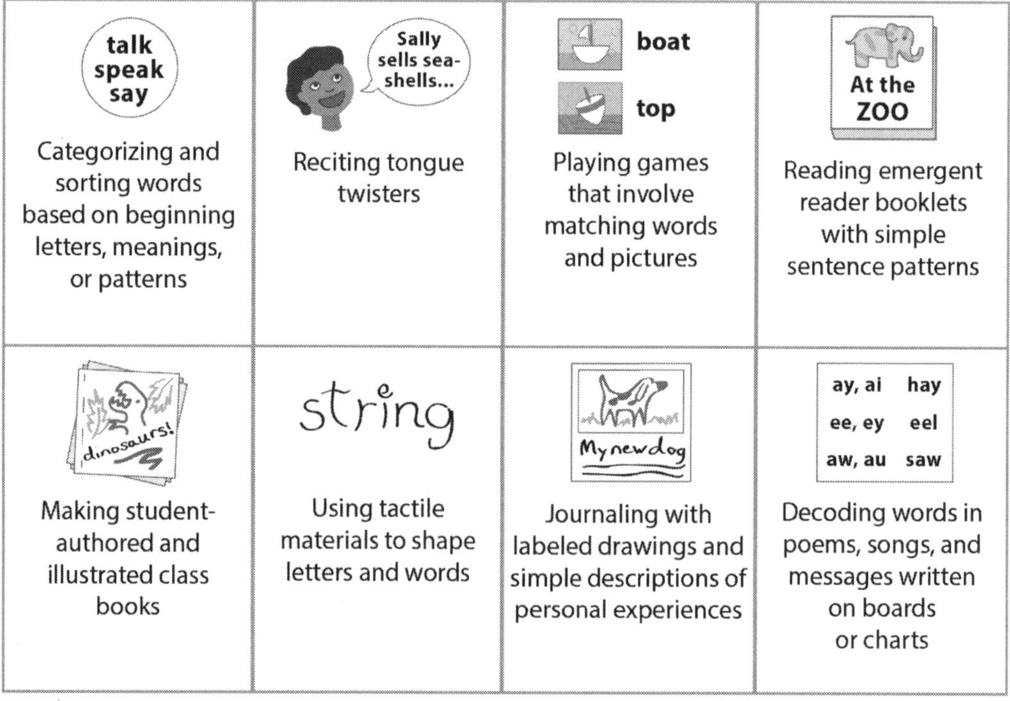


**Figure 3.3. Phonics Classroom Strategies**

Helping students practice phonics can involve a variety of strategies and activities, and these should always be developmentally appropriate for grade level and differentiated to accommodate students with varying needs and skills. English language learners will need additional practice with phonemes that are unique to English or simply not part of their home language. Students who come from a background with a language that does not use the Latin alphabet may need more background with the alphabetic principle than native speakers. Additionally, strategies such as visual cuing to indicate certain sounds may be needed to help hearing-impaired students master phonics.

Teachers may also need to provide extension and application activities for gifted students who may become bored with phonics study if they are already reading at a high level of proficiency. Frequently, these students can be accommodated within an existing lesson framework. For example, a teacher may aim for the bulk of her students to master two sight words per week from the Dolch list, but students who already know the whole list might practice spelling these words instead.

## SAMPLE QUESTION

5) **The word *elephant* is**

A. decodable.

B. a high-frequency word.

C. not composed of phonemes.

D. inappropriate for phonics instruction.

## FLUENCY

**Fluency** refers to the rate, accuracy, and expression of a piece when read. Fluency is an important measure of a student's reading development; lack of fluency will hamper overall comprehension as well as enjoyment of reading. Reading **rate** is a measure of speed and is generally calculated in words per minute. **Accuracy,** or the correct decoding of words, is generally entwined with rate when measuring fluency, as reading quickly but incorrectly is not desirable.

While fluency is not limited to oral reading, it is virtually impossible to assess fluency during silent reading, and most educators rely on frequent oral reading assessments to help determine student progress. While several standard measures exist, one of the most researched is the Hasbrouck-Tindal oral reading fluency chart. This chart is designed to measure progress over the course of the school year and from grade to grade and compares students in percentiles with their peers on a scale of words read correctly per minute. It is important to remember that all students will develop fluency on a different timeline, and assessments of fluency are most accurate when they are developmentally appropriate and when they are not presented as high-stakes testing situations.

In addition to rate and accuracy, **prosody**, or the overall liveliness and expressiveness of reading, is also a skill to nurture in students. Prosody may involve appropriate pauses and various changes in pitch and intonation based on punctuation and the overall meaning of the piece. Developing prosody in students should involve a combination of modeling by teachers—as they read stories, passages, and even directions aloud—and giving students plenty of opportunities for oral reading practice.

Educators may find it challenging to find time for oral reading assessment in the classroom as they balance multiple priorities. However, teachers must make time to listen to all students, regardless of grade level, read aloud with regularity. While examining written work and performance on independent or group practice activities may give some indication of a student's overall development, to get the fullest picture teachers must gather as much data as possible. Assessing student fluency through oral reading is seminal to an overall understanding of a particular student's learning situation.

Fluency is highly correlated with comprehension because students who struggle to read and decode individual words will have difficulty comprehending entire sentences and paragraphs. Additionally, students who read at a very slow rate may have trouble recalling what they have read. It is well worth the time investment to listen to students read aloud as much as possible.

SAMPLE QUESTION

6) **A second-grade teacher notices that his students often read in monotone during oral reading practice. Which strategy would best help his students develop prosody?**

A. setting aside timed oral reading each day

B. modeling an appropriate reading rate

C. using ability grouping for silent reading

D. having students act out a play from a script

# Literature and Informational Texts

## Genres

It is important that students of all ages be exposed to a wide variety of texts. **Informational texts**, or **nonfiction texts**, are texts about the world around us and generally do not use characters to convey information. Science and social studies texts fall into this category. These informational texts are often structured in such a way to organize information in a format that is accessible and meaningful to students.

As part of an introduction to different types of texts, a teacher might ask elementary-aged students to analyze elements of their textbooks or workbooks. Do they have bold headings to help the reader understand when new ideas are being introduced? Do they have **sidebars** to give readers additional information alongside the main body of text?

In contrast, **literary texts**, or **fiction texts**, are usually stories made up by the author. While they may contain true elements or be based on actual events, they usually include plenty of elements designed to keep and capture the reader's interest. They generally have **characters**, which may be real or imagined people, animals, or creatures, and a **plot**, or sequence of story events. The **setting** of fiction texts may be any time or place past, present, future, real, or imagined. While teachers may put a lot of focus on short stories that are highly accessible for young students, it is also important to expose children to other genres so that students get comprehension practice with texts that are unfamiliar at first.

In **drama**, most of the story is centered around dialogue between characters. They are usually separated into segments like chapters known as **acts** and smaller subsegments (generally with a consistent setting) known as **scenes**. Using drama in the classroom is a great way to get students interested in different types of texts. Consider setting up a simple **stage** in a kindergarten or elementary classroom as a natural outgrowth of a dramatic play center sometimes found in preschool classrooms. Building on students' innate curiosity and imagination, the possibilities are endless. Acting out dramas not only helps students work on expressive reading (prosody), but it also reinforces social and emotional learning as students analyze the emotions and actions of characters.

While poetry may be associated with older children, even young students can appreciate and recognize **rhyme**. Poetry with rhyme can help reinforce phonological awareness and is a natural outgrowth of many young children's love of song. **Meter**—or the rhythm, or beat, of the poem—can also be used to engage young students with different texts as a beat can be clapped to, stomped to, or even danced to! Many timeless books for children—such as *One Fish, Two Fish, Red Fish, Blue Fish* and *Each Peach Pear Plum*—have both rhyme and meter and give young children exposure to poetry. Young writers may even begin to write simple poems with one or two **stanzas**, or groups of **lines** similar to paragraphs. Students should be encouraged to recognize and create their own rhyming words as an additional outgrowth of phonological awareness. Asking students to name all the words they can think of that rhyme with dog, for example, will allow for continued practice with rhymes.

**The structural elements of literature** such as characters, setting, conflict, plot, resolution, point of view, and theme can be introduced alongside other literacy activities, even with students who are pre-readers. Consider bringing these elements into guided storybook sessions while asking questions such as:

- "Who are the characters on this page?" (characters)
- "Where does this story happen?" (setting)
- "Why was __________mad/happy/worried, etc.?" (conflict/plot)
- "What happened after______?" and "How was (problem) fixed?" (conflict/plot/resolution)

Although **point of view**, or the perspective from which the story is told (first person, *I, we*; third person, *he, she, it*, or *they*; sometimes second person, *you*), may be harder for very young students to grasp, teachers can begin introducing the basic concept of differing points of view by reading the **narrator's** part in one voice and each different character in a different voice and encouraging students to do the same. For older students, second-person point of view can be practiced by reading and writing letters: to other students, the teacher, or administrators or other school personnel.

## SAMPLE QUESTIONS

**7) Which of the following is an example of an activity that might be used with students to introduce informational texts?**

A. having students locate fiction books at the school library

B. having students examine the way their social studies textbook is organized

C. having students answer questions from different points of view

D. asking students questions about different characters in a story

**8) Which sentence is written in the third-person point of view?**

A. Harriet likes to go fishing on the weekends, though she has never caught anything.

B. I generally enjoy reading a variety of literature types, but I like historical fiction the best.

C. We need to determine the type of problem before we can think about solving it.

D. You really must stop calling me at all hours of the night; you are not being considerate.

## Key Ideas and Details

As students progress in their literacy and are able to decode longer passages with some consistency, by the second and third grade the focus will shift to the **comprehension** of many different types of passages. However, even students still practicing decoding and very young pre-readers can be given ample opportunities to explore the **central**, or main, **idea** of a story and make predictions about what might happen next. Questions such as "What was this book about?" and "What do you think character X will do next?" will help students make predictions and **summarize** or condense the main elements of a story.

As the stories read to students become more complex and as students begin reading their own stories, other literary elements can be introduced. Students of all ages generally enjoy stories with **themes**, or topics, to which they can relate or are already exploring. Integrated curriculums, or those that structure several cross-curricular units around a central theme, are popular in many early childhood and some lower elementary settings.

Even without a formal daily or weekly theme in the classroom, teachers can help students make connections by integrating texts from other domains such as science and social studies into literacy activities. For example, a unit on conservation might feature a story that includes a **moral**, or lesson, about the importance of conserving natural resources. Teachers might even encourage students to further explore their own interests and create their own integrated literary experiences by selecting and reading multiple works centered on a theme of their choosing.

Teachers may have students recall important **details** from a text or **analyze** the structure of a piece. Is it a narrative that tells a story, a description of something, or an essay designed to persuade? Can students make **inferences**, or logical conclusions, based on the text? Making inferences is an important skill in developing overall comprehension as it allows students to go deeper than the literal meaning and make conclusions based on previously obtained knowledge and experiences. Whenever teachers ask students to make an inference based on a text, they should be sure to ask them to support their inference with evidence. "How do you know this?" "What made you think this?" "Which part of the story/passage made you think this?" are all good follow-up questions for inferring activities.

As students advance in their comprehension skills, it is also important to ensure that students know that sometimes we all make faulty inferences and that we must constantly evaluate whether we are projecting our own beliefs and experiences onto a text that lacks support for a conclusion we drew. This foundational skill of making sound conclusions from texts will be the base upon which several future higher-level skills, such as identifying bias and providing counterpoints to an argument, will rest.

It is also highly worthwhile that students comprehend images embedded in texts. This helps students get the most from informational texts like textbooks and informational websites or educational software. Pointing out and helping students understand how visual elements promote a greater understanding of concepts or ideas that the author is trying to convey will help students be cognizant of these important elements that exist alongside text. Images can also aid struggling readers to decode. While students should not be reliant on pictures, most texts for young readers include ample images to aid in students' overall understanding and enjoyment, and these should be pointed out and discussed when appropriate.

### SAMPLE QUESTION

9) **John, a second-grade student, has an assignment to read a paragraph from his social studies textbook and write a sentence that states the central idea. What can John's teacher do to help him with this task?**

   A. ask John what he liked about what he read

   B. ask John to list all the details

   C. go over key vocabulary with John

   D. ask John what he thought was most important

## ORGANIZATIONAL STRUCTURES OF TEXT

Authors organize information in such a way as to get their point across as clearly as possible. They tend to use a text structure that suits their purpose. This structure may be a **sequence** of events, such as a news story recounting the days leading up to an important event, or a thorough **description** of something, as in the opening pages of a novel, which might describe the main character in finite detail.

Many historical texts are written in a **cause-and-effect** pattern where the cause is presented first and the result is discussed next. A chapter in a social studies text about the Industrial Revolution, for example, may follow this pattern as the Industrial Revolution is cited as the cause for a change in working and living conditions in many cities.

Other works may be organized in a **problem-solution structure**. This might be taught through a collaborative activity where students identify a problem in the classroom, school, or community and then write a letter to a decision maker outlining both the nature of the issue and a possible solution.

Students could also be challenged to **compare and contrast** or explain how two things from their everyday experience are similar and different. Charts and other visual/graphic organizers can help students organize their thoughts. A teacher may ask students, for example, what the differences and similarities are between first and second grade. This might even lead to a persuasive writing assignment about this topic.

While reading nonfiction texts is important, inciting a love of reading is often best accomplished through multiple exposures to high-interest fiction, both classic and contemporary. In order to facilitate deep comprehension of these narratives, teachers can help students understand key elements through a **plot diagram**. This graphic organizer helps students identify the **exposition**, or beginning, of the story, which sets up the reader for what is to come by describing the time, place, and main characters. The plot organizer will then help students move into the primary problem driving the story, or the **conflict**, and the **rising action**, or sequence of events leading to the eventual **climax**, or turning point, which is the apex of the diagram. The curve slopes sharply downward as the **falling action**, or results of the climax, unfolds. The diagram closes with the final **resolution**, or ending of the story. It is important to impart to students that the resolution might not always be happy, but all stories do have one.

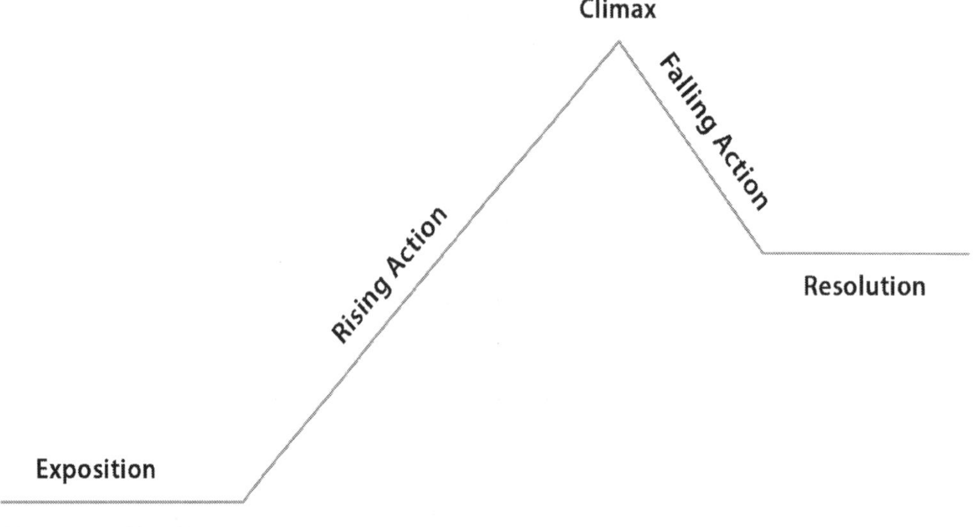


**Figure 3.4. Plot Diagram**

Introducing the plot diagram is easiest when students already have some background with a story. Teachers may draw on a popular children's movie or fairy tale to introduce these elements. If students are not struggling to comprehend a new text while being introduced to these elements, the understanding will likely come more quickly. Timeless stories with plots that students know by heart are ideal for an initial exploration of the plot diagram.

SAMPLE QUESTION

10) **Ms. Jones wants to introduce her first-grade students to new types of text structures they have not seen before. Which activity would best meet her goal?**

  A. ask students to go to the library and explain the different sections

  B. bring in magazines, pamphlets, newspapers, and other items for students to explore

  C. have students compare and contrast two different storybook characters they have read about

  D. divide students into groups and have them create a plot diagram about their favorite movie

## Point of View

A teacher may refer students to an evil character in a story they have just read or that the class has read together. "Why don't you like this character?" the teacher might query. The initial answers will generally be limited to the actions of said character and what he or she did or did not do that led to the story's conflict. The teacher might then remind students that the character is a creation of the author, so the real reason they like or dislike a character has to do with **point of view**, the perspective the author takes toward a character or subject. It is most likely the author's description, or point of view toward given characters, that makes students like or dislike them.

A discussion of point of view may begin to extend to the structural elements such as first person (author as narrator and generally protagonist), second person (author speaking directly to the reader), and third person (author uses third-person pronouns such as he, she, it, etc.). Teachers might help students associate certain pronouns with certain points of view but should keep in mind the developmental appropriateness of such exercises per the specific student population. It may be more appropriate to ask very young students questions like "Who told the story?" and "What was (character name) like?" to begin to introduce these concepts.

Point of view may also impact the reader's perspective of a text in its conveyance or non-conveyance of information. With first-person point of view, for example, the reader may empathize heavily with the protagonist's perspective because the reader feels that he or she knows the narrator well. Above all, the perspective the reader holds toward a character, setting, topic, or situation will heavily impact the way he or she perceives a work. Because of this, it is vital that students begin to differentiate between their own point of view, colored by their unique perspective, and that which is explicitly stated in the text. This is especially important in integrating literacy with socioemotional learning because we want students to be able to appreciate the myriad perspectives on a given issue or subject and understand that their own point of view may be one of many. Teachers can facilitate a discussion of this by asking students who their favorite or least favorite character in a piece was. Ideally, there will be divergent opinions, and this is an excellent opportunity to explain the ways in which many people can read the same story and have a different point of view.

SAMPLE QUESTION

11) **Some students in a kindergarten class are having trouble sharing classroom supplies. Which literacy activity might help students appreciate others' point of view?**

A. reading a story about a character who has to go without what he needs and asking students how they felt about the character

B. having students write a paragraph on how they can do a better job in sharing classroom supplies

C. asking students to distinguish between their flawed point of view and the point of view of the classroom rules, which are always correct

D. reading a fairy tale to students and asking them if they identify more with the evil or good characters

## Integrating Written, Visual, and Oral Information

Most children's earliest experiences with reading are with **picture books**. Timeless titles such as *Have You Seen My Duckling?* and *Pancakes for Breakfast* can be appreciated by young children and their parents alike, and being read to from a young age is positively associated with future interest in reading. Picture books help young children engage in "pretend reading" by recounting a story from memory or using a picture book to "read" to a sibling or parent. It is important that educators avoid relegating picture books to the discard pile too early or chide children for their enjoyment of **graphic novels**. Graphics have a place in enhancing interest and comprehension of texts and are prevalent in much of the written media that is consumed in daily life. In fact **visual** literacy, or the ability to comprehend visual texts, is an important predecessor to being able to comprehend more sophisticated written works.

DID YOU KNOW?

Reading to children has a strong correlation to future achievement. According to PISA (Program for International Student Assessment) results from fourteen countries, students whose parents read books to them during the first year of school averaged fourteen points higher on a reading assessment taken at age fifteen.

Teachers may use many types of **multimedia presentations** in the classroom, for example, Power Point, a Smartboard, or a simple white board. Adding visuals to aid in student understanding is important and may help students who process information most easily when it is presented visually. While long lectures are certainly not developmentally appropriate in an early childhood classroom, teachers might project images to use as a springboard for a discussion or writing prompt. Teachers may have elementary students create their own multimedia presentations on a story they have read or have preschool students use a tablet to record a scene they create using toy dinosaurs.

Many preschool classrooms have routine recordings of various **staged** productions as a natural outgrowth of the happenings at the dramatic play center. **Oral presentations** can also be excellent additions to the classroom routine and are easiest when students present about something they know; this generally takes the form of show and tell. In this way teachers can help students begin to process information coming from a variety of sources, both auditory and visual.

It is important that teachers help students compare multiple sources of information. They may take students to see a stage play based on a story the class read or show the film version or play an audio recording of a book. This helps students understand that visual and auditory information may not always match what the mind imagines from reading a story. The characters may look or sound different or the setting may be far from what was imagined.

Teachers might also help students compare multiple texts that seek to convey the same information. For example, one great activity might be to bring in a newspaper article in plain black and white font and have students compare it with an elaborately illustrated magazine article on the same topic. This helps reinforce the role of visual aids in understanding and may even prompt a discussion on the appeal of different types of texts to different audiences, as some readers may prefer the brevity and simplicity of the newspaper article.

Teachers will also want to draw students toward a comprehension of various visual elements embedded in their everyday texts, such as charts and tables in textbooks and on websites and even nutritional information on food packaging. It is essential that literacy is viewed as a complete capability to access written information and that activities be tailored to ensure students have multiple opportunities to practice understanding information presented in many different ways.

## SAMPLE QUESTION

**12) Mr. Johnson has a class of kindergarteners who are learning about using visual information to convey ideas. Which literacy activity might he integrate into a science unit on bugs?**

A. have students read multiple books on this topic and give oral reports to the class

B. have students go outside and find as many bugs as they can

C. split the students into groups and have them write a story in which a bug is the main character

D. have students create a bug picture book and present it to the class

## Text Complexity

Finding a balance between the complexity of a text and an individual student's current level of literacy development can be challenging. Many programs recognize this challenge and structure goal setting and student assessments in a growth-over-time approach. Regardless of the milestones laid out by a school or district, teachers should always aim for students to tackle ever more sophisticated texts as they develop the foundational skills they need to take on new challenges. However, this does not mean to push students beyond what they can decode. Giving students developmentally inappropriate texts may lead to a denigration of confidence and a lack of interest and enthusiasm for reading.

Many factors contribute to a text's complexity. Before determining appropriateness, texts should be evaluated qualitatively, quantitatively, and per their match to the reader. Quantitative measurements include anything for which a number can be calculated, such as **word frequency**, length of words and **sentence length**, average syllables per word, and so on. These quantitative calculations may result in a range or score being allotted to a text. The most popular of these is that calculated by MetaMetrics, a company that uses word frequency and sentence length in an equation that yields a score. MetaMetrics assigns scores to both readers and texts. Those assigned to readers typically come from standardized tests and measure a student's current level of reading ability; these are called reader measures.

MetaMetrics also assigns **Lexile ranges** to texts called Lexile test measures. While these ranges do not have a direct correlation to grade level in the strictest sense, charts can be used to glean the typical ranges for a given grade. The company purports that the best results come when the reader measure falls within a "sweet spot" range per the text measure.

More than likely, much of what students read (textbooks, passages in software programs, published children's literature) has already been assigned a Lexile text measure. Teachers can raise students' chances of enjoyment and comprehension of texts by ensuring that the Lexile text measure fits within the average range for the grade level and, more importantly, for the individual student's reader measure.

There are, of course, other metrics for measuring the readability of a text. Scales such as the Flesch-Kincaid Grade Level, the Gunning-Fog Index, and the SMOG index may also provide text analytics. A specific program or school may also use another proprietary tool such as Accelerated Reader Book Finder or Scholastic Book Levels.

Beyond the quantitative measures determined by Lexile and others are qualitative measures such as the layout of the text (illustrations, text size), the overall text **structure** (simple narrative chronology, more advanced argumentative essay), **sentence structure** (prevalence of simple or more complex sentences), **levels of meaning** (whether ideas are explicitly or implicitly communicated), and **knowledge**

**demand** (the cultural knowledge or other ideas that the reader must already know). The overall language and **vocabulary** of the text also generally fall under qualitative measures, although some quantitative scales measure the frequency of vocabulary with which students of a particular age or grade are unlikely to be familiar.

Table 3.3. Lexile Reader and Text Measures for Early Childhood

| **Grade** | **Reader Measures, Midyear**<br>***25th to 75th Percentile***<br>This is the typical range of reading ability for students in each grade. These measures are designed to help compare a student's level to a typical range; they are not intended to be standards. There are no reader measures for kindergarten students. Rather, text measures are descriptive of what is most appropriate for most kindergarten readers. | **Text Measures**<br>These text measures have been revised from previous measures to better align with the Common Core State Standards for English Language Arts to ensure that students will meet these standards and be "college and career ready" by the end of high school. |
|---|---|---|
| K | --- | BR40L to 230L |
| 1 | BR120L to 295L | 190L to 530L |
| 2 | 170L to 545L | 420L to 650L |
| 3 | 415L to 760L | 520L to 820L |

No singular measure of any text is sufficient to determine appropriateness for all students. Consider, for example, that Lexile ranges do not take into account the prevalence of mature subject matter and that overall appropriateness must always be considered. Teachers should also always keep in mind the need to differentiate literacy instruction in the classroom. The early childhood years present students with a wide range of previous pre-reading experiences, and educators often find themselves in classrooms of students with a vast array of reading abilities. While literacy development requires the reading of more and more complex texts, it does students little good to be constantly presented with inaccessible reading material. In fact, this can lead to the development of bad habits such as guessing at or skipping unfamiliar words instead of making a conscious effort to decode and waiting for the help of a teacher before confidently trying an unfamiliar word or text.

Whatever strategy a given program employs to address individualization of reading instruction (pull-out, push-in, small groups, intervention teacher, etc.), teachers must strive to find a just-right level of text complexity where students are challenged but not frustrated. Teachers must also rely on their own judgment and knowledge of their students alongside any formal tools used to help measure text complexity.

SAMPLE QUESTION

13) **Which of the following is the best way to differentiate instruction in a first-grade reading classroom?**

A. practice oral reading only with the more advanced students so those struggling will not feel uncomfortable

B. use only texts on the lower end of the first-grade Lexile range to ensure they are accessible to all students

C. set aside time for students to engage in silent reading with a teacher-selected book based on student ability and interests

D. conduct additional phonics drills with the students who need help with decoding while the other students do a science experiment

# Writing

## Developmental Stages of Writing

In their overall plan for developing literacy in students, teachers should give students plenty of opportunities to practice writing alongside reading and analyzing texts. It is important to ensure conscious writing instruction and practice as research suggests that this is sometimes an overlooked component of early childhood literacy curriculum. Some studies even suggest that many pre-kindergarten and kindergarten students spend less than three minutes a day on writing practice.

Learning to write involves three distinct and previously mentioned components: conceptual knowledge, procedural knowledge, and generative knowledge. In helping young students develop conceptual knowledge of writing, teachers should focus on activities that show students the link between print and its intended purpose. Environmental print is a great resource for helping students develop this knowledge as teachers point out classroom signs and posters or those in the school building and on the playground. They can further build early conceptual knowledge by having students **draw** or **scribble** to communicate their own feelings and ideas.

QUICK REVIEW

What are concepts of print? How can teachers encourage print awareness in their classrooms?

Procedural knowledge involves the nuts and bolts of writing. Procedural knowledge-building activities are those that build awareness of basic letter formation, the knowledge that words are made up of letters, the knowledge that words have spaces between them, and the overall mechanics of writing. Procedural knowledge and the alphabetic principle are entwined, and the letter sounds and names should be reinforced when consciously instructing correct letter formation.

Additionally, procedural knowledge of writing will coincide with the development of fine motor skills. Fine motor skills development in the classroom cannot be overemphasized, particularly in a preschool or kindergarten setting. As in any part of emergent literacy, teachers will have students with widely divergent levels of fine motor proficiency. It is essential the classroom provides a variety of opportunities for students to build these skills through the use of manipulatives such as alphabet boards and puzzles and a variety of writing implements such as crayons, markers, and pencils.

The mechanics of writing will generally involve explicit spelling instruction, and this will likely be part of a program's curriculum. It is important to view spelling as part of a developmental continuum and not overemphasize correct spelling too early when preschool students are still forming mock letters or letter strings. However, a standard **continuum of spelling** can be referenced to tailor spelling instruction appropriate to grade level while always keeping in mind the differing developmental levels within the classroom.

### Table 3.4. Continuum of Spelling

| | |
|---|---|
| By the end of first grade, most students should be able to correctly spell short words with . . . | short vowel sounds with a consonant-verb-consonant (cat, dog, pin) pattern [CVC]<br>vowel-consonant pattern (up, egg) and [VC]<br>simple consonant-vowel pattern (go, no) [CV]<br>consonant blends and digraphs in simple and high-frequency words (chat, that) [CCVC] |
| By the end of second grade, most students should be spelling words with . . . | final consonant blends (rant, fast, bend, link) [CVCC]<br>regular long vowel patterns (ride, tube) [CVC]<br>double consonant endings (lick, fuss)<br>more complex long vowel patterns (suit, fail)<br>r-controlled vowels (near, bear, hair, are) |
| By the end of third grade, most students should be able to spell words with . . . | diphthongs (coil, soon, enjoy, wow)<br>soft g's and c's (dice, hedge)<br>short vowel patterns (head, sought)<br>silent consonants (tomb, known, gnaw, wrote)<br>advanced digraphs and blends (phase, character, whose)<br>contractions<br>soft g's and c's (dice, hedge)<br>short vowel patterns (head, sought)<br>silent consonants (tomb, known, gnaw, wrote)<br>advanced digraphs and blends (phase, character, whose)<br>contractions<br>two-syllable words<br>compound words<br>words with suffixes that show number or degree (fastest, foxes) |

Table 3.4. Continuum of Spelling (continued)

| | |
|---|---|
| By the end of third grade, most students should be able to spell words with . . . | special spelling rules such as doubling the final letter on CVC words when adding certain suffixes (napping, saddest) |

Explicit spelling instruction will generally begin with simple consonant-vowel-consonant (CVC) patterns and progress as students learn new phonics structures. Practice with homophones, or words that have the same pronunciation but a different spelling and meaning, should begin in third grade, or sooner for some students. Common homophones include there/their/they're, *to/two/too*, and so on. It is important to point out to students that software applications that might detect spelling errors in other words often fail to pick up on spelling errors with homophones, so students should be extra vigilant when editing and revising writing containing these words.

It is also important to balance more explicit spelling practice with time to allow students to practice the third part of emergent writing, generative knowledge. In this domain students learn to write for a purpose that goes beyond simply forming a word and other mechanical concerns. While preschool students may not be able to write their own stories, teachers at this level can still give students practice by having them dictate a story that the teacher writes for them and perhaps even reads back to the class.

As students master more of the procedural knowledge of writing, they can begin generating more pieces on their own. Students generally progress from writing letter strings and word-like structures under a picture they have drawn to writing and spelling simple words to constructing sentences to constructing stories. It is important that the communicative purpose of each be emphasized to help students construct the generative knowledge of writing. A teacher might ask, for example, a student to talk about his or her picture and include an explanation of the letter strings underneath. The student has likely included them to describe or name the picture.

SAMPLE QUESTION

**14) Which word has a CVC pattern?**

A. gap

B. onto

C. drink

D. and

## Types of Writing

Once students are generating their own written pieces, it is prudent to expose them to different types of writing both as readers and writers. **Expository** writing is usually used to inform readers or give a description and may be anything from a recipe in a cookbook to a paragraph in a science or social studies textbook. Expository writing may also be highly **descriptive**, using many rhetorical techniques to describe a person, place, societal problem, or any topic of interest. **Persuasive** writing usually presents an argument and attempts to convince the reader of a certain perspective on the issue. In contrast to expository writing, **narrative** writing tells a story.

Students are primarily exposed to narrative texts in the preschool and early elementary years, and they may be somewhat unfamiliar with other rhetorical techniques. Teachers might introduce descriptive writing by reading a few sentences in a product advertisement and having students imagine what the item is like before showing them the ad. They might then have students write their own description of something they find on the playground or the school cafeteria. Practice with persuasive writing can be particularly engaging. Students might write about a subject of personal interest, for instance a letter to the principal to convince her to allow pets at school, or even a letter to a teacher to persuade him to stop assigning homework!

Students should also practice identifying the rhetorical conventions used in types of literature they encounter. Is a sidebar on a science worksheet attempting to persuade students to recycle? Is a paragraph in a story giving a detailed description of a place? Pointing these things out and engaging students in analyzing the intended purpose of everything they read and write will help them appreciate the need for multiple types of writing.

### SAMPLE QUESTION

**15) Mr. Dale's third-grade student Sarah is working on a short descriptive paragraph describing her physical appearance. Sarah is having trouble generating ideas for her writing. Which of the following questions could Mr. Dale propose to help Sarah?**

A. What do you want to write about?

B. What color is your hair?

C. How many red shirts do you have?

D. What do you want to persuade readers about?

## THE AUTHORING CYCLE

Students should understand that writing is a process and that even professional writers go through several phases before their finished product is released. This **authoring cycle** generally includes several phases in which ideas are transformed into written form to effectively communicate meaning. Students first need to **brainstorm** ideas. This can take many forms, and teachers might have the entire class generate ideas for writing topics and record them on the board or screen as an initial step.

Students can then create their own webs or **outlines** to organize their ideas. This initial planning can help students organize their overall point and supporting details. These activities can be based on a book they have read, where they take a stance on the work (e.g., "I liked the book," "I did not like the book," "My favorite/least favorite part was...") and then list the reasons why or why not. Students might also write a simple expository piece in which they introduce an overall topic and then use supporting details to inform the reader. Brainstorming activities can also help students organize the events they wish to recount when writing narratives.

After the brainstorming is complete, students draft their piece and link their ideas together with an introductory statement, support, and concluding section or statement. With scaffolding, students must then go through a **revision** and **editing** process in which they strengthen their piece through the addition of more supporting details and connecting words (because, also, then) and proofread for capitalization, end marks, and spelling.

Teachers may aid students in the revision process by providing a simple checklist to help students ensure they have met certain criteria. One simple revision checklist is the **COPS** mnemonic. This stands for **C**apitalization, **O**rganization, **P**unctuation, and **S**pelling and is used with success in many early elementary classrooms. Teachers may also employ peer and/or teacher feedback as part of the overall revision process. Receiving feedback helps reinforce that the overarching purpose of writing is to communicate ideas, so the perceptions and suggestions of multiple readers must be taken into account when revising a piece.

Students should also **publish** their work after the final copy is created, particularly if the writing project was significant in scope. Having students read their work aloud is one simple and immediate way to publish a piece, as is posting it on a classroom or school bulletin board. Teachers may have students organize and bind their work into a simple book with string or brads or collect student work into a class-wide literary sampler.

If a teacher uses student portfolios in the classroom, he or she may have students prepare their piece for inclusion into a digital or physical folder. This may involve transcribing the piece digitally, adding illustrations, or matting it on construction paper. Teachers should also emphasize to students that seminal to the idea of publishing is sharing the work with others. This is a great way to build a home–school connection while encouraging students to share their work with parents. Teachers should also show student work samples or portfolios at parent conferences to further build the home–school connection.

## SAMPLE QUESTION

**16) Which option is NOT a way to publish student writing?**

A. hosting a poetry night where students read their work aloud

B. submitting a student-authored essay to a writing contest

C. asking students to type their piece on the computer

D. having students trade a bound book they have created with a friend to read and enjoy

## CHARACTERISTICS OF EFFECTIVE WRITING

As students revise and examine their own writing and that of others, they should be mindful of what makes written communication effective. Above all, successful writing that communicates well has a central **focus**, or main idea. Brainstorming and other prewriting activities can help students maintain focus as they plan a piece. While much of the professional writing to which students are exposed will already be thoroughly edited to ensure a consistent focus, asking students to identify the author's focus across a broad range of texts is a solid strategy that spans capacity building in both reading and writing capability. Additionally, students should identify how the author uses details, examples, and other support as part of overall **concept development**. Students should be critical of how authors support their arguments and whether the evidence is sufficient. This can then be parlayed toward a critical reflection of their own writing and whether they have adequately proven a point.

A knowledge of basic text **organization** will also help students become critical readers and effective writers. While there are many text organizational structures, most effective writing has an introduction, several supporting details organized in a logical sequence, and a conclusion that wraps up the focus of the piece. Having students practice labeling these parts in various texts is an effective strategy, but simply pointing out the beginning, middle, and end of a story can introduce even very young children to the idea of text organization. As students edit and revise their own work, they should pay heed to their own organization of ideas to ensure that the reader will be able to follow a logical pattern in which the information is presented.

> QUICK REVIEW
>
> What are the steps in the authoring cycle?

Each piece of writing also has a unique **style**, or approach. Style can describe the author's choice of words. Style also includes sentence and paragraph structure. Both word choice and structure can make a piece formal, informal, or somewhere in between. One part of selecting a style is the intended **purpose** and **audience**. Teachers should always draw students' attention toward the reader of their piece. A more formal style, for example, would be called for in writing a letter to the principal advocating for a longer recess than would be necessary when writing a note to a friend. Students should also consider the style of pieces they read to determine why the author might have chosen a particular style convention: Did the writer intend to argue a point to a hostile audience? Inform a group of third graders about the difference between income and expenses? Was the style formal or informal?

**Mechanics** are the structural elements of writing and include punctuation, capitalization, spelling, grammar, and general conventions of usage. Like most procedural knowledge of writing, this proficiency may vary significantly from student to student and grade level to grade level. A kindergarten class, in particular, may be focused on a unit about capitalizing the first word in a sentence, whereas a second-grade class may be working on forming the past tense of verbs.

Teachers must also ensure they do not presume knowledge of Standard English conventions among students for whom English is not a first language. Correct use of prepositions, irregular verbs, and pronouns may be particularly challenging for these students until they become more experienced in common usage patterns. Teachers should always aim for growth versus perfection when helping students develop skills in editing their writing for errors in mechanics, as these skills continue to build throughout a student's schooling.

SAMPLE QUESTION

17) **Which of the following would most likely employ a highly formal writing style?**

A. a cookbook

B. a romance novel

C. a legal document

D. a short story

## Digital Tools

Increasingly, early childhood programs and schools are incorporating digital learning tools into their curriculum. Many schools have one or more subscriptions to various educational technology platforms that may enhance student learning and **digital literacy**, which is defined as the ability to find, use, and create digital information. **Media literacy**, a key part of digital literacy, is the ability of students to access, analyze, evaluate, and communicate information in both digital and physical form.

Some students may have extensive experiences with accessing digital information at home through previous use of computers, tablets, or phones. However, a similar level of digital literacy among students cannot be assumed, and teachers should explicitly direct students in strategies for gathering and assessing the usefulness of digital information. While the internet has created an unlimited platform for disseminating information, students must be taught early not to trust all sources equally and how to determine the validity and usefulness of a given source.

DID YOU KNOW?

There are many intentionally fake sites on the internet designed to help students practice determining whether online information is legitimate. One example is found at https://zapatopi.net/treeoctopus, where students can learn about the Pacific Northwest Tree Octopus.

Digital tools also provide an excellent way to differentiate literacy instruction through the use of adaptive software programs that target practice for each student's current skill level. Technological tools can also aid students with special needs or limited English proficiency as they navigate the day-to-day activities in the classroom. Devices and applications such as those that allow nonverbal children to communicate and those that help English language learners quickly translate new words may become indispensable learning aids.

Teachers should also incorporate **digital tools** into the writing process as appropriate. This may include the use of word processing or presentation software to aid in student drafting and revising and even perhaps the use of digital storytelling sites, which help students create and publish visual stories. The classroom or school may even have a website or social media page for publishing student-created content. Before publishing any student work online, however, always check with administration and secure necessary parental consent.

## SAMPLE QUESTION

18) **A first-grade teacher is trying to convince Mr. Walker, her co-teacher, to incorporate more technology into his lessons to meet new district standards. Mr. Walker did not grow up with technology and does not think his students need it. What is one argument that the teacher might propose to Mr. Walker to help him see its value?**

A. Students play video and computer games at home, so they should use technology at school, too.

B. Technology may help him to differentiate instruction for struggling readers.

C. The district standards are always based on what is best for students, so he should heed them.

D. Technology is not bad as long as it is strictly controlled by the teacher.

## THE RESEARCH PROCESS

Research and library skills are an important part of developing overall student literacy. Generally, there are seven steps in the research process:

1. **Identifying and focusing on the topic**. This might be as simple as having students pick a topic they want to learn more about or develop a research question they wish to answer—before searching online.
2. **Finding background information and conducting a preliminary search**. This involves getting a general overview of a topic and possible subtopics. During this stage students may Google a topic or read the Wikipedia page devoted to a particular topic.
3. **Locating materials**. This could involve work at the library and online. Teachers should encourage students to explore a wide variety of possible resources. As appropriate per the research topic, students should also be encouraged to seek out **primary sources**, or firsthand accounts. Primary sources may be speeches or diaries, surveys or census data, photographs of an event, and several other media that give eyewitness accounts of an event. Many primary sources are available online, and many sites organize these sources into an accessible format for students. Of course,

many materials that students find will also be **secondary sources**, or non-firsthand accounts. These include the majority of books, articles, and web pages devoted to a topic.

4. **Evaluating sources**. Students need to determine if certain sources are useful and accessible to them. For example, a library database may generate results for articles in publications to which the library does not have a subscription. Some resources may be inaccessible to students as they may be overly technical or written for an older audience. Students should also make sure they have **credible sources** written by experts. This stage in the research process might be a good time to introduce the different types of information available on the internet and the qualities that help increase reliability (listed author, .edu or .org domain, publication date, etc.).
5. **Note taking**. Note taking may involve the use of formal note cards or simply jotting down main ideas. As developmentally appropriate per student age, teachers should ensure students understand the idea of **paraphrasing**, or changing the author's words into their own, as they take notes. Paraphrasing can help students prevent **plagiarizing**, or presenting someone else's words as their own work.
6. **Writing**. This includes organizing all the notes into sentences and paragraphs. Students need to be cognizant of the overall organization of their work as they introduce a focused topic, provide support, and write a conclusion. Depending on the age group with which teachers work, they may have students make a poster or use another outlet to present their research instead of a formal paper.
7. **Citing sources**. This may include in-text **citations** and preparing a bibliography. To simplify these elements for young students, teachers might use a simpler works cited/bibliography page where students simply list titles of books and authors. Students in the upper elementary grades may work to develop more sophisticated bibliographies in MLA style, as it is generally regarded as the simplest citation style and the one to which students are first introduced.

Of course, these steps may be greatly simplified for very young students and per the scope of the research project. However, even kindergarteners can gather information from sources to answer a simple research question, and first-grade students can contribute to a simple class-wide research project with teacher support. The key is introducing students to the various parts of the research process while providing scaffolding as needed to support students as they explore new outlets for their developing literacy.

SAMPLE QUESTION

19) **Mrs. Burns has an inquisitive kindergarten class. During a unit on flags, her students asked many questions about flags from other states and countries. Which research activity might be most appropriate for Mrs. Burns to plan for her students to further explore flags?**

A. direct them to conduct an online search for three primary sources on flags

B. take them to the library and have them use the database to find flag-related articles

C. have them write a paper on state flags citing two secondary sources

D. help students find pictures of different flags online and then talk about what they like about each one

## Speaking and Listening

Some students may be introverted and others more extroverted. However, all children need help to develop basic skills in speaking and listening to enable them to become effective communicators. There will be times when students must employ **passive listening** where they listen to a speaker or presentation without conversing. These occasions might be at school assemblies, when watching a movie, or when listening to a storyteller. Passive listening, so long as it is done intently, is not necessarily bad; it just implies a lack of two-way communication. In fact, some occasions, such as being a respectful audience member, will require students to employ passive listening skills.

**Active listening**, on the other hand, should be employed whenever there is two-way communication. Active listening is used in many positive behavioral support programs, so if a school or program employs one of these, active listening may become a skill about which teachers are daily reminding students. The goal of active listening is to ensure that the listener has correctly understood the speaker. This is often extended to include an understanding of and empathy with this speaker. Generally, active listening involves making appropriate **eye contact** with the speaker, waiting for the speaker to finish, and then responding in a way that shows understanding.

Not only should teachers be active listeners to ensure they understand what students are thinking and feeling, but they should also encourage students to employ these techniques whenever they are listening to directions or holding conversations. Active listening can also help students avoid conflict with each other as they refrain from interrupting and practice valuing the thoughts and opinions of others.

Part of listening and responding may involve different **types of questioning** as listeners check for understanding. Speakers generally employ either open-ended questions ("What does your house look like?"), which require a significant response, or closed-ended questions ("Do you like fried chicken?"), which generally require only a simple one-word answer. Speakers may even ask rhetorical questions, which do not require a response but are designed to make the listener think.

An even deeper type of questioning comes from **metacognition**, or an awareness of one's own thinking. Teachers can help students think from a metacognitive perspective by teaching them to ask themselves questions both about their content knowledge ("Have I seen this before?" "Do I know this or need more practice?") and from a socioemotional perspective ("Am I feeling cranky because I am tired or hungry?" "How would I feel if that happened to me?").

During more formal speaking situations, especially those in which the audience is primarily involved in passive listening, several other measures must also be considered. **Audience awareness** involves being aware of those to whom one is speaking and their level of engagement and interest. One way to increase engagement both in formal and informal speaking situations is through appropriate volume and **articulation**, or clarity of speech. It may help teachers to periodically self-assess their own classroom speaking and listening by asking themselves questions such as "Am I keeping an appropriate volume or raising my voice frequently?" and "Am I asking students enough open-ended questions and using active-listening techniques?" Modeling effective communication for students is an important way to help teach these skills.

SAMPLE QUESTION

**20) Which of the following is an active listening strategy that can be taught to pre-kindergarten students?**

A. emphasizing proper articulation

B. maintaining eye contact

C. using open-ended questioning

D. practicing oral presentations

# Language

## Parts of Speech

Understanding the structure of language is an important part of effective oral and written communication. Students may not consistently use parts of speech correctly in their writing and speaking until well into their elementary years. Recall that within oral language development are phases in which children leave out needed articles, prepositions, and other linking words. Once speech becomes fully developed and students are generating their own sentences and paragraphs, basic rules of grammar can be introduced. Many structured language arts curriculum resources begin with a study of the eight parts of speech and their function within a sentence.

**Nouns** are words that indicate a person, place, thing, or idea. They may be either common (*student, teacher, room, school*) or proper (*Blanca, Ms. Robinson, Idaho, Frederick Douglass Elementary School*). **Common nouns** are not capitalized, but **proper nouns** must be capitalized. Nouns may also be singular or plural, and students will need practice in forming the plural form of nouns by adding either *–s* or *–es*.

**Pronouns** are words that take the place of nouns. They may either serve as subjects (*I, you, he, she, it, we, they*) or as objects (*me, you, her, him, it, us, them*) and are known as **subject pronouns** or **object pronouns**, respectively. Pronouns should always have an **antecedent**, or noun to which they refer. Pronouns must agree in number, person, and gender with their antecedents. Pronoun errors are frequent in developmental writers, and ambiguous pronoun references, lack of pronoun-antecedent agreement, and incorrect use of subject and object pronouns are all common mistakes.

As discussed above, pronouns generally also indicate the perspective or person in which a piece is written. First-person writing generally uses pronouns such as *I*, *me*, *we*, and *our*, and second-person writing uses the pronoun *you*. Third-person texts use a variety of pronouns such as *he*, *she*, *it*, and *them*. Shifts in pronoun person are common in student writing, and teachers need to provide help to students who unnecessarily change point of view in a writing assignment.

**Verbs** describe an action or state of being or occurrence. They can be action verbs, which like their name implies, describe actions such as *walk*, *eat*, and *speak*, or linking verbs, which describe states of being or link a subject to additional information (*is, become, seem*). Some verbs may be action verbs or linking verbs depending upon their specific use. If verbs are merely linking a subject to further information, they are considered linking verbs, but if they are expressing an action, they are considered action verbs.

This soup tastes bad.

In this sentence, the verb *tastes* links the subject *soup* to its predicate adjective *bad*, so *tastes* is being used as a linking verb.

I taste the soup.

In this sentence, *taste* is describing an action, so it is an action verb.

**Helping verbs** always appear alongside another main verb and show the tense (*will* be, *had* eaten) or possibility (*may* be, *could* last, *might* enjoy) of another verb. Helping verbs are used to **conjugate**, or change, many verbs to different **tenses**. Unnecessary shifts in tense from present to past or future are prevalent in student writing, and English language learners and native speakers alike will need lots of practice with forming challenging tenses such as the present and past perfect and challenging irregular past tenses with verbs such as *to lie*.

**Adjectives** modify and describe nouns, and their use is essential to descriptive writing. Student errors with adjectives generally include using an incorrect comparative or superlative form ("He is tallest than me!") or confusing adjectives and adverbs ("She eats hungry/She eats hungrily.").

QUICK REVIEW

What are the major phases of oral language development?

**Adverbs** modify adjectives, verbs, or other adverbs and frequently end in *–ly*. Student errors with adverbs are similar to those with adjectives and generally involve incorrect use of comparatives and superlatives or using adjectives and adverbs interchangeably.

A **preposition** is a word that expresses a relationship between words, and it usually comes before a noun or pronoun. Prepositions help form links in speech and writing, and student errors most frequently involve their omission. Additionally, English language learners may find using prepositions challenging, particularly when they are part of colloquial expressions (e.g., driving me *up* the wall, a pig *in* a poke, etc.).

A **conjunction** joins words or sentence parts together. There are both coordinating conjunctions (*and, but, or, nor, for, yet, so*), which join two independent clauses to form compound sentences, and subordinate conjunctions (*before, while, because, as*, etc.), which join dependent clauses to independent clauses to form complex and compound-complex sentences.

Table 3.5. Subordinating Conjunctions

| | |
|---|---|
| **Time** | after, as, as long as, as soon as, before, since, until, when, whenever, while |
| **Manner** | as, as if, as though |
| **Cause** | because |
| **Condition** | although, as long as, even if, even though, if, provided that, though, unless, while |
| **Purpose** | in order that, so that, that |
| **Comparison** | as, than |

An **interjection** expresses a spontaneous feeling and is usually followed by a comma or exclamation point. *Oops*, *whoa,* and *hmm* are examples of common interjections.

**Determiners** are not parts of speech in themselves but have a similar function: explaining what a noun refers to. They may be adjectives that are used as articles such as *a*, *an*, and *the*; possessive adjectives and pronouns (*my, his, ours, your*); demonstrative pronouns such as *this*, *that*, *these*, and *those*; or any other words that quantify, distribute, or show a difference (*a little*, *half*, *other*, *such*, *quite*).

HELPFUL HINT

Students can use the mnemonic PAPA N VIC to remember the eight parts of speech.

Like prepositions, determiners are challenging for English language learners. In some languages, determiners are used in only some situations and not others, and some languages lack certain types of English determiners entirely. English language learners who struggle with determiners might benefit from being paired with a native speaker for peer review to help insert needed articles into a piece.

Additionally, variations exist across all parts of speech in different languages. American Sign Language, as just one example, does not use what we might think of as conjugated verbs to show tense; rather, a sign indicating now, next, before, and so on is inserted into the beginning of the sentence to show the intended meaning. It is important for teachers to understand that grammatical knowledge will be more challenging for some students, and they should strive to ensure the classroom is a place where all students are being supported in their learning.

## SAMPLE QUESTIONS

**21) Which of the following is a preposition?**

A. our

B. from

C. has

D. so

**22) Which of the following skills do students need to master before they can determine whether an adjective or adverb is most appropriate to use in a sentence?**

A. understanding the difference between a noun and a verb

B. understanding the difference between a noun and a pronoun

C. understanding the function of prepositions

D. being able to form compound sentences

## CONSTRUCTING SENTENCES

Good writers use a variety of sentence structures to convey their meaning. While young students will generally start with **simple sentences** consisting of a single, independent clause, students should be encouraged to write more advanced sentences as appropriate. **Compound sentences** are made when two independent clauses are joined together using a comma and coordinating conjunction; a semicolon, either alone or with a transitional expression such as however or moreover; or a colon. Generally, a semicolon alone is only used to join two closely related independent clauses ("My mother likes chocolate; she is a chocoholic."). A colon is generally only used to introduce a second independent clause which is an example or elaboration upon the first ("I have only one thing to say to you: I am very disappointed.").

**Complex sentences** are formed when a dependent clause is joined to an independent clause with a subordinating conjunction, relative pronoun, or other word. A **dependent clause** is so called because it cannot stand on its own as a sentence, unlike an **independent clause**. The dependent clause may be added anywhere: the beginning, the middle, or the end of the sentence.

> My mother, *who is a gardener*, likes to spend most of her time outdoors.

In this sentence, the dependent clause is "who is a gardener," beginning with the relative pronoun *who*.

> *Because she likes to spend most of her time outdoors*, my mother is a gardener.

Here, the dependent clause is "[b]ecause she likes to spend most of her time outdoors," beginning with the subordinating conjunction *because*.

> My mother is a gardener *as she likes to spend most of her time outdoors.*

In the sentence above, the dependent clause is "as she likes to spend most of her time outdoors," beginning with the subordinating conjunction *as*.

**Compound-complex sentences** are merely compound sentences with one or more dependent clauses ("My mother is a gardener, but she does not like to spend time outdoors because she has allergies.").

### SAMPLE QUESTION

**23) Which of the following is a compound sentence?**

A. Jeremy likes to fish by the ocean because he finds it peaceful and relaxing.

B. I wish I could buy a new car, but I do not have enough money right now.

C. Jenny is a writer, and she writes for thirty minutes every day because she has to keep motivated.

D. While the train slowly chugged along the tracks, my little dog stared curiously out the window.

## Varieties of English

Early childhood teachers will likely have students whose home language is not English. It is important to preserve and respect multiple languages within the classroom while helping all students understand the nuances that exist within the English language. A **dialect** is a special way that a given group speaks, and having characters speak in different dialects is an important literary device that authors use to convey meaning. Characters may speak in a Southern dialect or in a Boston or Midwestern style. It might be challenging for students to read dialogue written in dialects with which they are unfamiliar, and teachers may need to scaffold learning with these texts.

An **accent** differs from a dialect in that vocabulary and grammar are the same, but pronunciation is different. There may be families at school, for example, who speak English in a British or Southern accent.

A **register** is a speech pattern that is affiliated with a certain social group or situation. Registers may be associated with an age group or ethnic group, and while they have no intrinsic level of correctness or incorrectness, social constructs may cause some people to associate certain registers with being formal or less formal or even from a lower social strata. Many people, and likely many students, will engage in a practice known as code switching, where they will switch between a home language or register and more formal or standard language in different situations. It is important that teachers avoid responding in a negative or judgmental way to the different dialects, accents, and registers that may be used in the everyday oral communications within the classroom.

Texts that students read, particularly narrative ones such as dramas and stories, will often feature a variety of dialects, accents, and registers to aid in the author's development of characters and setting. Poetry may use certain conventions with which students are unfamiliar. Rather than focusing on a thorough explication of poetry, a better strategy is helping students understand how certain language contributes to the overall purpose of the piece through creation of rhythm, rhyme, or visual imagery. Writers of academic work and other formal published pieces tend to employ a more formal usage of language than that found in everyday conversation. Teachers should strive to help students distinguish the differences between written and spoken language in a variety of contexts and situations.

Students will be exposed to a wide variety of vocabulary in a literacy-rich classroom, and teachers can further aid vocabulary acquisition through incorporating new words and new meanings into the daily routine. Some vocabulary acquisition will involve learning **content-specific words** that require students to first understand the vocabulary of the subject before applying the knowledge. Consider that even a kindergarten student must master dozens of basic math terms before applying them. For example, *triangle*, *hexagon*, and *rectangle* must all be learned intrinsically before a student can separate or sort items by shape. Additionally, third graders must learn terms like *habitat*, *natural resource*, *metric system*, and *variable* to apply them to science and math assignments.

Student vocabulary must also grow to include the various homonyms, or **multiple-meaning words**, that exist in the English language. The word *interest*, for example, might mean one thing as it applies to a math unit on saving money and another when used in a freewriting assignment on a topic of *interest*.

SAMPLE QUESTION

**24) Which of the following is an example of code switching that a student might employ to switch between registers?**

A. speaking Creole at home and English at school
B. using less formal language with friends than with teachers
C. speaking Spanish with friends and English in the classroom
D. turning off a French accent when in less formal situations

## Meaning of Words and Phrases

One helpful way to help students learn new vocabulary is through etymology. Many **root words** in English come from Latin or Greek. For example, the Greek root *chrono*, meaning time, makes many common words: *chronology*, *chronic*, *chronicle*, and so on. Many English words are made by adding an **affix** to a basic root word. If this affix is added at the beginning, it is known as a **prefix** (*anti*–, *un*–, etc.), and if it is added to the end of the word, it is known as a **suffix** (–*less*, –*able*, etc.).

Using this decoding strategy, when students encounter a new or challenging word, they can look for familiar prefixes, suffixes, or roots and ask themselves if the new word is like others they know. This can help students determine meaning from likening a new word to a previously learned word. For example, a student who knows the meaning of the affix *mid*– as in *middle* and *midway* can then apply this knowledge to a history passage with the word *midcentury*. Prefixes and suffixes can also help students identify parts of speech. For example, words ending in –*er* and –*est* are generally adjectives.

Teachers can further challenge students by exposing them to words that go beyond a **literal meaning** to a more figurative description. **Figurative language** includes simile, metaphor, hyperbole, and personification.

**Similes** compare two unlike things using the words *like* or *as*:

His throat was as dry as the Sahara Desert.

**Metaphors** are constructed by comparing two unlike things:

The carpet was sandpaper beneath my feet.

**Hyperbole** is an extreme exaggeration:

My feet are the worst smelling things in the entire school.

**Personification** involves giving a humanlike quality to a nonhuman:

The sea speaks and sings its mystery.

Figurative language may be challenging for students to understand at first, so they will need plenty of teacher support when first introducing this concept.

Above all, teachers should emphasize to students that there are multiple ways to glean the meaning of new words in context, and teachers should encourage students to try multiple strategies. Are there pictures on the page that might help? What context clues can be used? What point do students think the author is trying to make? Do students see any prefixes or parts of the word that they know? These are all guiding questions that will help students deepen their ability to learn new words from reading a variety of texts.

QUICK REVIEW

What is the difference between a prefix and a suffix?

SAMPLE QUESTION

**25) Which of the following uses hyperbole?**

A. The grass was as green as a crayon.

B. The ocean was as vast as the line at the DMV.

C. He was the best dancer in the entire world.

D. My mother is the best cook I know.

## TONE

**Tone** refers to the overall attitude of a piece of literature. It may be influenced by the author's feelings toward the subject matter or audience. The tone of a book on financial independence may be enthusiastic and positive as the author is trying to instill confidence and positivity into the mind of the reader. The tone might be formal, as in a paper a teacher writes to present at a literacy conference, or less formal, as in a note written to a colleague to thank her for help with lunch duty. Students should be encouraged to determine the tone of different pieces they read.

The **word choice**, or author's choice of specific vocabulary to impart meaning, will likely influence tone. A highly formal essay written for a sophisticated technical audience may include lots of vocabulary that students will not understand and contribute to an overall tone of seriousness. A book designed to entertain a young audience may have more simple vocabulary and an overall humorous tone.

Teachers might further ask students to consider why the author chose certain words or presented them in a certain order. **Syntax**, or the arrangement of words into sentences, can have a tremendous impact on a text. Several short, simple sentences might create anticipation: "It was dark. It was raining. My friend drove up." Longer and more complex sentences may create a more formal and sophisticated feel to a piece.

QUICK REVIEW

Consider the venerated character of Yoda in *Star Wars*. What impact is his inverted speech pattern ("Find them I will") intended to have on the audience? Does it make him sound more wise or experienced, for instance?

SAMPLE QUESTION

**26) Which of the following does NOT contribute to the tone of a piece?**

A. the author's attitude toward the subject

B. the inclusion of highly sophisticated vocabulary

C. the use of highly complex sentence structures

D. correct capitalization for proper nouns

## Children's Literature

Children's literature is an integral part of the early childhood classroom. A well-stocked library, even within a preschool classroom, can encourage students to take an interest in books. Access to children's books also aids in print awareness as students learn which way to hold the book and turn the pages from the story's beginning to its end. Further, it helps children understand that books contain information and ideas. This is usually first demonstrated to very young children through picture books. Since children are often initially drawn into a story through its graphic appeal, having several highly visually appealing books on hand is very helpful.

Beyond simply allowing young children to explore a classroom library on their own, one time-tested instructional methodology is class-wide storybook reading. In preschool and kindergarten classrooms, this often takes place during circle time. Any number of positive learning experiences can take place when the teacher reads a book to the class. Children's literature is most frequently developed intentionally to lead to the following outcomes:

- Students have their interest piqued by new topics or themes.
- Teachers can introduce a new topic or unit through storybook reading before an integrated unit.
- Teachers can introduce new vocabulary.
- Students can develop cognitive skills as they follow a sequence of story events.
- Teachers can encourage students to make predictions and form opinions about characters.
- Students can be exposed to targeted skills such as alphabet knowledge, letter-sound correspondence, and numeracy skills.
- Through storybooks that rhyme and have repeated words and rhythm, students can develop phonemic awareness.

Storybook reading to young children is best when it is interactive and enables them to make connections with the text. For this reason, it is essential that the reading be purposeful. Early childhood teachers should point out elements of print as appropriate (title, author, dialogue, key words, and so on) as well as ask guided questions throughout. **Repeated readings**, or reading the same book more than once, are also very helpful in preschool and kindergarten classrooms. Research shows that repeated readings allow children to connect more deeply with the story, follow its sequence, and make more in-depth opinions about characters as they relate the story to their own lives.

A broad cultural perspective, which might not be present in some classrooms that lack diversity, can be conveyed through children's literature. Classic stories, legends, and folktales from almost every cultural tradition are now widely available and can help familiarize students with the language, dress, and customs of various cultures. Children's books highlighting elements of culture (such as respect for differences and holidays) are available in fiction and nonfiction titles. Many nonfiction books for children contain purposeful elements such as illustrations, simple vocabulary, and even graphic novel–style layout to aid in student interest and understanding.

Class-wide **read-alouds** are an important instructional strategy to bridge sensitive or controversial topics. Some research has shown that when children experience a topic through a storybook, they feel more emotionally safe than when the teacher presents the same information topically. A wealth of children's literature on various social studies topics from segregation to transgender identity is widely available and carefully written to explain sensitive issues in a way that young children can understand. Books depicting characters who experience discrimination or marginalization also help young students develop socially and emotionally as they are encouraged to empathize with the book's characters.

Books with a moral or lesson also help socio-emotional development and can reinforce this type of learning as teachers connect stories to real-life scenarios. Books with themes of sharing, forgiveness, patience, and even prosocial behaviors such as avoiding biting and hitting can all be very useful in introducing, reinforcing, and integrating socio-emotional learning.

Of course, some children's books are very widely read and available in almost all school libraries. Many of these books illustrate several seminal themes in early childhood children's literature: use of animals or nonhumans as characters, emphasis on social learning, picture/text correlation, rhyme and rhythm, and a simple and predictable sequence of events. Many of these are classics that have been passed down from generation to generation. Some of the most commonly read works of children's literature are listed in Table 3.6 below.

Table 3.6. Common Works of Children's Literature

| **Author** | **Important Works** |
|---|---|
| A.A. Milne | *Winnie-the-Pooh*<br>*When We Were Very Young* |
| Hans Christian Andersen | *The Ugly Duckling*<br>*Thumbelina*<br>*The Princess and the Pea*<br>*The Emperor's New Clothes* |
| Brothers Grimm Fairy Tales | Numerous, including:<br>*Beauty and the Beast*<br>*The Bremen Town Musicians*<br>*Cinderella*<br>*Goldilocks and the Three Bears*<br>*Hansel and Gretel*<br>*Little Red Riding Hood*<br>*Rapunzel*<br>*Sleeping Beauty*<br>*Snow White* |
| Margery Williams | *The Velveteen Rabbit* |
| Beatrix Potter | *The Tale of Peter Rabbit* |
| Jean de Brunhoff | *The Story of Babar* |
| Dr. Seuss | *Numerous, Including:*<br>*The Cat in the Hat*<br>*Green Eggs and Ham*<br>*Hop on Pop*<br>*One Fish, Two Fish, Red Fish, Blue Fish*<br>*Horton Hears a Who!* |
| Crocket Johnson | *Harold and the Purple Crayon* |
| Sam McBratney | *Guess How Much I Love You* |
| Margaret Wise Brown | *The Runaway Bunny*<br>*Big Red Barn*<br>*Goodnight Moon* |
| Maurice Sendak | *Where the Wild Things Are*<br>*In the Night Kitchen*<br>*Little Bear (illustrated)* |
| Michael Bond | *A Bear Called Paddington* |
| Russell Hoban | *A Birthday for Frances* |

| Author | Important Works |
|---|---|
| Robert McCloskey | *Make Way for Ducklings*<br>*Blueberries for Sal*<br>*Homer Price* |
| Bill Martin | *Brown Bear, Brown Bear, What Do you See?* (with Eric Carle)<br>*Chicka Chicka Boom Boom* |
| Eric Carle | *The Very Hungry Caterpillar* |
| Ruth Krauss | *The Carrot Seed* |
| Vera Williams | *A Chair for My Mother* |
| Don Freeman | *Corduroy*<br>*A Rainbow of My Own* |
| H.A. Rey | *Curious George* |
| Donald Crews | *Freight Train*<br>*Ten Black Dots*<br>*Truck* |
| Leo Lionni | *Swimmy*<br>*Frederick*<br>*Little Blue and Little Yellow* |
| Arnold Lobel | *Frog and Toad Are Friends* |
| Shel Silverstein | *The Giving Tree*<br>*Where the Sidewalk Ends* |
| Gene Zion | *Harry the Dirty Dog* |
| Bernard Waber | *Lyle, Lyle, Crocodile*<br>*Ira Sleeps Over*<br>*The House on East 88th Street* |
| Laura Numeroff | *If You Give a Mouse a Cookie* |
| Watty Piper | *The Little Engine That Could* |
| Ludwig Bemelmans | *Madeline* |
| Virginia Lee Burton | *Mike Mulligan and His Steam Shovel*<br>*The Little House* |
| Wanda Gag | *Millions of Cats*<br>*The ABC Bunny* |
| Marcus Pfister | *The Rainbow Fish* |
| Ezra Jack Keats | *The Snowy Day*<br>*Peter's Chair* |
| Munro Leaf | *The Story of Ferdinand* |

| Table 3.6. Common Works of Children's Literature (continued) | |
|---|---|
| **Author** | **Important Works** |
| Tomie dePaola | *Strega Nona*<br>*Pancakes for Breakfast* |
| William Steig | *Sylvester and the Magic Pebble*<br>*Doctor De Soto*<br>*Shrek!*<br>*Amos & Boris* |
| Mercer Mayer | *There's a Nightmare in My Closet* |
| Arlene Mosel | *Tikki Tikki Tembo* |
| P.D. Eastman | *Go, Dog. Go!* |

## SAMPLE QUESTIONS

**27) What type of classroom library would a toddler classroom most likely include?**

A. It would likely not include a library, as toddlers cannot yet read.

B. A library with soft-bound and board picture books.

C. A library with books that rhyme and introduce numeracy skills.

D. A library of leveled-reader books.

**28) Which of the following was written by Hans Christian Andersen?**

A. *Tikki Tikki Tembo*

B. *Chicka Chicka Boom Boom*

C. *The Giving Tree*

D. *The Ugly Duckling*

# Answer Key

**1)** A. Incorrect. The student will likely not retain this information, and the purpose of the writing center is practice and not perfection since the student is in the invented spelling stage.

**B.** **Correct**. Practice is essential to developing writing and spelling skills, so praise is in order because the student chose this activity. Further, the student is likely in the normal and necessary invented spelling stage.

C. Incorrect. While hand-over-hand guidance may be appropriate in some cases where motor skills are still developing and students are reticent to write, this student has already written the words. Erasing and rewriting the invented spelling is unnecessary and may be discouraging.

D. Incorrect. This invented spelling is a normal stage, as students develop more accurate spelling skills through practice.

**2)** A. Incorrect. This is a recall and comprehension gauging question. It is not related to print awareness.

**B.** **Correct.** Knowing the difference between a letter, word, and sentence is an important component of print awareness.

C. Incorrect. This is a motor skills and alphabet knowledge question.

D. Incorrect. This is a letter-sound correspondence question.

**3)** **A.** **Correct.** This would help students to practice identifying both letter sounds and the initial sounds of words.

B. Incorrect. This would help students master overall phonological awareness, but not the alphabetic principle or onsets in particular.

C. Incorrect. This activity is more concerned with concepts of print.

D. Incorrect. This is phoneme deletion, a strategy to work on phonemic awareness, not onsets and the alphabetic principle.

**4)** A. Incorrect. This strategy would make a new word, not the word the student is struggling to read.

B. Incorrect. In phoneme blending, the student is given the sounds and must then say the word.

**C.** **Correct.** This is the strategy of "sounding out."

D. Incorrect. This will help promote phonological awareness but will not help the student read the word.

**5)** **A.** **Correct.** The word *elephant* can be decoded using phonics strategies.

B. Incorrect. *Elephant* is not one of the most frequently used words in English.

C. Incorrect. Phonemes are sounds, so each word has phonemes.

D. Incorrect. This word is illustrative of many sound structures.

**6)** A. Incorrect. Timed reading does not necessarily develop expression.

B. Incorrect. Prosody refers to expression, not reading rate.

C. Incorrect. Prosody is part of oral reading.

**D. Correct.** This would give students practice reading expressively.

**7)** A. Incorrect. This pertains to fiction texts, not informational texts.

**B. Correct.** This activity would help students see the structure of an informational text with which they are familiar.

C. Incorrect. This would pertain to fiction texts, not informational texts.

D. Incorrect. This would pertain to fiction texts, not informational texts.

**8) A. Correct.** This is a sentence written in third person with the appropriate third-person pronoun *she*.

B. Incorrect. The pronoun *I* indicates that this sentence is written in first-person point of view.

C. Incorrect. *We* is a first-person plural pronoun, so this sentence is written in the first person.

D. Incorrect. The second-person pronoun *you* indicates that this sentence is written in the second person.

**9)** A. Incorrect. This will not necessarily aid John in identifying the central idea.

B. Incorrect. This might be a start, but if the assignment is to identify the central idea, the teacher will want John to limit himself to only the most important or overall idea.

C. Incorrect. This will not necessarily help John generate the main idea.

**D. Correct.** This will help lead John to the central idea of the paragraph.

**10)** A. Incorrect. This activity might expose students to different books but not necessarily different text structures.

**B. Correct.** This allows for hands-on learning and will help Ms. Jones explain how these different texts are structured for their intended purpose.

C. Incorrect. This will help students compare and contrast characters, not text structures.

D. Incorrect. This will not expose students to different text structures.

**11) A. Correct.** This might help students look outside their own point of view to that of someone else and integrate socioemotional and literacy learning.

B. Incorrect. This is not developmentally appropriate for a kindergarten class.

C. Incorrect. This is not a literacy activity and might be a challenge for egocentric kindergarteners.

D. Incorrect. This does not help students see things from a different point of view.

**12)** A. Incorrect. This does not help students understand visual information.

B. Incorrect. This might help students understand more about bugs but is not literacy related.

C. Incorrect. This does not help students understand visual information.

**D.** **Correct.** This helps students understand how the visual representations of bugs in their picture book aid in an understanding of bugs.

**13)** A. Incorrect. All students need oral reading practice to develop fluency, rate, and prosody.

B. Incorrect. This will fail to challenge more advanced students and may be too challenging for others.

**C.** **Correct.** This method ensures each student is reading a text appropriate for his or her current skill level.

D. Incorrect. This might be seen as a punishment and might decrease student confidence.

**14)** **A.** **Correct.** The pattern is *g* (consonant), *a* (vowel), *p* (consonant).

B. Incorrect. This word has a vowel-consonant-vowel pattern.

C. Incorrect. This word has a consonant-vowel-consonant-consonant pattern.

D. Incorrect. This is a vowel-consonant-consonant pattern.

**15)** A. Incorrect. This will not help Sarah as she has already been assigned a topic.

**B.** **Correct.** This question will help Sarah understand the type of things she needs to describe.

C. Incorrect. This question will not help Sarah describe her appearance.

D. Incorrect. This is a descriptive and not persuasive writing assignment.

**16)** A. Incorrect. This is a way to publish student writing as publishing implies sharing the work with others.

B. Incorrect. This is a way to share the work with others.

**C.** **Correct.** This does not necessarily share the piece with others; it merely formats it in a different way.

D. Incorrect. This allows others to read the piece.

**17)** A. Incorrect. Cookbooks are written for a broad audience and are not highly formal as they need to be accessible by multiple readers.

B. Incorrect. Romance novels are generally written in a unique style, but it is not highly formal.

**C.** **Correct.** Because legal documents must be very specific and not leave room for interpretation, a highly formal and precise style would be used.

D. Incorrect. While some short stories are written more formally than others, this is not a consistent style choice for the genre as a whole.

**18)** A. Incorrect. This reasoning probably will not be convincing.

**B.** **Correct.** This is one benefit that may help his students and that he might have a hard time arguing against.

C. Incorrect. He likely already disagrees with these standards as he does not want to implement them.

D. Incorrect. This is a general statement and does not directly reference how technology might help his students.

**19) D.** **Correct.** This activity scaffolds students learning and helps them begin to develop research skills. The other activities are not developmentally appropriate for a kindergarten class.

**20) B.** **Correct.** This is a core part of active listening and can help pre-K students focus on a speaker. The other activities are not a part of active listening.

**21)** A. Incorrect. *Our* is a pronoun.

**B.** **Correct.** *From* is a preposition.

C. Incorrect. *Has* is a verb.

D. Incorrect. *So* is a coordinating conjunction.

**22) A.** **Correct.** Because adjectives modify nouns and adverbs modify verbs, adjectives, or other adverbs, this is a foundational understanding that must precede a discussion of when an adjective or adverb is most appropriate. The other choices are not relevant to adjective versus adverb use.

**23)** A. Incorrect. This is a complex sentence, with the dependent clause "because he finds it peaceful and relaxing."

**B.** **Correct.** Two independent clauses are joined with a comma and the coordinating conjunction *but*.

C. Incorrect. This is a compound-complex sentence, with the dependent clause "because she has to keep motivated."

D. Incorrect. This is a complex sentence, with the dependent clause "while the train slowly chugged along the tracks."

**24)** A. Incorrect. While switching between languages is code switching, it is not switching registers.

**B.** **Correct.** This is switching between two different social situations—changing registers.

C. Incorrect. This is code switching with a language, not a register.

D. Incorrect. One usually cannot turn off an accent.

**25)** A. Incorrect. This is a simile.

B. Incorrect. This is a simile.

**C. Correct.** This is an exaggeration.

D. Incorrect. This is a literal statement, not an exaggeration.

**26)** A. Incorrect. The author's attitude contributes to tone.

B. Incorrect. Word choice contributes to tone.

C. Incorrect. Syntax contributes to tone.

**D. Correct.** Capitalization does not necessarily contribute to tone and should be relatively standard.

**27)** A. Incorrect. Though toddlers cannot yet read, a classroom library is still crucial to encourage children's interest in books and to help them develop pre-reading skills.

**B. Correct.** These books are very appropriate for a toddler classroom since they are more durable and less likely to tear while very young children explore them.

C. Incorrect. While some rhyming books might be read by the teacher to the class, the classroom library should include books that students can explore on their own.

D. Incorrect. Leveled readers would not be appropriate for a toddler class.

**28)** A. Incorrect. This work was written by Arlene Mosel.

B. Incorrect. This work was written by Bill Martin.

C. Incorrect. This work was written by Shel Silverstein.

D. Correct. Hans Christian Andersen wrote *The Ugly Duckling*.

# Mathematics

## Emergent Mathematics

Children cultivate math skills from a very young age. **Emergent mathematics** refers to how young children develop math skills over time through intellectual development and interaction with their environment.

Skills such as **counting** and skip counting, which involve rote memorization of numeric words in a proper order, are some of the most important math concepts introduced to young children. **Skip counting** is a form of counting where numbers are not consecutively recited by one. Skip counting can occur in twos, threes, or in any fixed pattern. As children learn counting, they may not quite understand the concept of one-to-one correspondence in **numeration**.

**One-to-one correspondence** is the ability to say one number for each object pointed to or touched consecutively. For instance, when counting out "one, two, three, four" using **counters** or other objects, children who have not developed the concept of one-to-one correspondence may skip an object or count it more than once. Placing objects in a line and using counting motions like pointing or clapping while saying each number out loud helps correlate each number to an object.

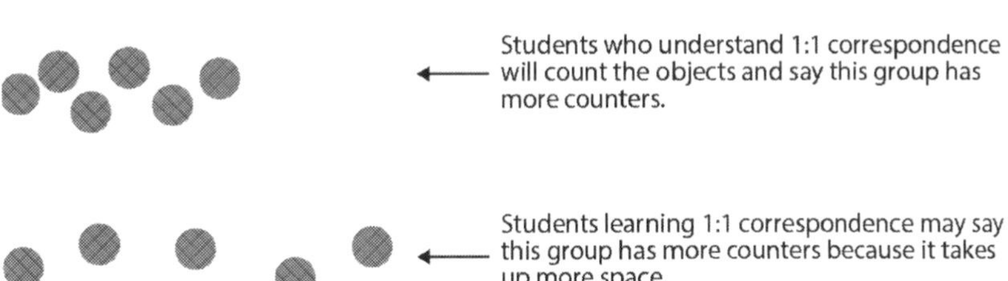


**Figure 4.1. One-to-One Correspondence**

**Pattern matching**, **grouping**, **sorting**, and **sequencing** are concepts in early math development that aid in understanding numeration. As children begin to categorize objects in their environment by how they are alike or different, a natural sense of order occurs. Since many fundamental math skills cannot be directly taught at a young age, **manipulatives** in the form of toys, puzzles, games, or even general household items provide excellent practice material. Toy blocks can be grouped or sorted by color, shape, or size; clothes can be arranged or sequenced by **pattern**; toys can be put away while counting each one.

Many children love using their fingers to count. In the past, using fingers was not considered an acceptable convention, but research has shown that children who count with fingers are better at quantitative tasks, as it is a natural sensory activity linking movement with brain activity. Counting on fingers is easily accessible, quick, and free.

Children revel in repetition, so the more such chores are undertaken, the better their recognition of crucial skills like number conservation. **Number conservation** refers to the understanding that a number of objects remains the same even when the objects are rearranged. A child putting away five stuffed animals will recognize that the quantity does not change regardless of which animal is put away first.

> HELPFUL HINT
>
> Help students connect counting to cardinality: When counting objects in a set, the last word said is the number of objects in that set.

Over time, a child maturing in age and cognitive development will have the ability to mentally conduct numeration in various ways. One such way is by **subitizing**—the capacity to view a small number of objects and immediately recognize how many there are without counting. Another numeric skill involves mastering one-to-one correspondence, which leads to an understanding of **cardinality**—finding out how many objects are in a group or set.

## SAMPLE QUESTIONS

1) **Chris puts away his ten stuffed animal toys every night. He learns that the quantity does not change regardless of which animal is put away first. Which of the following concepts is the child learning?**

   A. skip counting

   B. number conservation

   C. sorting

   D. pattern matching

2) **Kelly helped her mother bake chocolate chip cookies. After they were cool and placed on a plate, she immediately exclaimed that there were five cookies. Which of the following skills is Kelly demonstrating?**

A. sequencing
B. sorting
C. skip counting
D. subitizing

## Numbers and Operations

As children mature, they can gradually perform mental math and use numbers in everyday situations. But if children were to randomly manipulate numbers, they would not comprehend which number is relevant in a circumstance. They need to be introduced to deeper concepts to understand the true relevance of a number.

These deeper concepts include understanding place value, using the four basic mathematical operations with whole numbers, and fractions.

### Place Value

A **digit** (0 to 9) is a symbol used to make numbers. For instance, 5,182 is made up of the digits 5, 1, 8, and 2. The value of the position of each digit in a number is called its **place value**. In the number 5,182, the digit *5* is in the **thousands** place, *1* is in the **hundreds** place, *8* is in the **tens** place, and *2* is in the **ones** place.

A **place value chart** is a good visual aid to show children how to understand the value of digits using pictures or objects like base-ten blocks. The chart has place values listed right to left in the way numbers are typically formed. The chart also aids in reading and writing multi-digit numbers accurately, as each digit is placed in a column that correlates to its value.

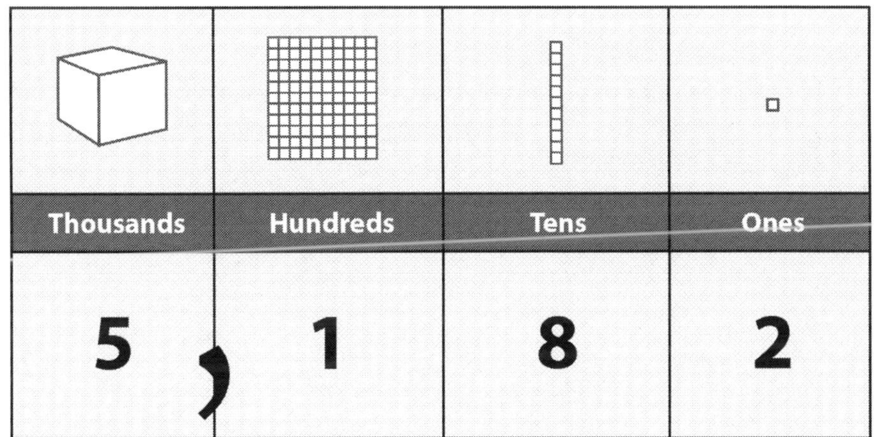


5000 + 100 + 80 + 2 = 5,182

**Figure 4.2. Place Value Chart**

Another way to express a number is by decomposing it. **Decomposing** a number breaks it down into individual parts. For instance, 6,417 can be decomposed to 6,000 + 400 + 10 + 7. Similarly, **composing** a number involves adding the individual parts. So, 9,000 + 400 + 30 + 1 can be written as 9,431.

COMMON STUDENT ERRORS

- misunderstanding how to expand numbers (306 = 30 + 6)
- decreasing the number in the specified place when rounding down (163 → 150).

Rounding is a useful skill. When working with large figures, for instance, it is easier to work with values rounded to the nearest ten or hundred; it is not always necessary to work with an exact number. **Rounding** a number makes it simpler to work with.

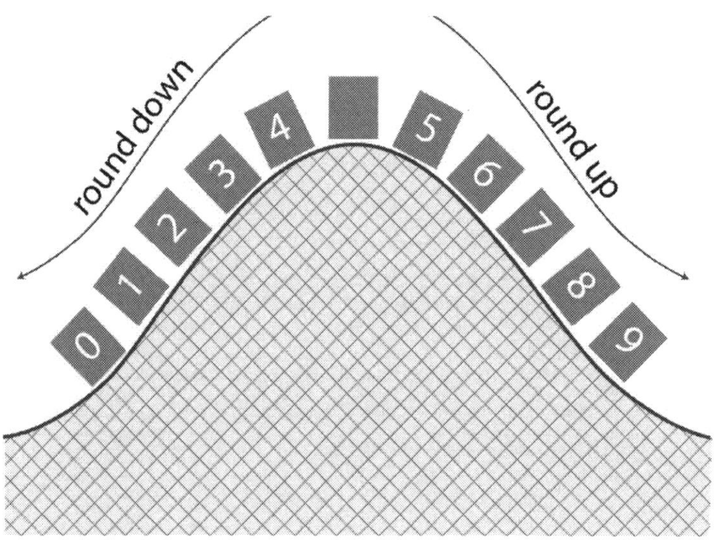


Figure 4.3. Rounding

STUDY TIP

You can use the following rhyme to teach rounding rules: Find the number, look next door. Four or less, let it rest. Five or more, raise the score.

Using whole numbers makes it easier to explain rounding. **Whole numbers** are numbers 0, 1, 2, 3, 4, and so on. They do not include negative numbers, decimals, or fractions. Rounding a whole number like 83 to the nearest ten gives 80, because 83 is closer to 80 than it is to 90. But 87 will be rounded up to 90. Similarly, rounding the number 345 to the nearest hundred is 300 since 345 is closer to 300 than it is to 400. Rounding the number 5,782 to the nearest hundred will be 5,800, because the hundreds value of 782 is closer to 800 than it is to 700.

## SAMPLE QUESTIONS

3) **In which of the following scenarios would it be appropriate to use rounding?**
   A. A window repairer measures windows that need glass replacement.
   B. A teacher is ordering pizzas for a school party with one hundred students.
   C. In a marathon, winners take first, second, and third prize.
   D. A man is paying for a shirt at a store and needs to know the amount.

4) **Two students in a class were asked to round the number 30,409 to the nearest thousand. Sam says it will be rounded to 31,000, and Paul says it will be rounded to 30,400. Which student is correct?**
   A. They are both correct.
   B. Sam is correct.
   C. Paul is correct.
   D. They are both incorrect.

## OPERATIONS WITH WHOLE NUMBERS

The four basic operations in math are addition, subtraction, multiplication, and division.

The concept of addition can be explained to children through visuals, such as two groups of blocks. Students can count the number of blocks in the first group and the number of blocks in the second group. After combining the groups together, the students should count all the blocks; they have just **added** the two sets of blocks together.

There are many ways to introduce addition: using counters or manipulatives, a **number line**, or paper and pencil. Counters provide a hands-on approach to counting out amounts, much like using fingers to count. As children learn to count out each amount before adding, they reinforce one-to-one correspondence.

Number lines help children visualize addition in the form of measurement and help them understand what the answers of addition and subtraction mean. For an addition equation like 6 + 3, take the first **addend**, 6, on the number line. Then "jump" three spaces to the right, landing at 9. In a subtraction equation like 10 – 4, mark 10 on the number line. Then "jump" four spaces to the left, landing at 6. Eventually students can use the number line with negative numbers, fractions, and decimals.

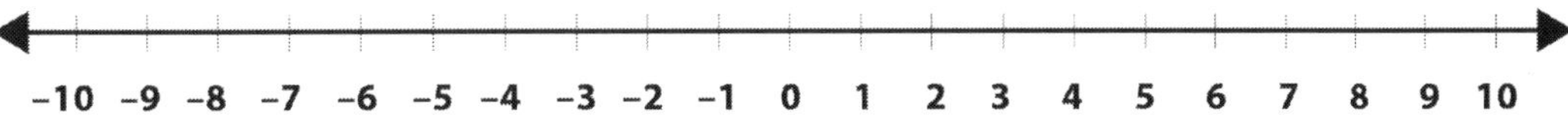


**Figure 4.4. Number Line**

Helping children get the gist of addition involves familiarizing them with common symbols like the addition and equal signs (+ and =) and words such as *addends*, *plus*, *all together*, *in all*, and *sum*. Once they understand these, they can progress to simple paper-and-pencil exercises with addition sentences or equations such as 3 + 4 = 7.

After children have achieved a certain level of familiarity with the above, they will be able to learn different strategies for addition, such as counting forward or backward, skip counting, grouping, and using doubles. **Grouping** refers to viewing numbers in a sequence that makes logical sense. For example, there are many ways to group numbers to add up to 10: 1 and 9, 2 and 8, 3 and 7, 4 and 6 all add up to 10. Using **doubles** is a type of grouping where the two numbers used in an addition equation are the same: 2 + 2, 3 + 3, 4 + 4, and so on. Both these strategies help children strengthen number sense and expand their thinking.

COMMON STUDENT ERRORS

- always subtracting the smaller number from the larger number (953 – 27 = 934)
- thinking that subtraction is commutative (9 – 4 = 4 – 9)

Subtraction can be explained as the inverse or opposite of addition because the two operations cancel each other out. Terms such as *minuend*, *minus*, *take away*, *left*, *remaining*, and *difference* should be introduced.

An everyday scenario can help get the concept across: "You have ten blocks and you give me three. How many blocks do you have left?" Children count out ten blocks and then move three blocks away. After they count out the seven remaining blocks, they have **subtracted** 3 from 10. They can understand a simple subtraction equation, 10 – 3 = 7.

| X | 0 | 1 | 2 | 3 | 4 | 5 | 6 | 7 | 8 | 9 | 10 |
|---|---|---|---|---|---|---|---|---|---|---|---|
| 0 | 0 | 0 | 0 | 0 | 0 | 0 | 0 | 0 | 0 | 0 | 0 |
| 1 | 0 | 1 | 2 | 3 | 4 | 5 | 6 | 7 | 8 | 9 | 10 |
| 2 | 0 | 2 | 4 | 6 | 8 | 10 | 12 | 14 | 16 | 18 | 20 |
| 3 | 0 | 3 | 6 | 9 | 12 | 15 | 18 | 21 | 24 | 27 | 30 |
| 4 | 0 | 4 | 8 | 12 | 16 | 20 | 24 | 28 | 32 | 36 | 40 |
| 5 | 0 | 5 | 10 | 15 | 20 | 25 | 30 | 35 | 40 | 45 | 50 |
| 6 | 0 | 6 | 12 | 18 | 24 | 30 | 36 | 42 | 48 | 54 | 60 |
| 7 | 0 | 7 | 14 | 21 | 28 | 35 | 42 | 49 | 56 | 63 | 70 |
| 8 | 0 | 8 | 16 | 24 | 32 | 40 | 48 | 56 | 64 | 72 | 80 |
| 9 | 0 | 9 | 18 | 27 | 36 | 45 | 54 | 63 | 72 | 81 | 90 |
| 10 | 0 | 10 | 20 | 30 | 40 | 50 | 60 | 70 | 80 | 90 | 100 |

**Figure 4.5. Multiplication Chart**

An extremely useful technique in relating addition and subtraction is a fact family. Just like people, numbers have relationships with each other under certain circumstances. For example, 5 + 2 is the same as 2 + 5. They both add up to 7. Understanding that can help children deduce that 7 – 2 = 5 and 7 – 5 = 2. The same three numbers have an addition and subtraction relationship. This relationship is called a **fact family**. A fact family like this one always gives two addition equations and two subtraction equations.

Multiplication and division are also inverse operations and are typically introduced at a point when a child can comfortably identify numbers up to 20 and is familiar with addition and subtraction. They can begin to understand terms such as *multiplier, factor, product, multiply,* and *times.*

Multiplication is basically repeated addition, so 5 × 3 is the same as 5 + 5 + 5. A **multiplication chart** can help students learn the multiple of small whole numbers. In the chart, children can just focus on the diagonals (2 × 2, 3 × 3, 4 × 4, etc.) and the section either above or below the diagonal (because of the commutative property of multiplication, which states that 5 × 3 is equivalent to 3 × 5).

It is no surprise that children develop concrete understanding with the aid of visual representations, such as cookie dough laid out on a baking tray, seats in a movie theatre, or a dozen donuts in a box. They are commonly arranged in rows and columns, which is called an **array**. Arrays can help explain multiplication using rows and columns: The number of rows and columns each refer to the factors used in a multiplication equation.

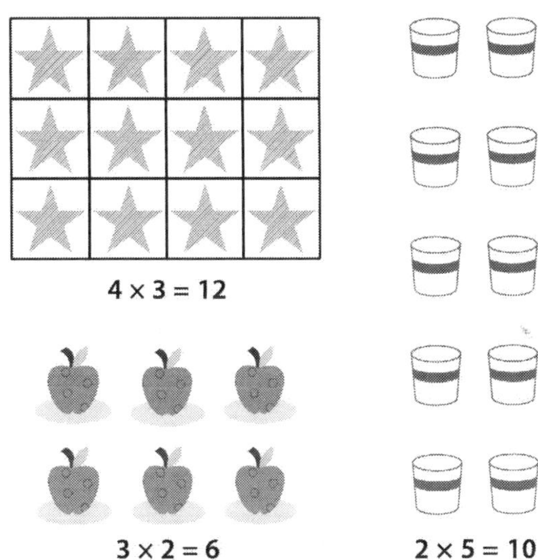


Figure 4.6. Arrays

Just as addition and subtraction are related in fact families, multiplication and division have a relationship too. **Division** is the act of splitting into equal parts or groups. For example, if three friends wish to share a pizza cut into nine slices, how many slices would each friend get? The terms *divisor, dividend, quotient, divided by,* and *remainder* are used in division. In this example, $\frac{9}{3}$ (or 9 ÷ 3) equals three wholes. If a number does not completely divide to give a whole number, the division will result in a **remainder**. For example, sharing twelve cupcakes with five

DID YOU KNOW?

Multiplication charts have long been a common resource in EC classrooms, but recent research suggests that arrays and other visual representation of multiplication are more effective teaching tools.

friends $\left(\frac{12}{5} \text{ or } 12 \div 5\right)$ will result in two whole cupcakes per friend with two left over, or a remainder of 2.

Arrays can also be used with division problems. In Figure 4.7, seven people are to share fourteen pizza slices. How many slices will each person get? The division equation is written as $14 \div 7 = 2$. The fourteen pizza slices are split into seven equal groups. That results in two slices per person.

QUICK REVIEW

How could you use manipulatives to teach students about remainders?

Multiplication and division are inverse operations and related through fact families. For instance, $3 \times 6$ is the same as $6 \times 3$. They both multiply to give 18. Now, using these same numbers, a child can deduce that $18 \div 3 = 6$ and $18 \div 3 = 6$. The three numbers have a multiplication and division relationship. A fact family such as this one always includes two multiplication equations and two division equations.

$14 \div 7 = 2$

**Figure 4.7. Using Arrays for Division**

## SAMPLE QUESTIONS

5) **Selena had seven pencils. She gave two pencils to her friend Amy. How many pencils does she have now?**

   **Which of the following problems has the same mathematical structure as the problem above?**

   A. Selena brought three friends to the end-of-summer party. Amy brought two friends. How many friends did they bring together?

   B. Selena brought ten carrot sticks for lunch. How many carrots sticks were left after she ate six?

   C. Selena earned two stickers every school day this week, Monday through Friday. How many stickers did she earn?

   D. Selena has seven markers. Amy has three more markers than Selena does. How many markers does Amy have?

6) **A teacher is passing out candy to a group of students. There are six students in the group, and each student will get two pieces of candy. How many pieces of candy does the teacher need?**

**Which of the following arrays shows the solution to this problem?**

A.

B.

C.

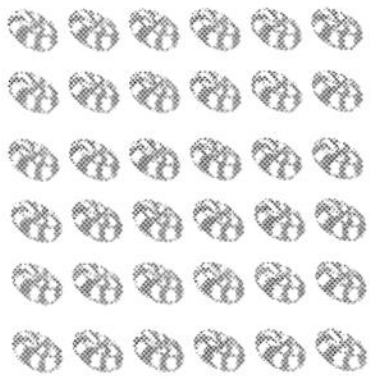

D.

# FRACTIONS

A fraction can be described as part of a whole. The top number of a fraction is called the **numerator**, and the bottom number is the **denominator**. The numerator represents how many of the parts are taken, and the denominator represents how many equal parts the object is split into. A fraction is the division of the top number by the bottom number.

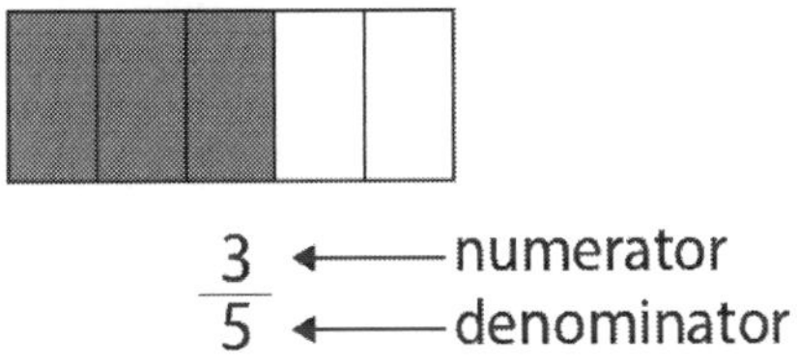

For early learners, a **visual fraction model** is a pictorial way of understanding fractions. It could include objects, shapes, or figures divided into fractions.

$\frac{3}{5}$ ← numerator / ← denominator

Figure 4.8. Visual Fraction Model

A **unit fraction** is a fraction in which the numerator is 1, such as $\frac{1}{6}$ or $\frac{1}{10}$. While the numerator stays 1, the denominator is the number that determines whether the value of a unit fraction decreases or increases. Consider the following two figures.

Rectangle A is divided into 4 equal parts, and rectangle B is divided in two parts. The unit fraction in A is $\frac{1}{4}$ and the one in B is $\frac{1}{2}$. Visually it is clear that $\frac{1}{4}$ is smaller than $\frac{1}{2}$. Rectangle A has been divided into more equal parts than rectangle B; hence its unit fraction is smaller.

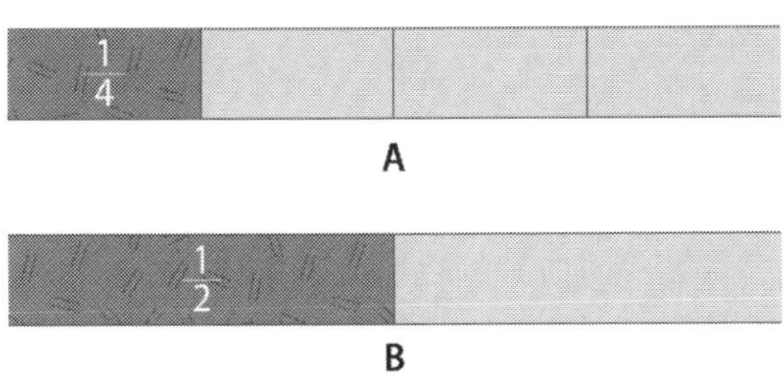


Figure 4.9. Comparing Unit Fractions

The math operations of addition, subtraction, multiplication, and division can be executed on fractions just as on whole numbers, but with a few modifications. When adding or subtracting two fractions, the denominator is important. For fractions with like (same) denominators, simply add or subtract the numerator and write the final answer over the same denominator. For example, $\frac{3}{10} + \frac{5}{10} = \frac{8}{10}$ and $\frac{5}{6} - \frac{1}{6} = \frac{4}{6}$.

For fractions with unlike (different) denominators, first find a common denominator. When two or more denominators are the same or brought to the same number, that number is called a **common denominator**. A common denominator can be found by finding the smallest whole number that is divisible by both denominators. Another way is to simply multiply denominators together to result in a common number.

> COMMON STUDENT ERRORS
>
> - thinking that the fraction with the larger denominator is larger $\left(\frac{1}{5} > \frac{1}{3}\right)$
> - adding the numerators and the denominators $\left(\frac{1}{3} + \frac{2}{5} = \frac{3}{8}\right)$
> - misunderstanding the relationship between the fraction bar and the decimal $\left(\frac{3}{5} = 3.5 \text{ or } 0.35\right)$

After finding the common denominator, the two fractions can be rewritten with the new denominator and added as usual. For instance, when adding $\frac{3}{4}$ to $\frac{1}{8}$, the denominators 4 and 8 have 8 as a common multiple. 4 goes into 8 twice (4 × 2). 8 is the smallest whole number divisible by 4 and 8. So, $\frac{3}{4}$ can be brought to the common denominator of 8 by multiplying both the numerator, 3, and the denominator, 4, by 2. This addition equation can now be expressed as $\frac{6}{8} + \frac{1}{8} = \frac{7}{8}$.

Similarly, in a subtraction equation like $\frac{3}{5} - \frac{1}{15}$, the denominators 5 and 15 have 15 as a common multiple. 5 goes into 15 three times. So, $\frac{3}{5}$ can be brought to a common denominator of 15 by multiplying the numerator, 3, and the denominator, 5, by 3. This subtraction equation can now be written as $\frac{9}{15} - \frac{1}{15} = \frac{8}{15}$.

The following are examples of adding and subtracting fractions with like and unlike denominators.

**Addition:**

- $\frac{7}{11} + \frac{2}{11} = \frac{9}{11}$ (like denominators)
- $\frac{2}{9} + \frac{1}{3} = \frac{2}{9} + \frac{3}{9} = \frac{5}{9}$ (unlike denominators)

**Subtraction:**

- $\frac{9}{12} - \frac{2}{12} = \frac{7}{12}$ (like denominators)
- $\frac{5}{6} - \frac{1}{3} = \frac{5}{6} - \frac{2}{6} = \frac{3}{6}$ (unlike denominators)

Multiplying fractions requires the least work. Both numerators are multiplied, and both denominators are multiplied.

**Multiplication:** $\frac{4}{5} \times \frac{3}{7} = \frac{(4 \times 3)}{(5 \times 7)} = \frac{12}{35}$

In dividing fractions, first find the reciprocal of the second fraction. A **reciprocal** is found by swapping the numerator and denominator. After taking the reciprocal of the second fraction, simply multiply the two fractions as usual to arrive at the final answer.

**Division:** $\frac{1}{3} \div \frac{2}{5} = \frac{1}{3} \times \frac{5}{2} = \frac{5}{6}$

Multiplication and division can result in large numerators and/or denominators. Fractions should be **simplified**—or **reduced**—for ease of understanding by dividing both the numerator and denominator by their greatest common factor. The greatest common factor—or GCF—is the highest number that can divide exactly into two or more numbers. A **common factor** is a number that can be divided into two or more numbers. The factors of 6 are 1, 2, 3, 6, and the factors of 15 are 1, 3, 5, 15. Both 6 and 15 have common factors of 1 and 3. The largest of those common factors is called the greatest common factor.

In the fraction $\frac{8}{12}$, the numerator 8 and the denominator 12 have 4 as their greatest common factor (that is, 4 is the highest factor common to both numbers). After dividing both numbers, the reduced fraction is now $\frac{2}{3}$. $\frac{8}{12}$ and $\frac{2}{3}$ are called **equivalent** fractions because even though they are expressed differently, they represent the same quantity.

Fractions are not always less than 1. There are fractions where the numerator is larger than the denominator. These are called **improper fractions**. In such cases, decomposing a fraction can be useful. **Decomposing** fractions involves splitting them into smaller pieces. Consider the improper fraction $\frac{7}{5}$. This can be decomposed into a part equal to 1 and a part smaller than 1: $\frac{7}{5} = \frac{5}{5} + \frac{2}{5}$.

$1 + \frac{3}{5} = 1\frac{3}{5}$ ← mixed number

*or*

$\frac{5}{5} + \frac{3}{5} = \frac{8}{5}$ ← improper fraction

**Figure 4.10. Types of Fractions**

There are also fractions that contain whole numbers with a fractional part. These are called **mixed numbers**. For instance, $4\frac{2}{3}$ is a mixed number. This number can be decomposed as:

$= 1 + 1 + 1 + 1 + \frac{2}{3}$

$= \frac{3}{3} + \frac{3}{3} + \frac{3}{3} + \frac{3}{3} + \frac{1}{3} + \frac{1}{3}$

This results in six fractions with a common denominator of 3. Decomposing fractions can make addition and subtraction of some fractions more straightforward.

Many real-life circumstances involve fractions. For instance:

> Mom bought $\frac{5}{12}$ of a pound of chicken. Dad bought $\frac{1}{3}$ of a pound of chicken. Who purchased the larger amount?

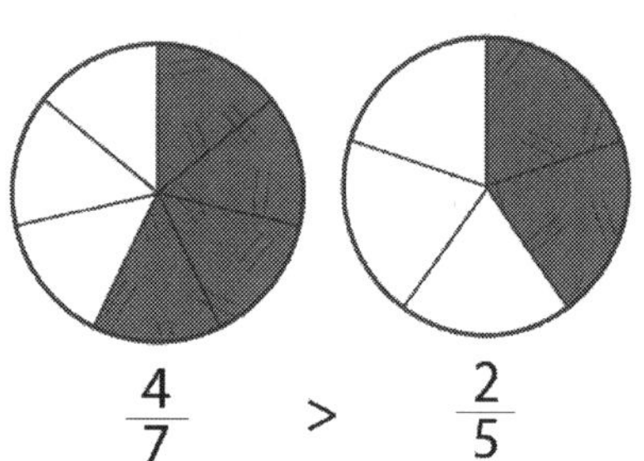


**Figure 4.11. Comparing Fractions**

First, bring both fractions to a common denominator (12 in this case). So, for Dad's chicken weighing $\frac{1}{3}$ pound (multiply both the numerator and denominator by 4), $\frac{1}{3} = \frac{4}{12}$. Upon comparison, $\frac{5}{12}$ is greater than $\frac{4}{12}$ since the numerator 5 is larger than 4. So, Mom purchased the larger amount.

Comparing fractions can also be done by using grid or **area models**.

## SAMPLE QUESTIONS

7) **Carla divides her pizza into eight equal slices and takes one slice. If the amount of pizza remaining is written as a fraction, the numerator will be which of the following values?**

   A. 1
   B. 7
   C. 8
   D. 9

8) **Which of the following is the best definition of decomposing fractions?**

   A. separating the numerator and denominator into individual numbers
   B. finding the reciprocal of a fraction
   C. splitting a fraction into smaller pieces
   D. creating equivalent fractions

## Ratios and Percentages

Fractions can be expressed in different ways—ratio, percent, and decimal. These different forms can all represent the same number. A **ratio** is a comparison of two numbers. As its definition indicates, a fraction specifies a part of a whole, but a ratio is an indicator of how much of one thing there is compared to another.

For instance, in a pouch containing eight blue and five red marbles, there are eight blue marbles to five red marbles—or a ratio to 8 to 5, also written 8:5. In a recipe that calls for six cups of flour and three cups of milk, the ratio of flour to milk is 6:3. Ratios are similar to fractions and illustrate the relationship between part and whole.

Another example is a classroom full of students. There are ten girls, eleven boys, and two instructors in a classroom. The following shows part-to-part and part-to-whole ratios.

| Part to Part | Part to Whole |
|---|---|
| Ratio of boys to girls: 11:10 or $\frac{11}{10}$ | Ratio of boys to all students: 11:21 or $\frac{11}{21}$ |
| Ratio of instructors to girls: 2:10 or $\frac{2}{10}$ | Ratio of girls to entire class: 10:23 or $\frac{10}{23}$ |

A **percent** is a type of fraction where the denominator is always 100, meaning it refers to parts per one hundred. Using 100 makes comparisons simple because the whole is always the same. A percent is easily identifiable by the percent symbol, %, added at the end. Students should first understand that 100% is considered all of everything. 100% of a class with thirty students refers to all thirty students. 50% refers to half—in this case, half of thirty, which is fifteen students ($30 \div 2 = 15$). Graph paper is a very useful tool in teaching percent to students.

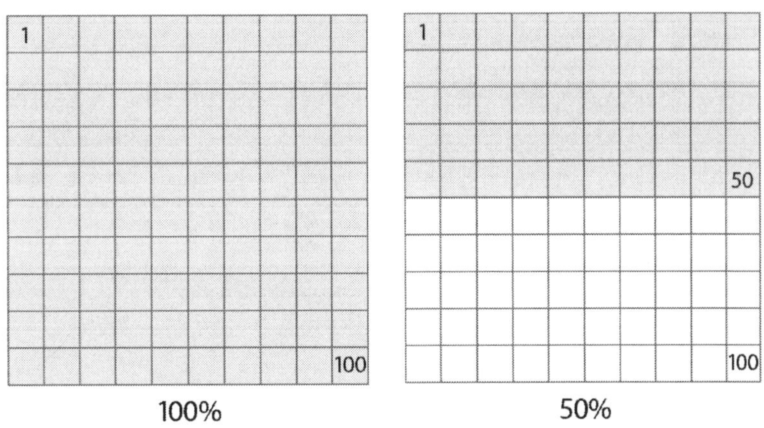


Figure 4.12. Drawing Percents on Graph Paper

A percent can be easily converted into a **decimal** by removing the percent symbol and dividing the number by 100. Also, dividing the numerator of a fraction by its denominator gives a decimal. The following example shows the progression of ratio to fraction to percent to decimal.

$$3:20 \quad = \quad \frac{3}{20} \quad = \quad \frac{3(5)}{20(5)} \quad = \quad \frac{15}{100} \quad = \quad 15\% \quad = \quad 0.15$$

**ratio** **fraction** *multiply to get a common denominator of 100* **percent** **decimal**

Figure 4.13. Relationship Between Ratios, Fractions, Percents, and Decimals

SAMPLE QUESTION

9) **A teacher is preparing a lesson with the objective of converting fractions to percents. Which of the following skills should students be able to perform before the teacher begins the lesson?**

A. comparing unit fractions

B. finding the reciprocal of a fraction

C. decomposing fractions

D. creating a common denominator

# Algebraic Thinking

Algebraic thinking is about simplifying mathematical ideas and developing the ability to express reasoning in age-appropriate ways. It involves the ability to identify, extend, describe, create patterns, manipulate properties, and implement order of math operations.

## Patterns

A pattern is a series or **sequence** that repeats. People's lives are a series of patterns—they wake up, get ready for work or school, make the drive back home, make dinner, etc. Then the cycle repeats.

Children are known to do well with structure and routine. The predictable nature of what comes next—patterns—in their day-to-day schedule helps them feel secure. Even babies can identify patterns soon after birth. An expectable routine of feeding, playing, and napping is based on patterns of repetition.

Children with a good understanding of patterns are enhancing their problem-solving, number manipulation, and counting skills. Identifying patterns is a vital skill in mathematical reasoning.

In math, patterns are sequences that repeat based on a rule. Common types of patterns in math are number patterns and shape patterns. These involve different numbers or shapes ordered and repeated according to a rule. Here is a game that can help children understand patterns. Using a box of blocks, the teacher lays out these colors in order:

Red, Blue, Yellow, Green, Red, Blue, Yellow, Green

Children should **predict** or guess the following pattern. For variety, the teacher can use different colors or a different number of blocks, or other items like crayons, beads, and beanbags. Sometimes children follow the pattern for a while and then begin to make up their own. They may feel bored or want to use their favorite color. Rather than correcting them, the teacher should reinforce the concept by encouraging them to try different patterns.

Recognizing patterns is not just a visual matching skill. Songs are full of repetition, and children gravitate toward catchy tunes. Many songs have an appealing hook that children love to repeat. Beating rhythmically on a drum or lid of a container with hands or spoons can give children practice with recurring musical pattern matching.

HELPFUL HINT

Teachers can use paint and paper to teach students about symmetry: Paint a picture on the top half of a piece of paper, then fold the paper in half while the paint is still wet. The image created will be a mirror image of the original painting. The painting as a whole is symmetrical, and the fold line is the line of symmetry.

There are also naturally occurring patterns in nature. Examples include trees, spirals, stripes, waves, and symmetries. **Symmetry** occurs when a shape looks the same when it has been flipped or turned. For example, a sunflower looks the same no matter how it is rotated around its center.

Children can find symmetry outdoors. Many flowers are symmetrical. Teachers should experiment with plucked flowers and encourage the children to find symmetry in them. The following are some symmetrical patterns in nature.

**Figure 4.14. Examples of Symmetry in Nature**

## SAMPLE QUESTIONS

**10) Which of the following has more than one line of symmetry?**

A. heart
B. circle
C. kite
D. the letter M

**11) Three-year-old Jess is playing with a box of that contains counters in five different colors. She takes a big handful of counters from the box and lays down a blue counter, followed by a red, then a yellow, then a green, then an orange. After a few minutes, she has five lines of counters, each following the same sequence of colors. What skill is she reinforcing?**

A. pattern matching
B. counting
C. sorting
D. identifying

## Properties and Order of Operations

As children become comfortable with addition, subtraction, multiplication, and division, they initially gain exposure performing these operations between two numbers. But what if an expression requires multiple operations? There are rules that dictate the order in which these operations are to be completed.

A math equation with multiple operations could include a combination of any of the four basic math operations plus parentheses and exponents. **Parentheses**, ( ), are symbols used to group things together. They take precedence in any math expression, and the operation(s) inside them must be performed first.

The next operation that takes precedence is exponents. An **exponent** is a number written as a superscript above a base number that indicates how many times to use that base number in multiplication. For example, $2^4 = 2 \times 2 \times 2 \times 2 = 16$. The exponent is 4 and the base number is 2. Sometimes it is phrased as 2 "to the power of" 4.

The general rule for the order of operations is:

- Any operation inside **P**arentheses is solved first.
- Any number with an **E**xponent is solved next.
- Then **M**ultiply and **D**ivide from left to right.
- Lastly, **A**dd and **S**ubtract from left to right.

The initials above spell the acronym **PEMDAS**.

At this point, children can be introduced to "tricks" and properties of math operations that will make problem solving easier. There are four basic properties of math operations.

The **commutative property** (for addition and multiplication) maintains that the order of the numbers in a math expression does not matter. For example, in addition, 5 + 4 and 4 + 5 have the same result, 9. In multiplication, 3 × 7 and 7 × 3 both equal 21. Switching the two numbers in an addition or multiplication equation does not change the end value. The commutative property does not apply to subtraction or division.

The **associative property** refers to the order a single operation (for example, addition) is done within a group. These groups are typically contained within parentheses. An addition equation like 3 + (9 + 5) can be written as (3 + 9) + 5 to equal 17. In multiplication, 6 × (2 × 4) can be written as (6 × 2) × 4 to yield 48. This property requires regrouping numbers. The associative property does not apply to subtraction or division.

The **distributive** property refers to distributing through the values within parentheses. For example, 3 × (6 + 2) can be rewritten as 3 × 6 + 3 × 2. (Remember that multiplication and division are performed before addition and subtraction.) Both equations produce the answer 24.

Addition and multiplication have a special property called the identity property. The **additive identity** is zero. This means any number added to zero remains the same and keeps its identity: $6 + 0 = 6$ or $0 + 2 = 2$. The **multiplicative identity** is one. This means any number multiplied by one remains the same and retains its identity: $130 \times 1 = 130$ or $1 \times 54 = 54$.

QUICK REVIEW

Which property is described in the statement $8 + 20 = 20 + 8$?

SAMPLE QUESTIONS

**12) Ms. Kyle's fifth-grade students were asked to write an equation depicting the additive identity property. Which of the following students is correct?**

A. Anna: $15 \times 4 = 4 \times 15$

B. Bob: $20 \times 1 = 20$

C. Michael: $18 + 4 = 4 + 18$

D. Jen: $27 + 0 = 27$

**13) Which of the following skills should students master before learning the associative property?**

A. order of operations

B. decomposing whole numbers

C. multiplication

D. adding fractions

## Geometry, Measurement, and Data

A good understanding of counting, basic math operations, and the properties and order of math operations leads to higher levels of algebraic thinking and problem-solving skills. Children can eventually work with problems involving geometry, measurement, and interpretation of data.

### MEASUREMENT

**Measurement** refers to numbers that show size or amount of some characteristic. The numbers can refer to characteristics like length, weight, time, money, or distance and are measured in specific units such as feet, pounds, minutes, dollars, or miles. A **unit of measurement** is the unit or term used to measure a characteristic. These units can be standard or nonstandard.

A **standard unit of measurement** is a defined, universal convention used to quantify the characteristic being measured. Examples include inches, miles, and meters (for distance) or ounces, pounds, and kilograms (for mass). A **nonstandard** unit of measurement refers to items not commonly used for measuring, such as paper clips, popsicle sticks, or an arm length.

Standard units of measurement can be classified into a number of systems. Most countries use the **metric** system, which uses units such as centimeters, kilometers, grams, and kilograms. In the United States, **US customary** units are used, including inches, feet, ounces, and pounds.

Children love measuring, especially **length** or **height**. They gain a degree of satisfaction in knowing the longest or tallest object in a group. They can use a nonstandard unit of measurement like a pencil or a stick to measure various things around the house or classroom. They can use a ruler to measure small items. They can now understand terms such as *length*, *how long*, *how short*, *width*, *tall*, *height*, and *inches*.

COMMON STUDENT ERRORS

- starting at the wrong end of the ruler or at 1 instead of at 0
- counting the lines instead of the spaces on a ruler

Another way to get them to practice math skills through measurement is by introducing them to metric mass, types of currency (money), and telling time.

People generally use the word *weight* to express how heavy or light something is. Weight is actually the measure of gravity pulling on an object, and **mass** is how much matter is packed into an object. Weight can vary depending on gravitational pull. For instance, the weight of an object on the moon is less than that on Earth because the gravitational pull is weaker on the moon. However, the object's mass remains the same. The standard unit of measurement for mass is kilogram.

Older children should be familiar with **money**: the denominations of US currency, skip counting, and converting currency. The four most-used coins and their values (penny = one cent, nickel = five cents, dime = ten cents, quarter = twenty-five cents) can be used to show conversions between values, such as the relationships between nickels and dimes, pennies and nickels, and nickels and quarters. Using play money is a great way to practice these types of calculations, which often involve skip counting.

The comfort of knowing what comes next in their day-to-day schedule has been shown to help children understand and manage **time**. However, teaching the concept of time to children can be a challenging undertaking.

Which type of clock is best to start with—analog or digital? The analog clock has moveable parts and can show elapsed time. It is also visually appealing. It can cover most of the concepts a child is expected to

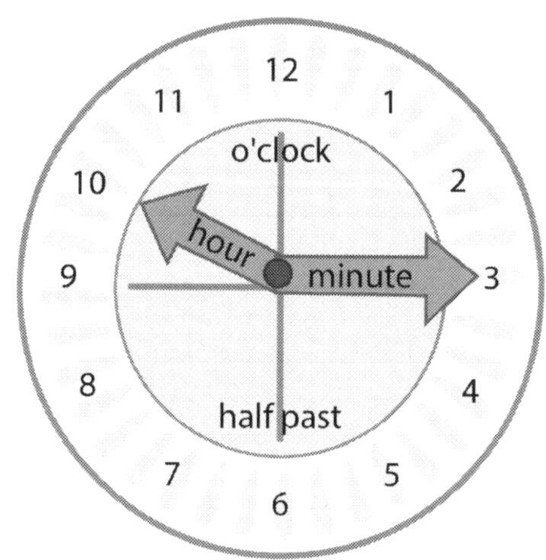


**Figure 4.15. Analog Clock Made from a Paper Plate**

know with regard to time. A digital clock may seem easier, but it is less useful for showing elapsed time or future time (like how many hours till dinner, or when to wake up in the morning, etc.).

An analog clock can introduce students to hours and minutes. The ability to count to sixty will benefit them in this exercise. Teachers can slowly introduce skip counting by fives (for the minute hand). Terms such as *hour, minute, o'clock, half past, quarter past*, and *quarter till* can be introduced concurrently. Once children are comfortable with the ins and outs of an analog clock, they can experiment with a digital clock. A fun activity involves matching time on a digital clock to an analog clock.

### SAMPLE QUESTION

**14) A kindergarten teacher asks her students to choose a nonstandard unit to measure the length of the classroom. Which of the following is the most appropriate nonstandard unit for the students to use?**

A. a carpet square
B. paper clips
C. a yardstick
D. popsicle sticks

## TWO-DIMENSIONAL SHAPES

Shapes can be described in various dimensions. A one-dimensional (1-D) object is just a point or points on a line. A common 1-D measurement is distance. A two-dimensional (2-D) object is a closed, flat figure with no depth and can be expressed on a **plane**—for example, a drawing of a triangle, square, or rectangle on a paper. It has length and width. A simple way to describe a three-dimensional (3-D) solid is something that takes up space—a ball, tree, house, or a car. It has height, depth, length, surface area, and volume.

Children's first drawings are probably replications of triangles, circles, rectangles, and squares—standard 2-D shapes. By age five, hand-eye coordination improves and drawings become more recognizable. This is a precursor to basic understanding of geometry. At this point, terms like *base, height, sides*, and many others become relevant.

An easy way to teach children to compose a 2-D shape is by first placing the corners—or vertices. For example, for a triangle, a student should draw three points on paper and join the points with lines. The triangle now has three corners and three **sides**. In more advanced geometry, children are ready to understand that the measure of the space between two lines that connect is called an **angle**. Another term to introduce is the bottom of a triangle, which is called the **base**. The measurement from the top of a triangle to its base is called the **height**.

Just like a triangle, a rectangle and a square can be composed by first placing the vertices and then connecting the points. Squares and rectangles are classified as **quadrilaterals**—four-sided figures with four straight sides. A square is a type of rectangle. Both have four right angles, but a **square**'s sides are all the same length, while a **rectangle** has two long sides and two short sides. The **length** of a rectangle is typically its longer side, while the **height** (or width) is its shorter side.

| Shape | Sides<br>Angles | Looks Like |
|---|---|---|
| Circle | no flat side<br>no angles | *clock* |
| Triangle | 3 sides<br>3 angles | YIELD<br>*yield sign* |
| Square | 4 sides<br>4 angles | Q W E R<br>A S<br>*keyboard keys* |
| Rectangle | 4 sides<br>4 angles | *TV* |
| Hexagon | 6 sides<br>6 angles | *white shapes in soccer ball* |

**Figure 4.16. Two-Dimensional Shapes Anchor Chart**

A circle is a 2-D shape with equal height and width (which is called the **diameter**). It is worth mentioning that half of a circle's diameter is called its **radius**. The radius is used to find area and circumference (the length of the circle's outline). However, a circle does not contain any corners or vertices, so a child trying to free draw a circle could very well end up with a misshapen circle. Sketching a circle is a challenge for young children as they do not have points or vertices to connect. One suggestion is to draw circles of different sizes on a paper and let the child trace over them. Another tip is to tie a pencil's end to a thread and secure the other end of the thread to a paper clip pierced into the center of a piece of paper. This will ensure that the thread stays taut as the child attempts to draw the outline of the circle. Advanced tools to draw circles include protractors, compasses, and stencils or templates.

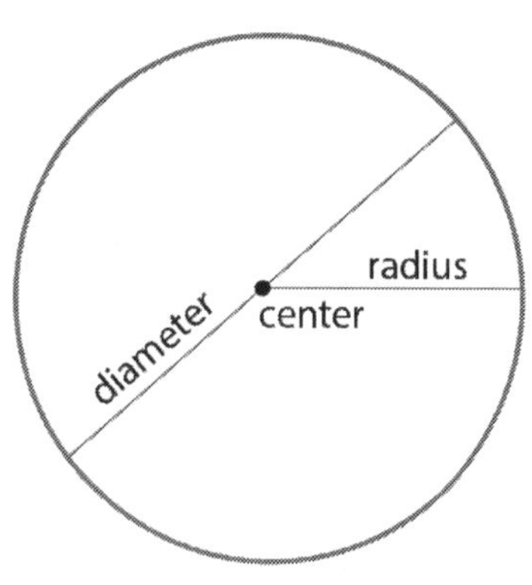


**Figure 4.17. Parts of a Circle**

A precursor to very advanced math topics like geometry, algebra, trigonometry, and calculus involves understanding the concept of area and perimeter of 2-D shapes. The **perimeter** is the length of the outline of a 2-D shape. The **area** of a 2-D shape is the amount of space inside it. Perimeter can be taught by letting students use nonstandard units of measurement like paper clips or toothpicks to measure the outline of an object like a book or a piece of paper. Unifix® or math cubes can be used to fill up the insides of a 2-D shape, introducing students to the concept of area.

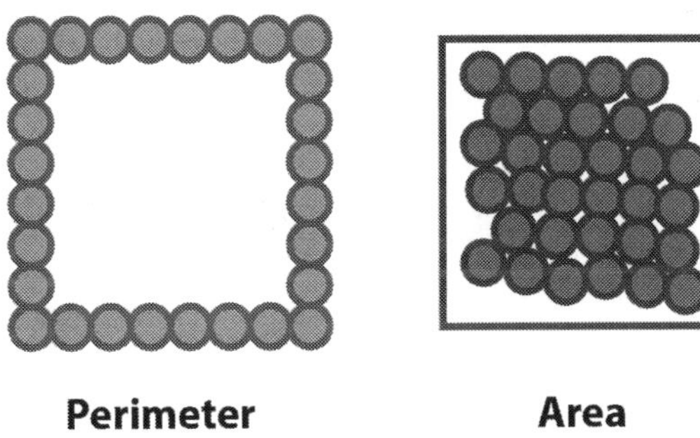


Figure 4.18. Using Nonstandard Units to Measure Perimeter and Area

## SAMPLE QUESTION

**15) A second-grade teacher has completed a lesson on categorizing types of two-dimensional shapes. She draws the figure below on the board and asks her students to give a possible name for the shape.**

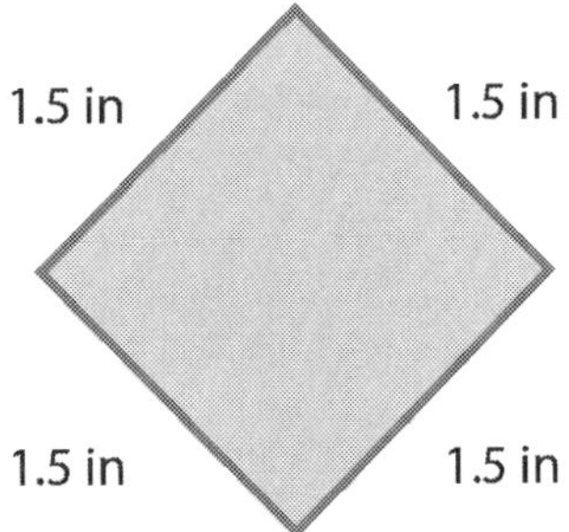


**Ari says it is a rectangle.**

**Edmundo says it is a square.**

**Donny says it is a quadrilateral.**

**Which student(s) correctly named the figure?**

A. Ari and Donny

B. Edmundo only

C. Edmundo and Donny

D. all three students

## THREE-DIMENSIONAL SHAPES

Three-dimensional (3-D) shapes have distinct attributes and characteristics. The main attribute differentiating 2-D shapes from 3-D shapes is that 2-D shapes are considered "flat," while 3-D shapes take up space—they can be held and are solid.

It is this attribute of 3-D shapes that associates them with objects in everyday life. For example, a beach ball is a **sphere**; sugar cubes are **cubes**; Egyptian pyramids are **pyramids**; a wedge of cheese can be a **prism**. Many of these 3-D solids are human-made. When discussing engineered 3-D solids with students, teachers should ask how students think engineers or designers created them. What types of measurements would they have to know to create these objects?

The **volume** of a 3-D shape is the amount of space it occupies. There are mathematical formulas for calculating volume depending on the shape. The **surface area** is the total area of every surface of a 3-D shape. The **face** of a 3-D shape is any flat, visible surface. For instance, a cube has six square faces. Its surface area is the area of all its six faces added together. A visual way for children to find the surface area of a 3-D solid is to flatten it into a 2-D shape (on paper). This flattened version is called a **net**. Figure 4.19 shows shapes and their nets.

QUICK REVIEW

What attribute is characteristic of a 3-D shape but not of a 2-D shape?

| Shape | Net | Faces Vertices | Looks Like |
|---|---|---|---|
| Sphere 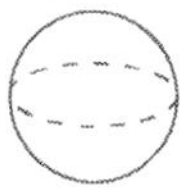 | can't be flattened | 1 curved face<br>no vertices | *baseball*<br>*balloon*<br>*the moon* |
| Cube 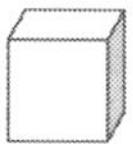 | 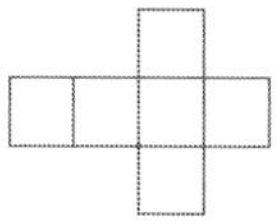 | 6 faces<br>8 vertices | *dice*<br>*ice cube* |
| Rectangular Prism 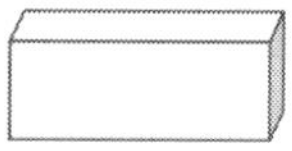 | 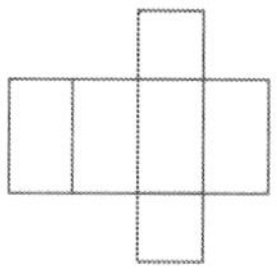 | 6 faces<br>8 vertices | *lego*<br>*book*<br>*box* |
| Pyramid 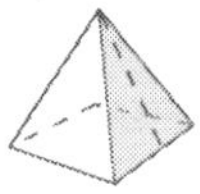 | 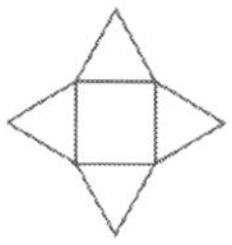 | 5 faces<br>5 vertices | *pyramids in Egypt* |
| Cylinder 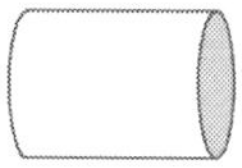 | 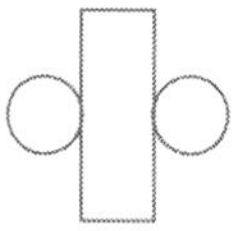 | 2 flat faces<br>1 curved face | *cup*<br>*soda can*<br>*marker* |
| Cone  |  | 1 flat face<br>1 curved face | *ice cream cone*<br>*party hat* |

**Figure 4.19. Three-Dimensional Shapes Anchor Chart**

## SAMPLE QUESTIONS

16) **Which 3-D solid has four triangular faces and one square face?**

A. pyramid

B. cube

C. rectangular prism

D. cylinder

17) **Which of the following shapes is produced when the net below is folded to make a 3-D shape?**

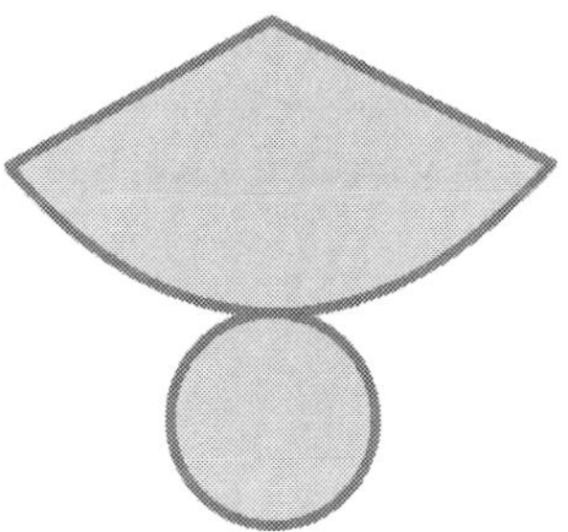

A. cylinder
B. cone
C. cube
D. pyramid

## COLLECTING, ORGANIZING, AND PRESENTING DATA

The world is filled with numerical information that needs to be collected, organized, and deciphered. Some examples of such numerical information are test scores of students in a classroom, income of people in an organization, or costs of airline tickets. Manipulating information or data is the basis for the science of statistical analysis. Data collection is the process of grouping and measuring information on specific topics. This data can be displayed in the form of pictures, charts, or graphs. A **graph** is an illustration of values or data. Graphs are useful because they are visual and can represent the data better than words and numbers alone. Graphs and charts may be considered compact and concise depictions of data.

A **bar graph** is a display of bars of different colors or sizes. The longer the bar, the larger the number represented. For example, the bar graph in Figure 4.20 shows the **comparison** of the number of students who chose dog, elephant, cat, giraffe, or koala as their favorite animal. It shows quantitative data and is best used to compare among different groups.

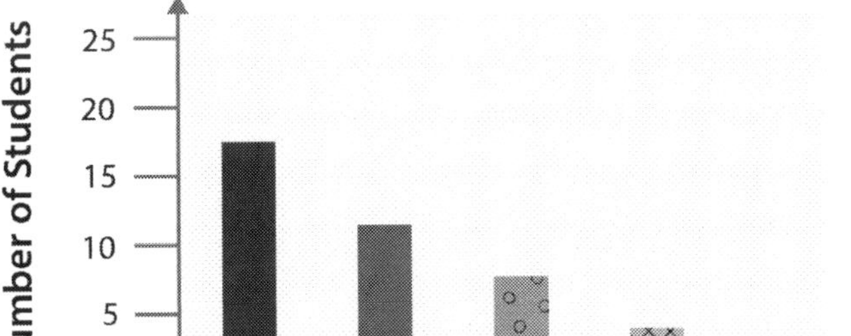


Figure 4.20. Bar Graph

A **line graph** is a type of graph that uses data values as points connected by lines. It is typically used to show how the variable being measured changes in value. The example in Figure 4.21 shows the math test scores of a student through middle school and high school years. A math score is marked for each grade and each point is connected by lines. It is a type of chart used to visualize the changes in the value of a variable over time.

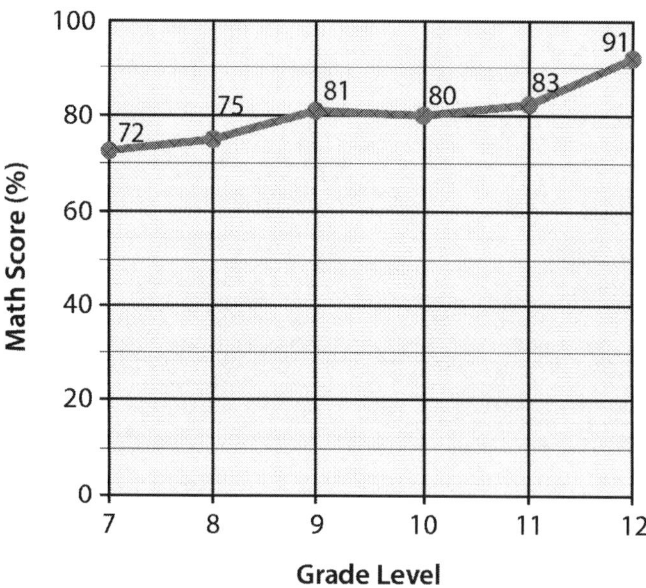


**Figure 4.21. Line Graph**

**Pie charts** are circular graphs. They look like a pie divided into slices. Pie charts are useful when showing quantities as parts of a whole. They are a common statistical graphic used in the business world. They can also be useful in a school environment. For instance, the pie chart in Figure 4.22 shows the number of textbooks classified by genre in a school's library. It shows quantitative data. The largest slice represents the category with the highest number of books. The entire circle represents all books in the library.

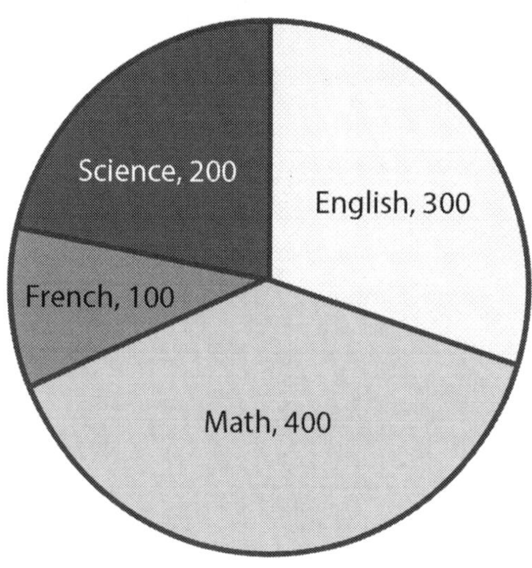


**Figure 4.22. Pie Chart**

**Scatter plots** are like line graphs, but their purpose is unique. They are used to show how one variable (or set) can be affected by another. In other words, a scatter plot shows the **correlation** between the two variables or sets of data being plotted. In Figure 4.23, student test scores are plotted against the number of hours spent studying. The more hours spent studying, the better the test scores. Both variables are increasing together, indicating a positive correlation.

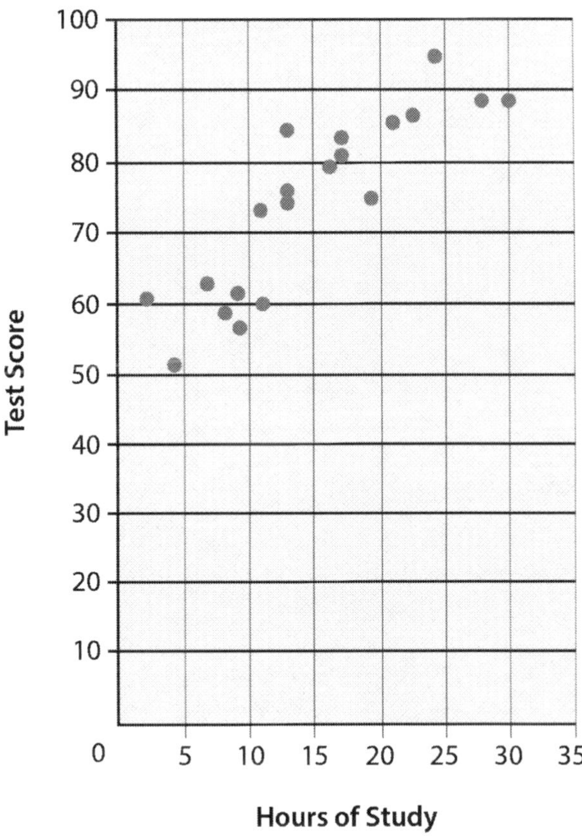


Figure 4.23. Scatter Plot

A **line plot** is a type of graph that shows data frequency along a number line. Take an example of student test scores. This is a list of test scores received by twenty students.

86, 84, 87, 81, 84, 89, 81, 87, 92, 91, 92, 88, 81, 86, 85, 84, 88, 82, 83, 86

To make a line plot, establish a range that includes all the data in suitable intervals. Then plot each number using a symbol (such as an X or an *).

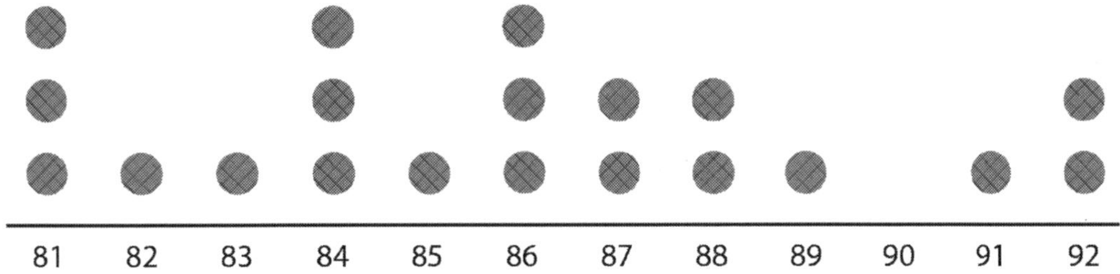


Figure 4.24. Line Plot

A **stem-and-leaf** plot shows data frequency among the categories of values that occur. These plots are useful for presenting the same set of data in the shape of a distribution. Using the same example of the twenty student test scores, first sort the data in ascending order.

81, 81, 81, 82, 83, 84, 84, 84, 85, 86, 86, 86, 87, 87, 88, 88, 89, 91, 92, 92

The *stem* consists of the highest (or first) place value digit of the data numbers (in this case, tens) and the *leaf* consists of all the other digit(s) (in this case, ones).

| Stem | Leaf |
|---|---|
| 8 | 1 1 1 2 3 4 4 4 5 6 6 6 7 7 8 8 9 |
| 9 | 1 2 2 |

**Figure 4.25. Stem-and-Leaf Plot**

To read a stem-and-leaf plot, simply connect the tens (first column) to the ones (second column).

How is all this data in the form of graphs, charts, and plots meaningful? Statistical tools such as mean, median, and mode give insight into viewing this data in specific forms.

The **average**—or **mean**—of a group of data refers to the sum of all data divided by the total number of data items. This is a way to measure what value best represents a sample of data. Think of the average as the "spokesperson" for the entire data set. For example, Li, Jess, and Antoine get allowances of $14, $20, and $17 respectively. What amount could serve as the "spokesperson" for the students' allowances? Find the average: (14 + 20 + 17)/3 = 51/3 = 17. Take the total amount received ($51), and divide that by the total number of people (3). The average of $17 is one way to describe the data set.

HELPFUL HINT

You can use the following rhyme to teach statistical terms:

*Hey diddle diddle,*

*The median's the middle.*

*You add and divide the mean.*

*The mode's the one you find the most,*

*and the range is the difference between.*

Again take the example of the twenty student test scores. If the scores were redistributed to ensure that each student has the same score, that score is referred to as the mean. Just as in calculating the average, first add up all the test scores.

86 + 84 + 87 + 81 + 84 + 89 + 81 + 87 + 92 + 91 + 92 + 88 + 81 + 86 + 85 + 84 + 88 + 82 + 83 + 86 = 1,712

Divide this by the number of scores (20). $\frac{1,717}{20}$ = 85.9, which is the mean score for each student.

When there are extreme values in a data set and the data is very spread out, the average could be skewed high or low due to the wide range of data. In this case, the mean may actually misrepresent the data. The **median**, which is the middle value of a data group, is a good substitute in this instance. Unlike the average or mean, the median is not affected by a very low or very high data value.

Using the same example of the twenty student test scores, here are the scores in ascending order:

81, 81, 81, 82, 83, 84, 84, 84, 85, **86**, **86**, 86, 87, 87, 88, 88, 89, 91, 92, 92

Since this is an even group of data, the median will be the average of the middle two values (in bold). The median here is $\frac{(86 + 86)}{2}$ = 86.

Another statistical tool is called the **mode**, which is the number or numbers that occur most frequently in the data. Here is a conceivable scenario for using the mode instead of the average. Say, for instance, a teacher is measuring the height of each of her fifteen fifth-grade students as part of a math unit on measurement. Most students are of similar height, but she has one exceptionally tall student. Finding the average height of the group of fifteen students will result in a skewed number because of the one tall student. So using the mode can be effective, as it will show where most of the student's heights lie. Unlike the average or the median, the mode is not unique. In a data set, there can be several different data values that occur at the same frequency. This will result in more than one mode. In the example of the twenty student test scores, the modes of the data set are 81, 84, and 86. They all occur three times.

The range is the difference between the smallest and the largest values.

## SAMPLE QUESTIONS

**18) A second-grade teacher has her students pick which genre of movie they like they best. Which of the following should the students use to present their data?**

A. line plot

B. scatter plot

C. stem-and-leaf plot

D. pie chart

19) **For a school project, Imani contacted an ice-cream store owner to collect data on ice-cream sales. She wanted to know which flavor customers purchase the most. The owner's response was chocolate. Which of the following statistical measures does chocolate represent?**

A. mode

B. mean

C. median

D. range

# Answer Key

**1)** A. Incorrect. Skip counting omits numbers in a pattern.

**B.** **Correct.** Number conservation refers to the understanding that the number of objects remains the same even when they are rearranged.

C. Incorrect. Sorting is the process of dividing items into groups based on their characteristics.

D. Incorrect. Pattern matching requires ordering or sorting by a pattern or design.

**2)** A. Incorrect. Sequencing is putting objects in a certain order.

B. Incorrect. Sorting is a way to categorize objects by how they are alike or different.

C. Incorrect. Skip counting omits numbers in a pattern.

**D.** **Correct.** Subitizing refers to the capacity to identify a small number of objects and immediately recognize how many there are without counting.

**3)** A. Incorrect. If the glass is expected to fit into the window frame, it should be measured exactly.

**B.** **Correct.** The teacher can estimate how many pizzas she will need by assuming each person will eat a certain amount and multiplying by 100.

C. Incorrect. Marathons are timed to the second, so exact timings need to be recorded.

D. Incorrect. Bills for consumer purchases include the amount of tax, so they are exact.

**4)** **D)** **Correct.** The number 30,409 rounded to the thousands place is 30,000. Sam rounded up instead of down, and Paul rounded to the hundreds place.

**5)** A. Incorrect. This is an addition problem ($3 + 2 = 5$)

**B.** **Correct.** This is a subtraction problem ($10 - 6 = 4$), as is the scenario in the question ($7 - 2 = 5$).

C. Incorrect. This is a multiplication problem ($2 \times 5 = 10$).

D. Incorrect. This is an addition problem ($7 + 3 = 10$).

**6)** **A.** **Correct.** Array A shows the operations $6 \times 2 = 12$, which is the number of students times the number of pieces of candy each student will receive.

**7)** **B.** **Correct.** Seven of eight pizza slices are left after Carla takes one, so $\frac{7}{8}$ of the pizza remains. 7 is the numerator of this fraction.

**8)** A. Incorrect. There is no need to separate the numerator and denominator.

B. Incorrect. Finding the reciprocal of a fraction is used when dividing two fractions.

**C. Correct.** Decomposing fractions is the process of splitting it into smaller pieces.

D. Incorrect. Creating equivalent fractions helps reduce a large fraction into a simpler form.

**9) D. Correct.** To convert a fraction to a percent, the student will need to convert fractions so they have a denominator of 100.

**10) B. Correct.** A circle has infinite lines of symmetry. The other shapes have one line of symmetry that cuts the shape vertically through the center.

**11) A. Correct.** Jess is matching the color pattern by creating lines of counters that match the original pattern.

**12)** A. Incorrect. Anna has written the commutative property of multiplication.

B. Incorrect. Bob has written the multiplicative identity property.

C. Incorrect. Michael has written the commutative property of addition.

**D. Correct.** Jen has written the additive identity property.

**13)** A. Incorrect. The associative property is a part of the order of operations and must be understood to master it.

B. Incorrect. Decomposing whole numbers is not a skill that is needed to understand the associative property.

**C. Correct.** The associative property addresses grouping addition or multiplication problems. To understand the associative property, students should know how to add and multiply.

D. Incorrect. While some associative property problems may involve fractions, most will involve whole numbers.

**14) A. Correct.** Students can lay carpet squares end-to-end to measure the length of the room.

B. Incorrect. Paper clips will be too short, making it difficult for students to get an accurate measurement.

C. Incorrect. A yardstick measures a standard unit (inches and feet).

D. Incorrect. Popsicle sticks will be too short, making it difficult for students to get an accurate measurement.

**15) D. Correct.** The figure is a quadrilateral, a square, and a rectangle: It has four equal, parallel sides and four right angles.

16) **A.** **Correct.** A pyramid has four triangular faces and one square face.

B. Incorrect. There are no triangular faces on a cube.

C. Incorrect. There are no triangular faces on a rectangular prism.

D. Incorrect. There are no triangular faces on a cylinder.

17) **B.** **Correct.** A cone has an enclosed slanted curve with a circular base.

18) A. Incorrect. A line plot is best used to track the frequency of data points.

B. Incorrect. A scatter plot is used the show the correlation between two variables.

C. Incorrect. A stem-and-leaf plot is best used to track the frequency of data points.

**D.** **Correct.** A pie chart is best used when comparing part of a whole (in this case genres of movies).

19) **A.** **Correct.** The mode is the most frequently occurring data value, which is chocolate.

B. Incorrect. The mean is the sum of all data values divided by the total number of data items.

C. Incorrect. The median is the middle value of a data group.

D. Incorrect. The range is the difference between the largest and smallest data value.

# 5

# Social Science

## Culture and Cultural Identity

### Cultural Perspectives

Students in almost any American classroom will have many different cultural perspectives. While all students will have to adapt to certain parts of the school culture such as behavioral and academic expectations, they will also be part of other **groups** outside of the school community that may have differences and similarities to the **shared experience** within the school. Most state standards provide support for children to learn about and appreciate these similarities and differences.

> DID YOU KNOW?
>
> Immigration patterns in the local community are often first observed in the classroom. Hispanic and Asian student enrollment in public schools in particular has grown by over five million students since the 1990s. The states with the most diverse student populations are Nevada, Florida, California, New York, and Texas.

The school and classroom are unique environments in that students are united in a common goal to grow and learn in a structured setting and are also somewhat separate in their own cultural experiences. All social groups and cultures share basic needs and wants like food, clothing, housing, and security, and they have some method for addressing the concerns of their members. However, what food, clothing, housing, and security look like may vary greatly among groups. A teacher might use the example of a Mongolian reindeer herder to illustrate this. While many Americans may find security in a stable home in one place, nomadic peoples, such as those who pick up their yurts to follow their herds of reindeer, may find security in a portable home that can adapt to the herd's migration.

A teacher might also show various examples of food and clothing that, while different from each other, still meet the physical needs of a community. Differences in a group of people's **physical environment** (part of the human environment that includes purely physical factors such as climate and vegetation) may dictate food, clothing, and housing choices, as people tend to use the resources most readily available. A teacher may point out the differences in clothing between those living in different climates and how housing and food may also vary based on a location's proximity to the equator. These discussions are easily integrated into science themes as well, and appreciation for differences while maintaining an understanding of unity in purpose to meet basic needs is essential.

Of course, the way in which different social groups are organized can vary greatly. This may manifest itself on a microlevel within a student's family, whereby certain gender roles are adhered to, or on a macro-level, in which there is a social custom in the community for neighbors to collaborate in providing after-school childcare. Additionally, the **social conditions**, or situation in society based on income, job, or education level, in which one finds oneself may vary across a larger group. For example, all residents of a certain American city may have some shared culture, but this may vary based on socioeconomic status. Higher-income individuals may frequent different stores and restaurants and live in and attend school in different communities.

Teachers will want to model respect for people across a broad social strata and various cultural backgrounds and avoid making direct comparisons that might imply a value judgment. Instead of saying, for example, "Sanya wears a sari, which makes it hard to run, and Jenny wears jeans, which are comfortable," teachers should say things like "Sanya wears a sari, and Jenny wears jeans."

Additionally, every effort should be made to make the classroom environment one in which many different cultural experiences and expressions are valued as part of the shared experience of the classroom. Strategies for this may involve inclusion of diverse cultural artwork in the classroom decor and reading stories from many different cultural and social perspectives. Teachers may also label items in the classroom in different languages representative of the home languages of students or invite families to share traditional food from their culture with the class.

## SAMPLE QUESTIONS

1) **Which of the following would be most useful for a teacher to show students to help them understand that housing is different in different environments?**

   A. an image of a New York apartment building and an igloo

   B. a drawing of a sprawling suburban home and a simple ranch house

   C. a picture of a Native American woman and man

   D. a photo of the White House and the Pentagon

2) **How might a prekindergarten teacher set up the classroom environment in a way that encourages appreciation for other cultures?**

   A. having multiple learning centers for subjects like literacy and art

   B. including a kimono and sari as part of the dramatic play center

   C. labeling all the classroom items with words such as chair, desk, board, and so on

   D. clearly posting the classroom rules where all can see

## COMPONENTS OF CULTURE

Every culture has elements of expression that make it unique. Certain **cultural norms**, or attitudes or behaviors that are considered normal, may vary significantly from culture to culture. For instance, typical greetings range from the handshake in the United States to kisses in France. Some cultural norms may be even more subtle. In the United States, where people are often focused on health and thinness, refusing a second helping of dinner might be commonplace; whereas in some cultures, refusing food and drink is considered a very rude practice. Even concepts of physical space and what is appropriate social behavior may vary widely. American travelers to some parts of Asia are often surprised at the size of hotel rooms or how closely people sit together on public transport.

While it is important for students to learn such cultural norms of American society as saying "please" and "thank you" and making eye contact when speaking, teachers should ensure that students are aware that cultural norms may vary considerably. As with any method of instilling appreciation for cultural differences, this lesson is often best taught through hands-on learning. A first-grade teacher might ask a parent to speak to the class about different cultural norms in her country, or a third-grade teacher might assign a class research project on different social customs around the world.

Another part of appreciating culture is an awareness of and respect for that culture's **language**. Since it is easiest for children to learn new languages when they are young, many early childhood programs offer class-wide instruction or language immersion in a second language such as Spanish or Mandarin. This instruction lends itself to a further exploration of the broader culture of Latin America or China and should be pursued to spark students' interest in other cultures.

> QUICK REVIEW
>
> What are some cultural norms that have shocked or surprised you while visiting other places?

Early childhood teachers will appreciate the overall differences in language among students and their families and should accommodate these differences. Teachers and schools may translate important information on websites or in news-letters into common home languages of the student population. This shows that the teacher and school respect the different languages spoken and also helps increase communication between schools and families.

DID YOU KNOW?

Mandarin is the most-spoken language in the world, with 12 percent of the world's population speaking it. It is followed by Spanish (6 percent), English (5 percent), Arabic (5 percent), and Hindi (3.5 percent).

The **artistic creations** of any given culture are also a great medium for student exploration. This exploration allows for integration of art and social studies and helps young students develop fine motor skills as well as an awareness of art in different cultures. Students may study and create any number of pieces specific to a given culture. For example, papier-mâché is a common art activity for young students that is often erroneously associated only with Europe. In fact, the ancient Egyptians and Persians also used the art form to great success. This single art project could be integrated into a broader unit on several different cultures. Similarly, piñatas, typically associated with Mexico, are used in many different cultures, including American birthday celebrations. Because art is enjoyed and appreciated by students of all ages, field trips to art museums and galleries are interesting and effective ways to expose students to art from a variety of cultures, both near and far.

**Music** is another fun and creative way to introduce students to different cultural, artistic expression. Many classrooms use music to help very young children develop oral language skills and an understanding of sounds and rhyme. Music can be chosen from an international selection geared toward a young audience. Moreover, students might study and even construct instruments from different cultural traditions as they learn about their use. Drums, maracas, castanets, and shakers can easily be made with simple materials. Soothing music from a different cultural tradition can be played in the background of the classroom if appropriate.

Incorporating **literature** from many cultural perspectives into the curriculum is another way to develop cultural awareness. A piece of literature shared with a third-grade class that includes dialogue written in a different dialect and set in a far-off place may spark interest and enthusiasm for further cultural exploration. A storybook read aloud to a kindergarten class followed by guided questions such as "Where did the characters live?" and "What do you know about this place?" may lead to a discussion of different places. There are a great many developmentally appropriate literary titles across a wide range of cultural themes that can easily be matched to a particular social studies unit.

## SAMPLE QUESTIONS

3) **Mr. Wyatt wants to suggest an activity to the art teacher to use as a springboard for his second-grade class's study of different cultural heritages within the United States. Which activity might be a good suggestion?**

A. students creating a replica of a Civil War cannon
B. students creating a painting in the cubist style
C. students making a simple Native American doll
D. students finger painting a landscape scene

4) **Which is NOT a cultural norm in the United States?**
A. washing hands after using the bathroom
B. shaking hands when meeting someone
C. arriving later than the scheduled time of a meeting
D. saying "thank you" when receiving a gift

## CULTURAL RELATIONSHIPS

Few individuals or cultures can provide for all of their needs without help. This leads to **interdependence**, whereby groups or individuals are dependent upon others to meet certain needs. Young children can best grasp this concept by understanding their own dependence on farmers and ranchers to produce the food they eat and on manufacturers to make clothing and products they use.

Elementary-aged students may begin to understand broader ideas of one nation's interdependence upon another. For example, some products not available in one country (like grain in some Middle Eastern countries) must be imported from other countries (like the United States). In exchange, the country with the desired resource receives a payment of cash or a necessary product. This example shows how interdependence leads to the import of grain to some Middle Eastern countries and to the export of grain by the United States. In return, the United States might receive petroleum from a Middle Eastern country.

All parts of the world have different natural resources and thus access to some goods but not others. In some parts of the world and even in some desert regions in the United States, it is impossible to grow food, making these areas dependent on others for their very survival. This makes trade relationships and alliances crucial to meet the most basic needs of a community.

Cultural communities that are **intradependent** are not reliant on outsiders to meet the needs of their members and are able to produce resources within their own communities. This does not mean these communities do not have specialists who provide specific goods and services. For example, the relationship between a farrier (a person who shoes horses) and the Amish community is one of intradependence. The farrier is able to meet the needs of other community members whose horses need shoes. However, he is likely not able to meet all of his own needs. He might rely on a carpenter within his community to make

STUDY TIPS

The prefix *intra–* means "within." The prefix *inter–* means "between or among." Intradependence happens within a group, and interdependence happens among different groups.

furniture for his home and a roofer to repair his roof. Intradependence is not very common in today's world. It is much more common for even developed countries like the United States to rely on other nations like China to produce certain manufactured goods, even though we have the capability to do so. Labor costs are lower in China, so the goods can be produced at a lower price.

Cultures may experience both **unity** and **diversity** simultaneously. For example, in the United States, people are unified under a common system of government and laws. However, there exists great diversity in ethnicity, religion, and language. One common idea is that of unity in diversity. That is, certain cultural groups are unified under some common purposes but have a diverse body. Some say that this is the case in the United States.

Some cultures are more heterogeneous, like many parts of the United States, where people of diverse cultural backgrounds can be found. Others are more homogeneous and have a single and very dominant culture. Since early childhood programs are found in both more and less diverse parts of the nation, and because some schools have a very homogeneous student population, it is vitally important to ensure all students have experiences that allow them to appreciate the different cultures throughout the nation and world.

Teachers in less diverse environments must make a conscious effort to ensure that diversity is appreciated as a construct even where it does not actually exist. Because research suggests that teachers in less diverse environments do not always seek out opportunities to teach about diversity, many state and national standards intentionally include these elements, like requirements relating to the types of literature that are mandated at certain grade levels. Using multicultural literature can be an excellent and authentic way to introduce students to ideas, beliefs, and customs they might be unfamiliar with. This is important to ensure that students will be successful and able to navigate not just their immediate environs but also the ever-shrinking world in which everyone lives.

Globalization, the process by which businesses and organizations operate on an international scale, is rapidly increasing. This increase has led to a **global culture**, in which certain norms and values are shared across a global scale. The development of a global culture has both negative and positive impacts, as shared understandings lead to more interconnectedness. But sometimes more dominant cultural constructs, such as American consumerism, may spread to the detriment of local culture. While the opening of American fast-food restaurants throughout the world may unite people in their love of french fries or a certain brand of coffee, it might do so at the expense of small local restaurants that preserve traditional cooking methods and foods. It is important for students to understand this dichotomy, as is age appropriate.

## SAMPLE QUESTIONS

5) **Which of the following is NOT an example of a downside to a shared global culture?**

   A. Local customs and dress may become extinct.

   B. Local businesses may go out of business.

   C. People may understand each other better.

   D. Local languages may be lost.

6) **How might a first-grade teacher introduce the concept of interdependence to her class?**

   A. by discussing trade agreements such as the North American Free Trade Agreement (NAFTA)

   B. by asking students to name the major exports of China

   C. by asking students to list all the items in the classroom not made in America

   D. by asking students where they got their shoes

# People, Places, and Environments

## SPATIAL THINKING

Humans have long been fascinated with geography and their place on the planet. Today, a person's geographic **location**, or exact position on the earth, is typically defined by latitude and longitude coordinates. However, even before the invention of these systems of measurement, explorers and cartographers made attempts to track location. Early **maps** and **globes** featured known land alongside *terra incognita*, or unknown land, which sparked interest in future maritime exploration. Today's maps and globes, both digital and physical, are far more complex and can help travelers navigate to very exact locations.

This precision is made possible by the geographical reference system of latitude and longitude. Latitude refers to the coordinates that specify the north-south position of a given point on the surface of the earth. These horizontal lines are usually marked and labeled on globes and include the equator—the line representing an angle of 0°—and four other named lines: the Arctic Circle at 66° north, the Antarctic Circle at 66°south, the Tropic of Cancer at 23°north, and the Tropic of Capricorn at 23°south. The climate of locations closer to the equator tends to be hotter because these areas receive more direct sunlight, while the climate of locations farther from it is colder because of the slant of the earth.

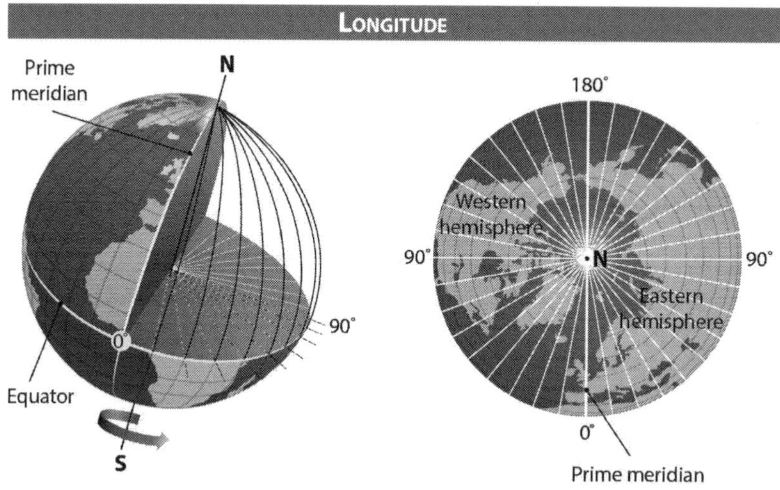


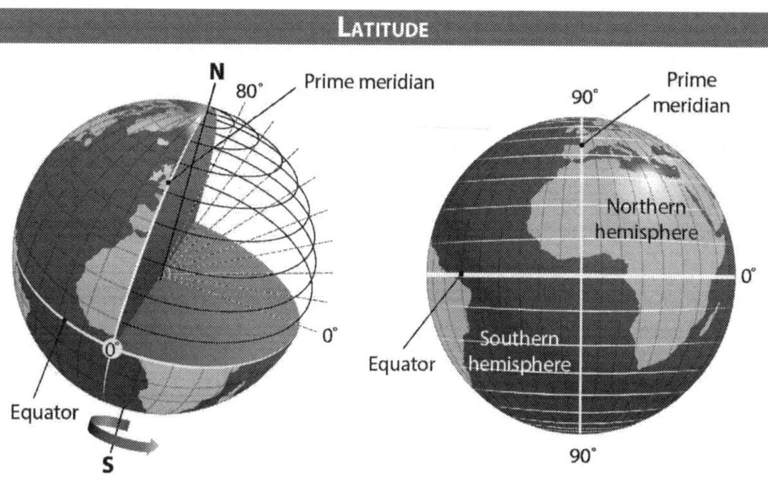


**Figure 5.1. Longitude and Latitude**

**Longitude** refers to the geographic coordinates that provide an east-west position on the earth's surface. This measurement far postdated the ability to calculate latitude, which could easily be calculated based on the position of the sun and stars. English clockmaker John Harrison invented a device in 1773 that calculated longitude, thereby ushering in a new wave of maritime navigation and exploration. Like latitude, lines of longitude have a central line at 0°, which is known as the **prime meridian**. While there was some initial controversy over where to designate the exact location of this line, it has now been firmly established at the Royal Observatory in Greenwich, United Kingdom. This is the origin of the term Greenwich Mean Time (GMT), or the solar time at this point.

In the past, calculating time on the entirety of the earth's surface was no easy task, as points on Earth seemed to elapse to a new day at different rates. With the establishment of the International Date Line halfway around the world from the prime meridian, however, a standard demarcation was made. This line is roughly based on 180° longitude; however, it deviates slightly to accommodate certain territories. The line shows what day it is based on a concept of Coordinated Universal

Time (UTC). Areas can be either ahead of or behind this time, as denoted by UTC+ or UTC–. This standard time system allows anyone to know what time and day it is anywhere on the globe.

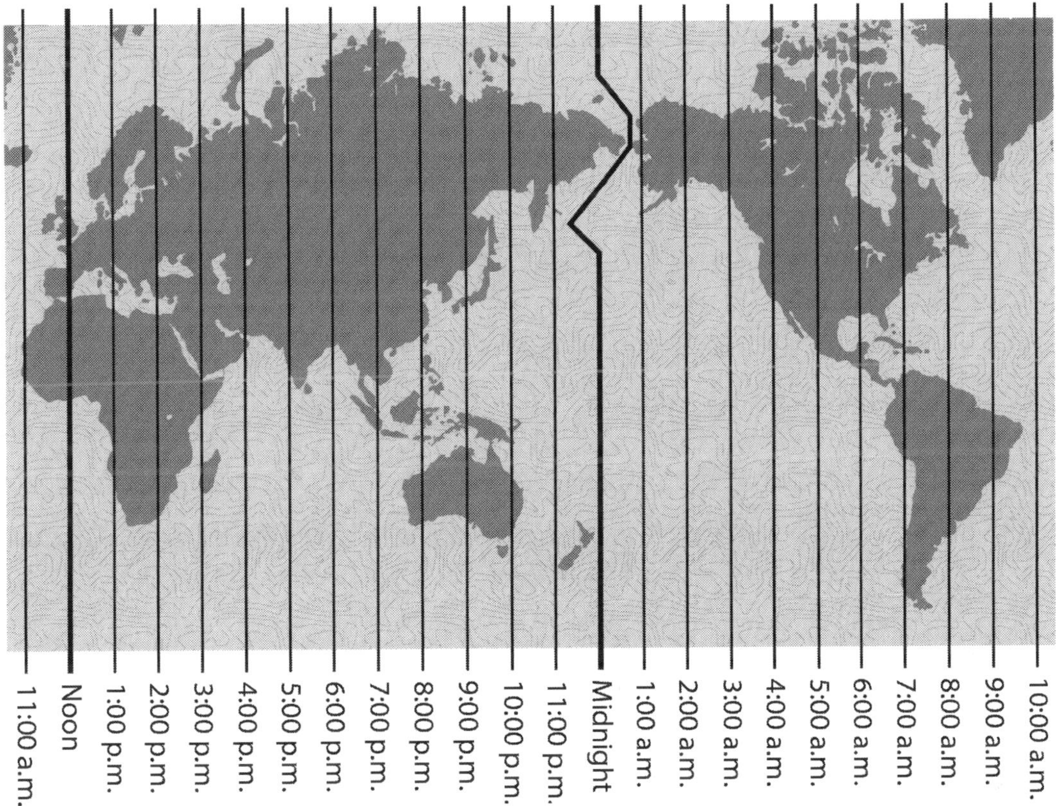


**Figure 5.2. Time Zones and the International Date Line**

While a globe is the most accurate representation of the earth's surface, it is not always practical or easy to transport. Unfortunately, no completely accurate flat map exists, though there are several standard map projections that minimize the amount of distortion. The first of these was the **Mercator projection**, developed in 1569 by Flemish geographer Gerardus Mercator. Its strength is its helpfulness in plotting a maritime course (certainly its primary use at the time), and its weakness is its gross distortion of the size of several landmasses, including Greenland, which looks as though it is larger than Africa (which is in fact fourteen times larger).

The **Winkel tripel projection** was proposed in 1921 in hopes of minimizing distortion in area, direction, and distance. This projection does minimize object distortion, but the lines of latitude are not totally parallel and are more curved than in actuality. Still, it is the map of choice for National Geographic, which has used this projection since 1998.

**The Robinson projection** was devised in 1963 at the behest of the Rand McNally map company. It is a compromise between the Mercator projection and the Winkel tripel projection in that, although there is some distortion, it is mostly near the poles, with some lack of accuracy in the lines of longitude.

Figure 5.3. Mercator Projection

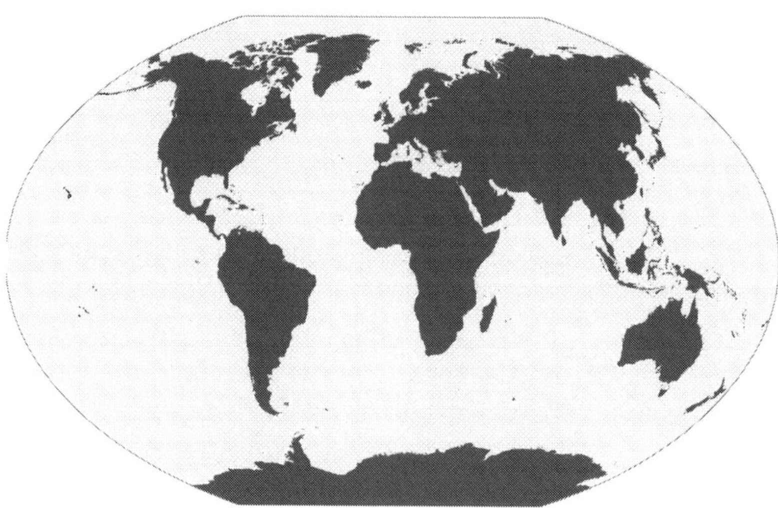

Figure 5.4. Winkel Tripel Projection

Other projections, including new digital map projections, abound. Students should know that no map projection is completely accurate, due to the shape of the planet, and that while flat maps might be good for identifying major regions, landmarks, and streets, globes are still the best tools for measuring precise locations and calculating one's global position. Newer digital maps like Google Earth might be even more accurate because they show changes in a map over time. An interesting activity for students of all ages is comparing the Google Street View of the area around the school with its physical reality. Teachers can spark discussion by asking if the digital map is accurate or what parts of the map may be outdated.

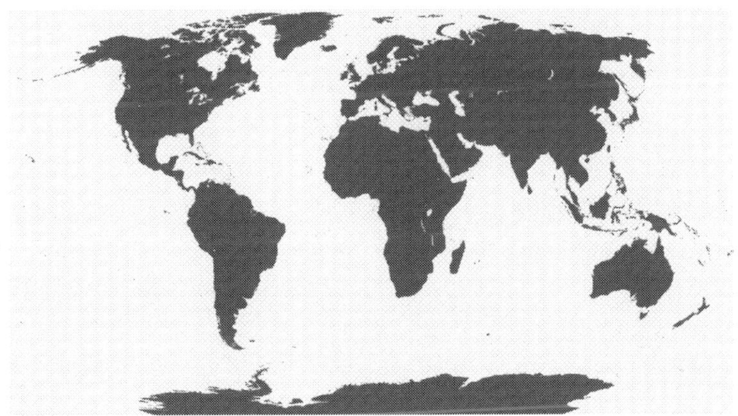

Figure 5.5. Robinson Projection

Globes are not practical to use when traveling, so students must be able to read and understand information on maps. In fact, many elementary students report that map-reading questions are the most challenging parts of standardized tests.

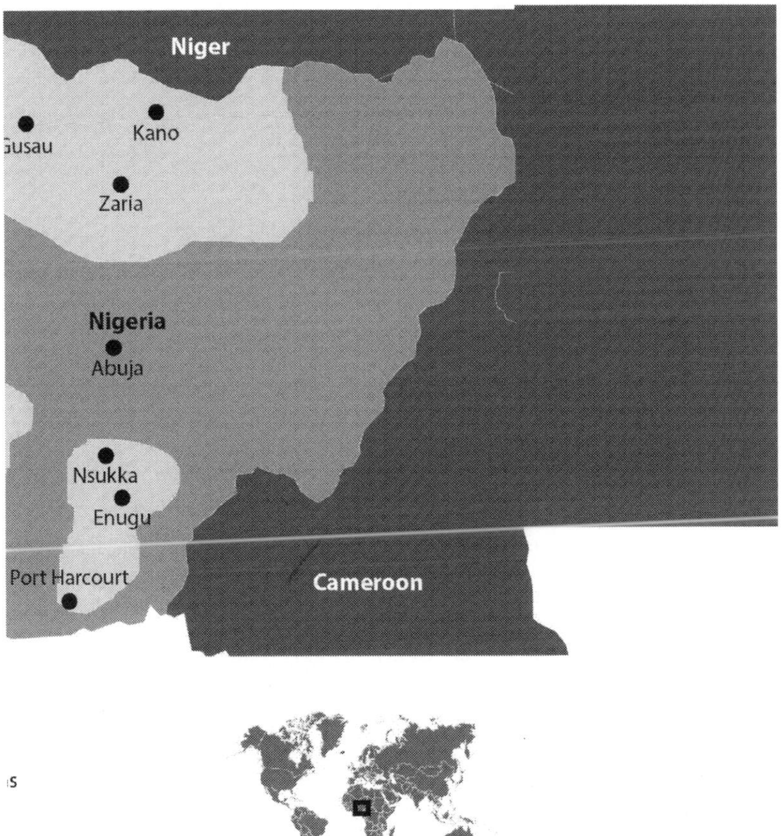


Figure 5.6. Parts of a Map

Perhaps this is because children do not practice this activity much in their daily lives, and turn-by-turn directional technology has now replaced traditional maps in many cases. Map reading is still an essential geographical skill that helps students understand their spatial position in relationship to other locations, as well as how to interpret and understand graphics designed to convey information.

Kindergarten students should be introduced to basic **directional terms** such as left, right, over, and under and should be able to locate basic locations in familiar environments like their school. They should also begin to recognize other major **landmarks**, or easily recognizable places, in their community. By first grade, students should be able to use the cardinal directions as illustrated by the **compass rose** with some fluency to find the location of objects and places. By second grade, students should start to use maps and globes to identify various locations, including being able to identify the map **title**, using the map's **legend** to understand what symbols or colors represent, using the **scale** to measure distances, and using a map's **grid** reference system to identify the coordinates of locations. Students should be afforded plenty of practice with maps and be given opportunities to use and make simple maps. This might take the form of a class-wide project to draw a map of the school in the second or third grade, or even a simple sketch of the classroom layout for kindergarteners and first graders. The key is making the map-focused activities as purposeful and relevant as possible to keep student engagement high and help them recognize and practice using and creating maps with purpose.

Maps are not the only type of graphic representations that students need practice with interpreting. Both **graphs** and **charts** are used in many different types of texts, and students need practice in extrapolating information from them. An appropriate chart for a kindergarten student may be a simple pictorial representation, while third-grade students will need significant practice with interpreting various bar and line graphs to meet both social studies and math objectives. The key is providing students with strategies to comprehend graphic information. Teachers can help students develop these skills by asking questions such as "What does ____mean/represent/stand for?" and "What information does ____ show?" and "What do you see in the row/column/pie?"

QUICK REVIEW

What types of things might you chart in simple pictorial form in the kindergarten classroom?

## SAMPLE QUESTIONS

7) **Which of the following is a landmark appropriate for a first grader to recognize?**

A. the Leaning Tower of Pisa

B. London Bridge

C. the Statue of Liberty

D. the Coliseum

8) **Which symbol on a map denotes north, south, east, and west?**

A. the compass rose

B. the scale

C. the grid

D. the Mercator projection

## GEOGRAPHIC PERSPECTIVES

**Regions** are the basic units of geography and describe areas of land that have common features. Regions can be based on political or cultural similarities but often are defined in terms of climate and vegetation. These regional differences affect human behavior and interaction with the environment. The major climate regions are listed as follows:

- polar: cold and dry year-round
- temperate: cold winters, mild summers, some forests and plains/prairies
- arid: hot and dry year-round and include some deserts (some deserts are found in cold tundra regions as well)
- tropical: always hot and wet, rain forests
- Mediterranean: mild winters and hot, dry summers
- tundra: cold year-round with three subtypes:
  - Arctic tundra is found in the far Northern Hemisphere and features a very desolate landscape. The ground is frozen in these cold desert regions, making it impossible for most plants to grow.
  - Antarctic tundra is found in Antarctica and features some desolate landscape and desert. However, some areas support plant life.
  - Alpine tundra is a mountainous region also without significant plant life.

These environmental conditions impact people in a variety of ways. People living on plains and prairies where there are few trees, for example, often have to build houses out of materials other than lumber. People living in mountain and desert regions may have to import food from other areas since the landscape makes farming difficult. People who live in particularly fragile environments, such as the rain forest, often use the intense biodiversity around them to develop innovative solutions to meet their needs, such as growing small batches of crops in the limited ground space and hunting a wide variety of animals. One challenge facing many of the world's geographic regions is the desire for economic development balanced with the preservation of natural environments. Destroying rain forests, for example, not only displaces animals but also forces their inhabitants to change their very way of life.

> QUICK REVIEW
>
> What is the climate of your local community? How does this impact your daily life and the lives of your students?

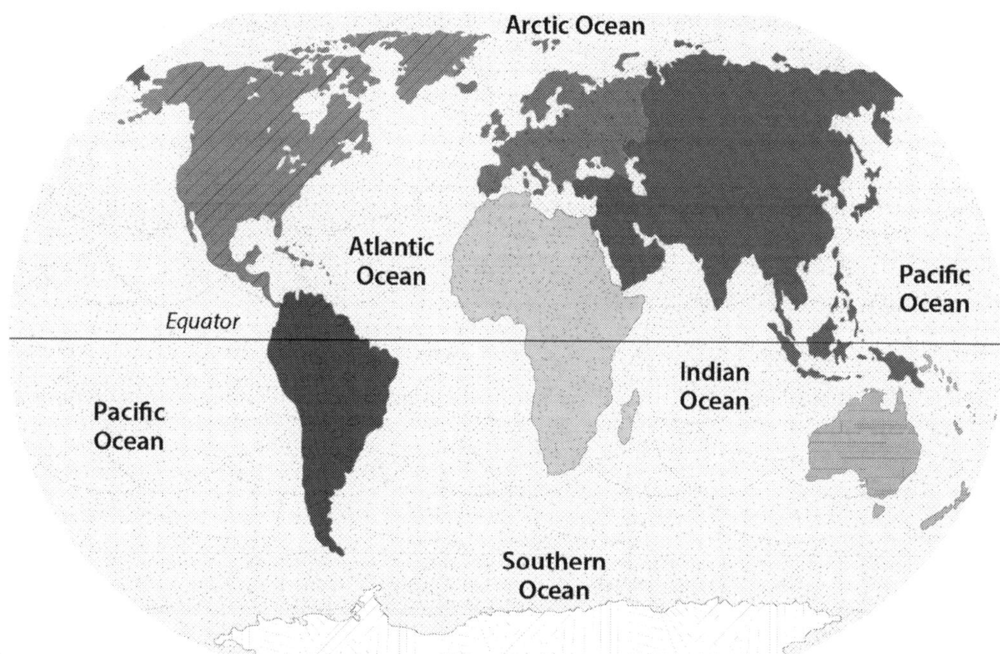


**Figure 5.7. The Continents and Oceans**

In addition to the six populated **continents** of North and South America, Asia, Europe, Africa, and Australia, there are two other large formations that account for the solid surface area of the planet. The North Pole is the northernmost point on the globe and is sometimes referred to as the Arctic. It is not a landform in the strictest sense because it is really a large sheet of ice that expands and contracts based on temperature. However, some definitions of "the Arctic" cover the entire region of the Arctic Ocean and inhabited areas such as parts of Canada and Greenland. The South Pole, on the other hand, is located on the continent of Antarctica and represents the southernmost point on the globe. Antarctica boasts no permanent residents, but it is, like the North Pole, an important location for research stations.

The surface of the earth is 71 percent water, and its continents are surrounded by five **oceans**: the Atlantic, Pacific, Indian, Arctic, and Antarctic. The Antarctic Ocean is also sometimes referred to as the Southern Ocean or the Antarctic Sea. These saltwater bodies are connected by **seas**, which are generally smaller than oceans, often surrounded partly or wholly by land, saltwater, and usually connect with their larger counterparts.

STUDY TIPS

Ensure that you can identify the Atlantic, Pacific, Indian, Arctic, and Antarctic Oceans on a map or globe without labels. Can you come up with a mnemonic device that would help students remember the names and locations of the oceans?

**Rivers** and their smaller cousins, **streams**, are flowing bodies of water that empty into seas and oceans and are generally freshwater. **Lakes**, like seas, are large bodies of water that are surrounded by land; though unlike seas, they are usually freshwater. While some lakes are natural, many are artificial and constructed for recreation. Most other bodies of water are naturally occurring and impact those in their vicinity. People who live near large bodies of water use the water source for food and transportation. Teachers whose programs are located near a body of water can ask students to consider the ways in which the body of water impacts the life of the community. Is fishing a popular local industry? Does the beach or lake promote tourism to the area?

### SAMPLE QUESTIONS

9) **What is the main distinction between rivers and lakes?**

   A. Rivers are surrounded by land, and lakes are not.

   B. Lakes are generally saltwater, and rivers are generally freshwater.

   C. Rivers divide continents, while lakes are within continents.

   D. Lakes do not flow, while rivers flow into seas and oceans.

10) **Mrs. Martin, who teaches first grade in the Arizona desert, wants to help her students understand how climate affects the way humans live in a given area. Which integrated social studies and science activity would help her class understand this concept?**

   A. showing them a video of people shopping for a new house in another state

   B. planting a few different crops in the school garden to see which ones grow

   C. bringing in a guest chef to talk to the students about different flavor profiles

   D. having her students design their "dream house" out of blocks

## HUMAN–ENVIRONMENTAL INTERACTION

Our planet is divided into political divisions based on governmental jurisdiction. The largest units of these are sovereign states or nation-states that are generally referred to as countries. Within these **countries** are smaller units known as **states**, provinces, counties, parishes, districts, and cities or towns. The United States follows a pattern of states subdivided into counties or parishes and then cities or towns. It is important that, as developmentally appropriate, students understand that **borders** between both countries and states are human constructs. While the lines of demarcation may be based upon physical boundaries such as rivers or mountains, these are political borders created by humans that do not exist organically.

There are two primary types of communities based on population density. **Rural** communities such as farms and villages contain a smaller population of people, and they often participate in an agrarian, or **farming**, lifestyle. Farming is a somewhat general term often used to describe the use of land or water for the production or obtainment of food. This includes **ranching**, which uses land to produce livestock, and **fishing**, which extracts food from bodies of water or raises fish in tanks. **Urban** communities are cities and towns where the economy is driven by business and the **trade**, or exchange, of goods and services.

While both urban and rural areas may be important to the overall economy, or wealth of resources, of a country or region, urban areas tend to be centers of commerce and production. Cities originally developed around markets later grew around factories as industry developed. Factories are large buildings where products are made, originally by humans and increasingly by machines controlled by humans. Some cities are known for a particular type of factory, such as the automotive production factories in Detroit, Michigan. Additionally, most cities have elaborate transportation networks that move people and goods from one place to another. People living in cities often have many public transportation options such as trains, subways, and buses. These options are more limited in rural communities because of remoteness and lack of population density.

Rural areas, however, produce many raw materials and crops that must be transported to manufacturing centers and cities for production and sale to consumers. Since those who rely on ranching and fishing require land to produce or procure their foodstuffs, they, too, tend to be located in areas remote from urban centers. A railroad system that uses trains to ship important commodities, and a **highway** system that uses **trucks** to transport goods are very important to the **transportation** network of rural and remote communities. Without such networks, interdependent relationships between communities would not be possible. This interdependence is often marked by raw goods and commodities such as cotton and soybeans being produced in rural areas and then shipped to urban areas for transformation into processed foods and clothing. These finished goods are then shipped and sold both to urban and rural communities.

Though transporting goods over water does not require the same type of transportation network as transporting goods over land, this method does rely on the construction of ports and canals, which might be highly relevant to the economy of a given community. Although generally more expensive, **airplanes** can be used to transport people and goods. In some very remote areas, such as rural Alaska, airplane travel is the only method of transportation available because road and rail networks do not exist. Even in urban areas, the reliance on **shipping** direct to the consumer has become very popular as more and more people rely on the internet to buy consumer goods.

One trend in the United States has been increasing urbanization, or the shift in population from rural to urban areas. Recent data from the US Census Bureau revealed that over 80 percent of Americans live in urban areas. In some very fast-growing cities, the pace of **construction** of new homes, schools, and roads is often unable to accommodate population growth. This creates many urban problems like traffic, school overcrowding, and lack of affordable housing.

The desire of people to move from a rural area to an urban one (or from any area to a new area) is generally the result of both push and pull factors. **Push factors** are situations that push people from their community. These could include drought, lack of educational or economic opportunity, or the loss of a job or livelihood. **Pull factors** are situations that pull people toward a new community. These factors could be the promise of a new job or the possibility of more educational or social opportunities. Some students may have experienced these factors in their own family's immigration to the United States. An existing network of extended family in the United States might have been a pull factor, for example.

Both urban and rural areas have advantages and disadvantages related to population density. High-population density in urban areas often leads to pollution, traffic, and crowded conditions. Conversely, life in a rural area may bring limited educational and economic opportunities and even less access to technological innovation.

In many developed nations, and particularly the United States, people strike a balance between urban and rural in the establishment of suburban communities. These communities, located just on the outskirts of major cities, give residents access to the city's economic resources while allowing them to enjoy some of the positive elements of rural life, such as open green areas and larger living spaces. Teachers with programs located in any of these urban, rural, or suburban communities must strive to help children understand that even within a country or state, humans live in many different types of places.

### STUDY TIPS

Create a chart comparing the advantages and disadvantages of urban and rural life. Then list the economic contributions that both urban and rural communities make to any society.

## SAMPLE QUESTIONS

11) **Ms. Annie is a pre-kindergarten teacher in a rural community in Iowa. She is reading a story to her students about a girl who is afraid of taking the elevator to her twelfth-floor Manhattan apartment. What question would be most appropriate for her to ask her students to help them understand the different environments people live in as described in the story?**

A. Is the story set in an urban, rural, or suburban environment?

B. Why is the girl afraid of taking the elevator up?

C. Is Manhattan an island?

D. What kind of house does the girl live in?

12) **Mr. Martin's third-grade student Hector is very interested in trains. Mr. Martin wants to make sure Hector's research project interests him and pertains to the assignment's topic of the American economy. Which topical suggestion might Mr. Martin make to Hector?**

A. trains throughout American history

B. the role of trains in cattle ranching

C. the invention of the steam engine

D. the decline of the American railroad

# Time, Continuity, and Change

## Chronological Thinking

Humans have long realized that there were others who came before them. **History**, or the study of past events, helps humans situate themselves in time. The strictest definition of history is the study of the past through the examination of written records; however, more contemporary definitions cite many other disciplines as being part of the overall study of history.

- **archaeology**: the study of human history through artifacts and remains
- **anthropology**: the study of human cultural development and evolution
- **sociology**: the study of human society

Many historians have found that an interdisciplinary approach often provides tremendous benefits, particularly when studying past cultures that did not leave any written accounts.

> QUICK REVIEW
>
> What sources can be used to study prehistory?

Students should be exposed to textual sources such as books, articles, and stories, as well as to other **historical data** such as timelines, maps, graphs, and tables. These sources should reference the entire expanse of human history, including what is commonly referred to as **pre-history**, or the period before humans left a written record of their experiences.

Children's understanding of history begins in late preschool when they start to understand concepts of time. Students at age four can begin to understand that a day is shorter than a month and a second is shorter than a minute. They can begin to grasp that their birthday is next week or that they went to the park yesterday. Teachers can reinforce this chronological knowledge by encouraging young students to use words that express time relationships, such as before, after, tomorrow, and so on. Teachers can also encourage young students to understand the distant past through concrete pictorial representations like ancient Egyptian artifacts, and they can make predictions about the future after reading stories or examining pictures with futuristic themes.

By kindergarten, most children begin to understand that some events happen at a certain time each day, such as art first, then center time, and finally recess. Calendar-tracking activities are generally very popular in kindergarten classrooms, as these aid in students' understanding of the passage of time. These activities may involve having students track and mark off time each day, week, month, or even year. This will help students in their eventual progression in the elementary years in grasping more advanced concepts of time such as centuries (one-hundred-year periods) and even millennia (one-thousand-year periods).

Many educators once believed that young children should not be exposed to unsettling parts of history, but the latest research indicates that it is far better to present a more balanced view of **key historical events**, even when presenting these events to a preschool audience. While it is not prudent to burden young children with the atrocities of **war** and genocide, it is most certainly not appropriate to present a historical event leaving out key events and concepts. For example, teaching first-grade students that the Pilgrims settled uninhabited land would be historically inaccurate and leave them with a gross oversimplification of a very complex event that sparked a series of interactions and future events. When talking of **natural disasters**, economic crises, or other upsetting events that are part of the elementary curriculum, it is vital to support students in their understanding that studying troubling historical events is part of the overall study of history.

One popular curriculum strategy is using fictional works on various topics of cultural and historical sensitivity as part of social studies. This can allow for troubling or difficult topics to be introduced and handled more readily than in a personal context. For example, a second-grade student might find it upsetting to discuss her own experiences with racism, but reading an age-appropriate book on segregation such as *These Hands* by Margaret H. Mason might allow her to discuss the concept safely in the context of the social studies curriculum.

Social studies teachers should make an effort to discuss current events in the context of students' everyday lives, as is age appropriate. Are their parents going to vote in the upcoming **elections**? Do students know the candidates who are running? These are excellent questions to spark discussion. Helping students maintain an awareness of current events will help them to develop an interest in staying informed and participating in the civic life of the community.

## SAMPLE QUESTIONS

**13) How can a kindergarten teacher help her students develop an understanding of chronology?**

A. directing students to make timelines showing major events in world history

B. having a classroom calendar that students use to mark off each day

C. explaining the concepts of year, century, and millennium

D. assigning students a project to write about the major events of their lives

**14) Miss Clark wants to incorporate visual/graphic literacy activities into her third-grade class's study of Native Americans. Which activity would be most appropriate?**

A. asking a Native American community member to visit the class and speak on her experiences

B. reading an age-appropriate story about the Navajo people to the class

C. having her students write an essay comparing two Native American tribes

D. giving her students a chart that shows the different regions in which certain tribes live

## Social Studies Tools

It is important for students to be exposed to a rich variety of both primary and secondary sources in their study of history and society. Graphic literacy is an important part of a social studies curriculum, and activities must be calibrated for age and grade appropriateness. Kindergarten students, for example, might create their own **map** of the playground, coloring in the locations of trees, play equipment, bathrooms, and so on. This will help them understand not only that the map represents concrete locations and objects but also that it can be used for directional purposes. Older students may create and even use more sophisticated maps. A second- or third-grade class might, with support from the teacher, work to create a map of the school or use a simple map to go on a school or classroom scavenger hunt.

Maps and globes can also be used to help students pinpoint their location in relationship to others. By first grade, most students should be able to identify their city, state, and the United States on a map or globe, though this will likely take explicit teaching. Second-grade students should be able to locate additional places such as the state capital, major cities within the state, the location of various oceans and bodies of water, and the location of Canada and Mexico. By third grade, students should begin practicing with a map grid system and various map symbols to enable them to use maps even when they are referencing unfamiliar locations.

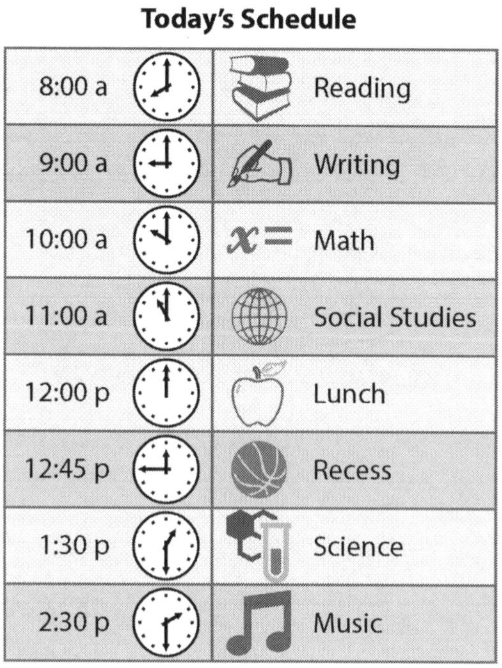

Students of all ages should also be exposed to **timelines**. In a preschool or kindergarten classroom, this might be as simple as the daily schedule posted in the classroom in both written and visual form. Visual schedules are very popular

**Today's Schedule**

|  |  |
|---|---|
| 8:00 a | Reading |
| 9:00 a | Writing |
| 10:00 a | Math |
| 11:00 a | Social Studies |
| 12:00 p | Lunch |
| 12:45 p | Recess |
| 1:30 p | Science |
| 2:30 p | Music |

**Figure 5.8. A Visual Schedule**

in many programs, and these graphics are the simplest form of a daily timeline. They might illustrate, for example, when different classes, lunch, and recess are set to occur.

Teachers might further reinforce the daily timeline by mixing up the elements of the daily schedule and asking students to put them back in the correct order. Older students in first or second grade may even be encouraged to create their own daily schedule or timeline that shows their activities before and after school. By third grade, students should begin creating and understanding historical events on a timeline.

Students will also need to be able to understand and interpret quantitative information in both **graphs** and **tables**. These will range in complexity based on student age and grade level but should be a common part of the social studies curriculum. Graphs showing increases, decreases, or back-and-forth changes over time help students understand changing economic or social conditions as well as basic mathematical concepts. Tables help students organize and compartmentalize information and details. Using graphs and tables in the social studies classroom will also integrate social studies, math, and science curriculum and help students make connections and use math skills to analyze graphic relationships in a social studies context.

QUICK REVIEW

What are some specific mathematical concepts that can be integrated into social studies units on using graphs and charts?

Another important, though relatively recent, addition to the historical record are **photographs**. Unlike many historical narratives, photographs are often **primary sources**, or historical artifacts in themselves. Photographs can make history far more interesting for young students, and any historical study in the early childhood grade levels should make use of as many photographs as possible. It is important, as part of visual literacy in the social studies context, that students examine photographs carefully for their implicit meaning. Teachers might ask the following questions when helping students evaluate historical photographs:

- Why do you think the photographer took this picture?
- When do you think this photograph was taken? Why?
- Do you think the person wanted his/her photo taken? Why or why not?
- What event is this photograph showing/documenting?

Additionally, photography might be a part of the early childhood classroom's own historical documentation. Preschool and kindergarten teachers using student portfolios as part of an overall assessment strategy might take and include photographs of students in these digital or physical records of student progress, if school policy permits. Students

DID YOU KNOW?

The National Archives (archives.gov) and the Library of Congress (loc.gov) have links to thousands of digital photograph collections in various online archives.

might also be encouraged to use photography to document class- or school-wide events. With the simplification of camera technology and the ease of use of most tablet computers, even prekindergarten students can take photos of an important school or class event. These photos can then be organized into a visual timeline (with the aid of the teacher) on a classroom bulletin board or even organized into a scrapbook. Taking and using photographs to document events will help students understand the role of photography in social studies. Teachers should always follow school policy regarding photography at school events.

## SAMPLE QUESTIONS

15) **Which activity would be most appropriate to introduce a timeline to a prekindergarten classroom?**

  A. creating a timeline of all the annual holidays and calculating when each will occur

  B. asking students to help place visual images of the day's activities into the proper order

  C. directing students to create a timeline of the major events of the Civil War

  D. encouraging students to keep a journal documenting their daily activity in order

16) **Mr. Fuller is in a parent-student-teacher conference with Lisa, his kindergarten student. He opens Lisa's portfolio to the page with pictures of her conducting show-and-tell, which he has arranged in order with the words FIRST, SECOND, NEXT, and LAST. He then asks Lisa to explain this page to her mother. Why is he doing this?**

  A. He wants to ensure that Lisa understands the purpose of the portfolio in documenting her progress.

  B. He thinks Lisa's mother will be impressed with her vocabulary development as she is describing the photos.

  C. This reinforces Lisa's understanding of chronology of events.

  D. This helps Lisa grasp that these photographs are primary sources.

# Civics and Government

## Civics Concepts

A well-managed early childhood classroom will introduce students to many different civics concepts through explicit teaching and everyday interactions. Basic concepts of **justice**, or fair treatment, will likely come up quite frequently when young children are involved. In the early childhood classroom, this more often involves ensuring each child gets his or her needs met versus treating each child in the exact same way. This often plays out in assessing the reason for or antecedent of a child's behavior. A teacher ignoring a child's inappropriate behavior might be acceptable if the reason for the behavior was desire for attention, but if attention-seeking was not the likely antecedent of the behavior and if there is a social lesson to be taught, ignoring the behavior may not be the best approach.

In helping students to understand the concept of justice, it is important to equate justice, as much as is possible, with a fitting consequence for an action. It might be just, for example, for Stephanie to be selected as the second-grade Pledge of Allegiance leader because of her excellent classroom conduct and high rates of homework completion. It might also be just for third grader Max to clean up the mess he made in the cafeteria after lunch, causing him to miss classwork and have extra homework. These are natural consequences for actions that represent the truest idea of justice.

As a social studies construct, justice generally refers to the justice system, in which people are held accountable for the consequences of their actions within society. This typically involves the role of the courts to ascribe particular penalties for certain illicit actions. Teachers can help students understand the basic tenets of the justice system at many grade levels. Preschool and kindergarten teachers might help students identify the role of community helpers like police officers, lawyers, and judges. First-grade teachers may ask students to declare whether they believe a character in a story is guilty or innocent of a given charge. Second- and third-grade teachers may explore the justice process even more deeply and hold simple mock trials or have students participate in mock criminal investigations. It is also important to point out, as is age appropriate, that in the United States, it is the **rule of law**, or the idea that it is the law itself, that governs, rather than government officials. In this way, the law empowers its agents in government to enforce it. It grants them no powers outside of it.

**Equality** is another important civics ideology that should be discussed in the classroom and in society. It is not always easy to achieve equality in a classroom with varying student needs and limited resources or in a society with many different people with varying needs and similarly limited resources. While there are differing opinions about whether all Americans truly enjoy equality in terms of the legal system, the justice system is founded upon the principle of equality before the law in which all people should be treated equally both in the creation and implementation of the law.

Unlike the concept of equality, in which all people are treated the same, the concept of **equity** involves giving individuals what they need to be successful. Classrooms are places where equality exists in some cases, and equity exists in others. For example, a teacher might promote equality by giving all her first-grade students ten spelling words each week. She might promote equity by giving her English-Language Learners a list of ten different words that are more appropriate to their current skill level.

There may be other parts of educational equity within a school or classroom as well. Many schools, realizing that hungry children cannot learn at the same rate as children who get enough to eat, offer free lunches to students who cannot afford to bring or purchase their own lunches. Students with Individualized Education Programs (IEPs) may have accommodations within the classroom such as scribes, interpreters, or educational aides to promote equity. Federal programs like Title I and the Every Student Succeeds Act (ESSA) are designed to promote equity in educational environments by ensuring that students with special needs or from disadvantaged backgrounds receive the support they need to take full advantage of educational opportunities. It is important that teachers take the tenets of these programs seriously and familiarize themselves with all of the resources available to their students and help students and family obtain the resources they need. This will help promote an equitable educational environment.

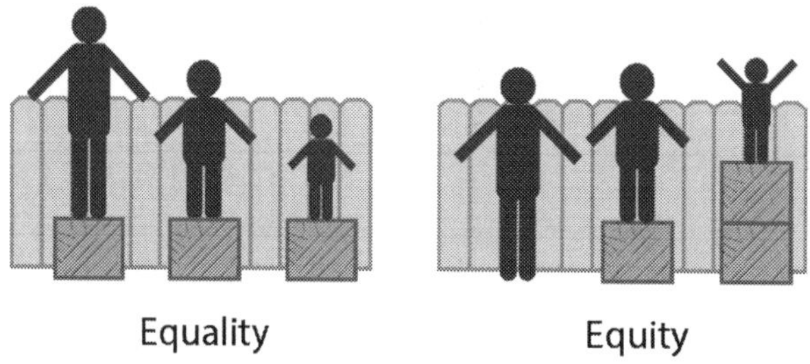


**Figure 5.9. Equality Versus Equity**

Teachers should also promote **tolerance**, or the acceptance of beliefs or behaviors that one does not necessarily agree with, as appropriate in the classroom and help students understand the need for tolerance in pluralistic American society. Freedom of religion is a core tenet of the United States, and many classrooms will have students with different belief systems. Helping students to be understanding and tolerant of the beliefs of others starts with accepting differences. While some students might not understand why certain dietary or dress restrictions are observed by their peers, part of promoting tolerance includes helping students understand that there are many different ways of doing things. The nonprofit organization Teaching Tolerance (tolerance.org) created a list of standards appropriate for each K–12 grade level that can be used as a reference to guide explicit instruction to help students develop tolerance.

## SAMPLE QUESTIONS

17) **Mrs. Rose has just welcomed a new third grader named Noor into her classroom. Unlike the other students, Noor wears a hijab. Mrs. Rose notices that one of the more vocal students has made some disparaging comments about Noor's "funny hat." What theme might Mrs. Rose consider for her next social studies lesson?**

A. tolerance

B. equality

C. equity

D. justice

**18) Mr. Haskell is always reminding his class that it is the classroom rules that govern the classroom, not the teacher. What concept is he basing this statement upon?**

A. justice

B. tolerance

C. rule of law

D. equity

## Civic Participation

Civic participation, or participating in issues of public concern, is important, but it is not practiced in many communities. Low turnouts, particularly at local elections, are evidence of this trend. However, this trend can be reversed by educating young people about how individuals in a society can help in the **decision-making** that affects their communities.

To participate in civic life, individuals must first be informed of the **issues**. Teachers can help their students keep up with current events on a local, national, and global scale through social studies lessons on contemporary issues. Teachers can point out that there are often different **points of view** on any given issue and that different groups bring different backgrounds and desires to any issue. A teacher may illustrate this by proposing an increase in social studies time and a decrease in math time. He or she might then ask the class to weigh in on the issue. Is everyone in favor? Why are some groups against this? Students are likely to have different points of view based on their ease with or interest in either subject. Often in civic matters, one must compromise, or meet those with a different point of view in the middle on an issue. This give-and-take is part of what makes democracy work.

In a representative democracy, such as that of the United States, power and authority in decision-making rest with elected officials who have been designated by the people. The process of electing officials and raising issues of public concern to these officials brings many different viewpoints, as illustrated by the example of students weighing in on the issue of more social studies and less math time. In this example, students approach the issue from an individual perspective: those who like social studies and dislike math would be in favor of more social studies time, while those who like math more may not be in favor. This perspective represents the individual needs of students. However, students must consider many perspectives on the issue. Would a decrease in math time leave students ill-prepared for state tests? Would students who need more math practice be at a disadvantage? These considerations might then lead to making a decision based on the overall needs of the group, which must be balanced with individual needs and preferences. This is a key part of the democratic process.

Students should understand their role as members of many different communities.

DID YOU KNOW?

Only around 55 percent of eligible Americans voted in the 2016 national election.

They must be advocates in their local community to ensure their schools, hospitals, roads, and local services are operating smoothly and efficiently. They should also appreciate their role in the larger city, state, and nation regarding their future ability to vote, organize, and have their voices heard.

Students should also understand their role as global citizens who must protect the natural resources and biodiversity of the planet. The topic of global **citizenship**, or actions taken to promote social, political, or environmental issues on a global scale, is easily integrated with science topics such as recycling, conservation, and environmental advocacy. Environmental protection is necessary for keeping the plant and animal life on Earth diverse. It is also vital since all living things, their environment, and the economy are interdependent. A teacher might discuss this concept broadly with younger students by explaining that we must protect the earth in order to continue using its resources such as food and water.

DID YOU KNOW?

The United Nations Educational, Scientific and Cultural Organization (UNESCO) has created learning tools and objectives for each grade level to promote global citizenship and education.

Older students might delve more deeply into this issue and examine the cause-and-effect relationship between lack of environmental resource protection and the local economy. For example, a community reliant on the shrimping industry might be severely impacted by pollution in the Gulf of Mexico. This action by humans on the environment impacts the shrimp in the Gulf, whose populations may die out or dwindle. This, in turn, impacts the local economy, as shrimping may no longer be possible. This can have all sorts of further consequences, as shrimpers may leave the community, forcing the businesses that served the shrimpers (grocery and clothing stores, restaurants, and so on) to also go out of business. In this way, the environment and the economy are interdependent, and an action on one will impact the other.

It is also worthwhile to point out that the American early childhood classroom is an increasingly diverse place. It is unreasonable to assume that all students in any given classroom have the same national identity or even US citizenship. Teachers should respect and encourage the civic growth of all students, regardless of citizenship status or country of origin. Respect for this diversity under a common shared identity as humans is another key component of global citizenship. Globally responsible students will understand that human dignity, or the inherent value and worth of all humans, must be preserved on both a local and global scale.

## SAMPLE QUESTIONS

**19) Ms. Sturgis happens upon two of her first-grade students in a heated argument about what game to play at recess. Which strategy might help her students learn to compromise?**

A. picking the game herself and telling the students which game to play
B. designating one student to decide which game to play
C. proposing that they join the kickball game already in progress
D. suggesting that they play one game for five minutes and the other game the next five minutes

20) **Which activity is associated with global citizenship?**
A. organizing a clothing drive to help a local shelter
B. serving on a jury
C. voting in a national election
D. recycling

## UNITED STATES GOVERNMENT

Understanding the basics of government will help children to grow up to be responsible citizens who select leaders fit for their office. The United States government is composed of three branches: the executive, legislative, and judicial. A system of **checks and balances** keeps each branch from having too much power.

The **executive branch** of government is made up of the **president, vice president**, and fifteen executive departments, including the Departments of Defense, Commerce, State, Justice, Labor, and so on. The executive branch enforces the laws. The president and vice president are elected members of the executive branch, but officials in other executive branch departments and agencies are appointed.

The legislative branch includes both houses of **Congress**: the Senate and the House of Representatives. The legislative branch makes the laws. Members of both the House and the Senate are elected, with each state electing two senators per state, and the number of representatives totaling 435 but varying in number based on state population. California and Texas have the most representatives at fifty-three and thirty-six, respectively, while some less-populous states have only one representative.

STUDY TIPS

The names of the different branches of government tell what they do. The executive branch is like the executive of a company—it ensures the "execution" of the company's objectives (like laws). The legislative branch "legislates," or deals in making laws. The judicial branch "judges," or interprets the laws.

The judicial branch comprises the federal court system, including the **Supreme Court**. The Supreme Court is made up of nine justices who are nominated by the president and approved by the Senate. The judicial branch interprets the meaning of the laws.

The federal government was formed by and operates based on the outline set out in the **Constitution**. In its interpretation of the laws made by Congress, the

Supreme Court frequently examines whether legislation is in line with this document. While the basic governmental framework has been laid out, the political actors are selected through citizens who **vote** in **elections**.

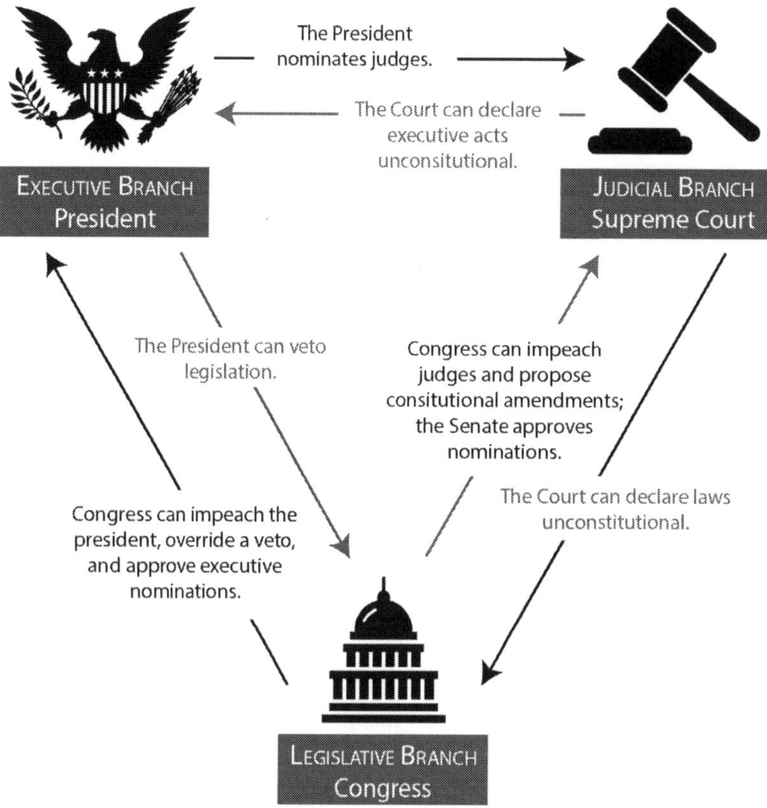


**Figure 5.10. Checks and Balances**

Early childhood classrooms are excellent places to encourage an understanding of representative democracy. Teachers might have the class vote on classroom issues such as what type of class pet to get. The early childhood classroom is also an appropriate environment for students to learn the role of government officials as servants of the public. Having special "classroom helpers" assigned to complete key housekeeping or administrative tasks can help students understand service to the classroom community. Assigning a student the responsibility of emptying out the pencil sharpener each day or collecting assignments, for example, can help students to appreciate the value in service to community, the foundation upon which all public service should rest.

## SAMPLE QUESTIONS

**21) Mr. Harrison wants to teach his third-grade class about how a written document, such as the Constitution, can outline the procedures an organization or country must follow. Which activity meets this goal?**

A. having students research the history of the Constitution

B. directing students to draft a "classroom compact"

C. asking students to compare their rules at home with the school rules

D. organizing a school-wide recycling program

**22) Which of the following is NOT an elected position?**

A. US senator

B. US representative

C. vice president

D. secretary of state

# Answer Key

1) **A.** **Correct**. This shows how housing is different based on environmental conditions.
   B. Incorrect. This difference is based more on income than environment.
   C. Incorrect. This does not pertain to housing.
   D. Incorrect. Only one of these is a house, and both are located in similar environments (both within the United States).

2) A. Incorrect. Learning centers do not necessarily pertain to cultural appreciation.
   **B.** **Correct.** These props help students appreciate the different types of clothing worn in different cultures.
   C. Incorrect. This would only help if the labels were in languages other than English.
   D. Incorrect. The classroom rules do not directly relate to the appreciation of other cultures.

3) A. Incorrect. This exposes students to American history, not necessarily a different cultural heritage.
   B. Incorrect. This exposes students to a different style of painting, not necessarily a cultural heritage.
   **C.** **Correct**. Mr. Wyatt could use this activity as a springboard for a unit about Native Americans and various parts of this cultural heritage.
   D. Incorrect. This exposes students to a different artistic technique and subject matter, not a different culture.

4) A. Incorrect. This is an important cultural norm that must be taught to students.
   B. Incorrect. This is an American cultural norm.
   **C.** **Correct**. This is not an American cultural norm, but it is a norm in some countries.
   D. Incorrect. This is an American cultural norm.

5) A. Incorrect. This is certainly a downside.
   B. Incorrect. This is also a downside.
   **C.** **Correct**. This is a definite advantage to a global culture.
   D. Incorrect. This is a downside.

6) A. Incorrect. This is far too advanced a concept for a first-grade class.
   B. Incorrect. This is also too advanced for the grade level.

C. Incorrect. First-grade students likely would not know this unless every item was labeled.

**D.** **Correct**. This question will help students see that they are dependent on others, since they cannot make their own shoes.

**7)** A. Incorrect. This is not common enough and would be challenging for a first grader.

B. Incorrect. This would also be very challenging for a first grader, especially one who has not traveled.

**C.** **Correct**. The Statue of Liberty is one of the most widely recognized American landmarks, and it would be appropriate for a first grader to recognize this symbol.

D. Incorrect. A first grader would be unlikely to have the background in Roman history to recognize the Coliseum.

**8)** **A.** **Correct**. The compass rose indicates the cardinal directions.

B. Incorrect. The scale shows the relative distance as indicated by the map.

C. Incorrect. The grid is a coordinate system that helps show location by points.

D. Incorrect. This is one projection used to show the globe on a flat surface.

**9)** A. Incorrect. Both rivers and lakes are surrounded by land.

B. Incorrect. Both lakes and rivers are generally freshwater.

C. Incorrect. Both lakes and rivers are within continents.

**D.** **Correct**. Rivers flow into seas and oceans, but lakes do not.

**10)** A. Incorrect. This is not pertinent to climate.

**B.** **Correct**. Because the school is in the desert, some crops will survive and others will not (or all will die), prompting a discussion about how people living in the desert grow only certain crops or must import food.

C. Incorrect. This activity does not pertain to climate.

D. Incorrect. Again, this project is not related to climate.

**11)** A. Incorrect. This is too advanced for a prekindergarten class.

B. Incorrect. This is a question about plot, not about different environments.

C. Incorrect. Prekindergarten students in rural Iowa likely would not know the answer to this question.

**D.** **Correct**. This will help lead students in a discussion about different types of houses such as apartments in urban areas.

**12)** A. Incorrect. This topic is not specifically about the economy, and Hector might choose to discuss other aspects of trains in American history.

**B.** **Correct.** This topic is pertinent to the role of trains in a subset of the American economy: cattle ranching.

C. Incorrect. This topic does not necessarily pertain to the economy.

D. Incorrect. This topic might have something to do with the changing American economy, but it is related more to other transportation options than to the economy.

**13)** A. Incorrect. This is not developmentally appropriate for a kindergartener.

**B.** **Correct.** This gives students a visual representation of the passage of time.

C. Incorrect. Kindergarten students would not understand this.

D. Incorrect. This would not be developmentally appropriate for a kindergarten class.

**14)** A. Incorrect. This activity does not promote visual/graphic literacy.

B. Incorrect. This activity promotes general literacy but not visual/graphic literacy in particular.

C. Incorrect. This activity promotes general literacy in writing ability but not visual/graphic literacy.

**D.** **Correct.** This activity will help her students use and understand social studies information presented graphically and aid in the development of overall visual/graphic literacy.

**15)** A. Incorrect. This activity is far too advanced for a prekindergarten class.

**B.** **Correct.** This activity helps students understand the daily chronology.

C. Incorrect. This activity is not developmentally appropriate for a prekindergarten class.

D. Incorrect. Again, this activity is far too advanced for this grade level.

**16)** A. Incorrect. It is unlikely that Lisa would understand the concept of the portfolio as assessment/documentation of progress.

B. Incorrect. Lisa might have the chance to demonstrate her vocabulary skills to her mother, but vocabulary is not Mr. Fuller's primary motivation.

**C.** **Correct.** This activity helps Lisa link the visual photographic representations with what she did first, second, next, and last.

D. Incorrect. This activity does not clearly demonstrate to Lisa that the photographs are primary soruces.

**17)** **A.** **Correct**. Mrs. Rose can help address this issue by promoting tolerance of different religions and styles of dress.

B. Incorrect. Equality does not necessarily pertain to this situation.

C. Incorrect. Equity does not pertain directly to this situation.

D. Incorrect. This situation is about tolerance of difference, not fairness.

**18)** A. Incorrect. This is not a statement about fairness so much as rule of law.

B. Incorrect. This is not a statement about tolerance.

**C.** **Correct**. Mr. Haskell is likening his classroom rules to laws that apply to everyone, even the teacher.

D. Incorrect. This is not a statement about equity.

**19)** A. Incorrect. This solution does not encourage compromise, since Ms. Sturgis solved the problem for the students.

B. Incorrect. This suggestion also does not encourage compromise and might be seen as unfair.

C. Incorrect. This idea avoids the issue and misses the opportunity to teach compromise.

**D.** **Correct**. This suggestion is a compromise in which both students give and take something.

**20)** A. Incorrect. This activity is being a good local citizen.

B. Incorrect. This activity is also being a good local citizen.

C. Incorrect. This activity is being a good national citizen.

**D.** **Correct**. This activity is part of global citizenship since recycling affects the entire planet.

**21)** A. Incorrect. Researching the Constitution's history does not directly address this goal, as there are many different parts related to the history of the Constitution.

**B.** **Correct**. This activity will help his students make the connection between the Constitution that outlines the rules our government must follow and a "classroom compact" that will outline the rules the classroom must operate within.

C. Incorrect. Comparing home and school rules is not related to a written document, as it is unlikely that the rules of the home are written.

D. Incorrect. A school recycling program is more about global citizenship than understanding the Constitution.

**22)** A. Incorrect. US senators are elected.

B. Incorrect. US representatives are elected.

C. Incorrect. The vice president is elected.

**D.** **Correct**. The secretary of state is appointed by the president.

6

# Science

## Scientific Inquiry

**Scientific inquiry** refers to the methods used to understand the fundamental concepts and processes within the disciplines of physical science, life science, Earth and space science, engineering and technology, and others. Scientific inquiry requires an understanding of basic science skills, including observation, description, and classification. For example, when conducting an experiment, students formulate questions, test hypotheses, and communicate information to help explain the world.

It is very important that early childhood educators make a conscious effort to include evidence-based scientific teaching into their classrooms. Many in the field of early childhood education once believed that these concepts were too abstract for young children to grasp and should be saved for higher grades. Current research suggests quite the opposite, and the national push for science education and the creation of the Next Generation Science Standards for grades kindergarten through twelve put science education in the forefront.

> DID YOU KNOW?
>
> STEM jobs are projected to grow at a much higher rate than other occupations through 2020. Introducing scientific concepts in early childhood can help prepare students for this economy.

### Unifying Scientific Concepts

A major idea behind scientific inquiry is **unifying scientific concepts**. Unifying scientific concepts provide students with themes across scientific disciplines to help them understand the natural world. Some of these concepts are:

- **Evolution**: Evolution is a theory that explains how living species change over a period of time and how they have come to be the way they are today. While dinosaurs are a favorite topic of interest in many early childhood classrooms, and not all state and national standards reference evolution explicitly, current research indicates that teaching evolution early (kindergarten through second grade) might have strong benefits. Most notable among these is helping students to clear up misconceptions or questions that they may have.

- **Systems**: Systems are sets of connected parts that work together to form a whole. The human body, a lake, and a classroom terrarium are all examples of systems that students can easily grasp. Much of early childhood science education revolves around the interrelationship of living things and how they work together. This organization can be observed on a broader level when students take a field trip to a nature conservancy or even in the microcosm of a fish tank in the classroom. Part of a foundational understanding of the concept of systems is the idea that all living things have a role to play. A teacher in a preschool classroom with a class pet might point out, for example, that the pet is entirely dependent upon humans to feed and care for it, just as students are dependent upon their parents to meet their own basic needs.
- **Cycles**: Cycles are the sequences of changing states of systems. The life cycle of the butterfly is a very popular and easy way for very young students to be introduced to this concept. The water cycle, the life cycle of a plant, and many others are great ways to increase students' knowledge and interest in the cyclical nature of all living things.
- **Organization**: Each part of a system has a purpose, and those parts work together in a specific way. For example, the human body must maintain a state of **equilibrium**, or balance, among component parts and systems. The inner ear is a system that balances opposing actions. If the inner ear does not maintain equilibrium, the balance is off, and the person will feel dizzy or fall. There is also organization among groups of living things in which schools of fish, herds of buffalo, and even families of humans work together to reach common goals.

## SAMPLE QUESTION

1) **A first-grade teacher wants to help her students understand that living organisms often start off in one form and then grow and change over time to meet their needs. Which class-wide project would be best to help students meet this objective?**

   A. planting seeds and then observing plants as they grow

   B. asking students to make a poster for the classroom about the water cycle

   C. taking a field trip to the zoo to observe different animals and their young

   D. picking vegetables from the school garden to make a salad that the whole class enjoys

## THE SCIENTIFIC PROCESS AND BASIC SCIENCE SKILLS

A major part of scientific inquiry is the scientific process. The scientific process is how science is performed. It includes basic science skills and the scientific method. The first step in the process is for students to think of the **purpose** of the experiment and ask a **question** that defines the problem or issue to be resolved.

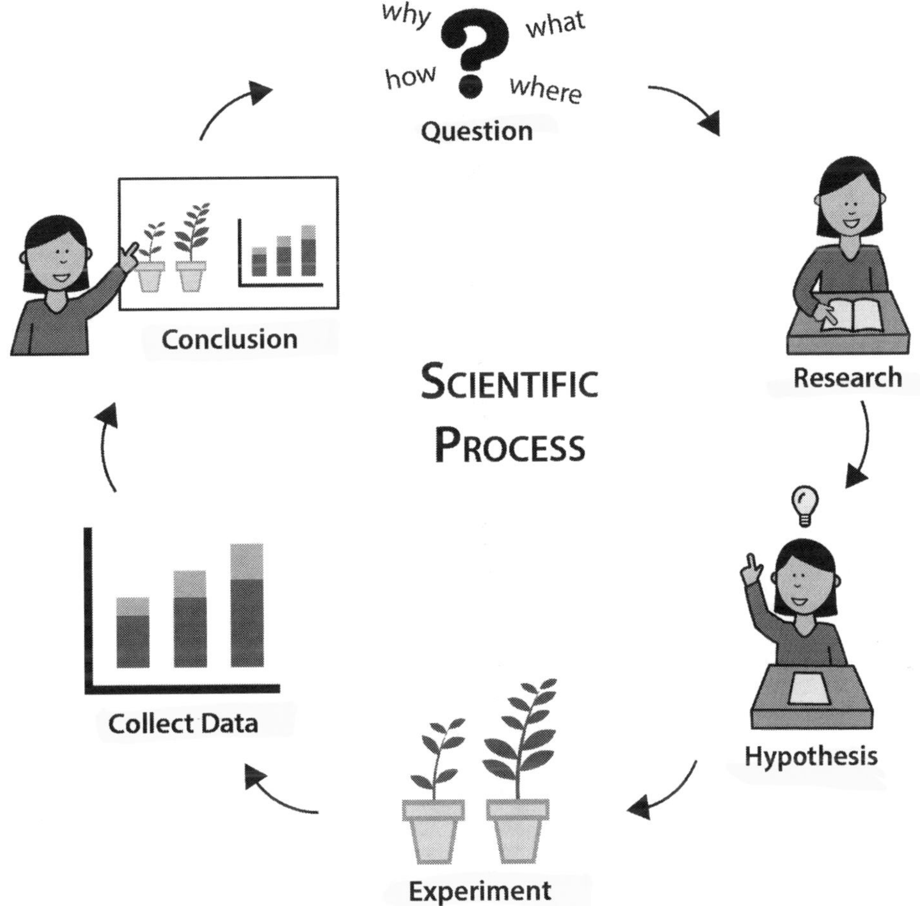


Figure 6.1. The Scientific Process

For example, students may want to see what will happen when they put celery in water with food coloring. They might ask: "What will happen to celery when it is placed in a cup of water with blue food coloring?" After creating a question, the students conduct an investigation, or **research**, the topic. The students might check to see if someone else has asked the same question, or they may do further research on the very nature of celery. Then the students form a **hypothesis**, which is a prediction about what will happen during the experiment. The students' hypothesis might be: "Half of the celery stick will turn blue, and the other half will stay green."

The next step in the scientific process is the **experiment**. An experiment tests the hypothesis in controlled conditions. While the students conduct their experiment, they should be **collecting data**, or gathering and measuring information from the experiment. They should also **classify** their data, or sort it into different groups.

After the experiment, students will **analyze** the data, draw a **conclusion**, make **inferences**, and create an **analysis**. This means that the students will determine what the data means, explain what happened during the experiment, and show the results of the experiment. In the example above, students might notice that the celery stick completely changed color after a week. They might infer that because the water is blue, and the celery needs water to live, the blue water travels up the celery stick, making it blue.

The last part of the scientific process is **representing findings** from the experiment. In other words, the students must share the results of the experiment—the **evidence**, or the reasoning, that either supports or disproves their hypothesis.

Table 6.1. The Scientific Process

| Step | Example |
|---|---|
| Purpose/question | Which type of soil is the best to use for planting? |
| Hypothesis | Sandy soil is the best to use for planting. |
| Experiment | Gather three planters. Put sand in one, dirt soil in one, and clay in the other. Add a plant to each. Observe what happens to the three plants. |
| Record observations | The plants start to grow. The plant in the sandy soil is shorter than the plant in the dirt soil. The plant in the clay soil is the shortest. |
| Draw a conclusion | Dirt soil is the best soil to use for planting. |

Encouraging students to discover through the scientific method is particularly important and can be integrated into several other parts of the overall curriculum. For example, prekindergarten students at a block center might be encouraged to develop a hypothesis as to what might happen if more and more blocks are stacked in varying configurations and then test their hypothesis by stacking the blocks in different ways. Second-grade students learning a new computer drag-and-drop coding program might first form a hypothesis as to what will happen if they drop pieces into a certain order; then they test this theory.

Integrating inquiry-based learning—allowing children to use their natural curiosity to explore the world around them—throughout the school day can often be done with less effort than it might at first appear. First-grade students observing bugs on the playground at recess, for example, might be encouraged to explore the topic further during library time by checking out books on the subject. Third-grade students learning responsible global citizenship might use scientific inquiry to see how many families they can encourage to begin

QUICK REVIEW

Can you think of a scientific experiment that would be appropriate for students in pre-K, kindergarten, first grade, and second grade?

recycling in a school-wide recycling program through different targeted awareness and outreach campaigns.

The opportunities for integration of scientific principles are virtually limitless, and teachers should use them. Research suggests that not only is a child's interest in scientific fields best developed in early childhood but also their language and literacy development often occur best in a scientific context as they hear and use new language used to describe the world around them.

## SAMPLE QUESTIONS

2) **What makes a good hypothesis?**

   A. The hypothesis is written clearly.

   B. The hypothesis is written as a question.

   C. The hypothesis is testable.

   D. The hypothesis describes the experiment.

3) **Mr. Martinez wants to integrate more science concepts into his existing second-grade reading curriculum. Which activity would be best?**

   A. using words, like *mammals* and *habitats*, as part of an existing vocabulary lesson

   B. encouraging students to make observations of things that are happening in the classroom

   C. asking students open-ended questions

   D. reading a book to the class about a young man who wants to be a scientist

# Physical Science

Physical science is any science that deals with inanimate matter or energy. Physical science investigates the basic phenomena of the physical world. Topics in physical science include:

- the properties of objects and materials, such as the states of matter (solid, liquid, gas)
- forms of energy, such as light, electricity, heat, and magnetism; forces, such as pushing and pulling; and phenomena, such as the reflection and absorption of light and the production and conduction of heat
- motion, or the change of position of objects when a force is applied

## MATTER

**Matter** is a substance that occupies physical space. **Atoms** are the basis of all matter in the universe. Any object or material that contains atoms and takes up space contains matter.

Objects can be measured by mass and volume. **Mass** is the amount of matter an object contains. **Volume** is how much space it takes up. For example, a table tennis ball and a golf ball have about the same volume, but the golf ball has more mass. Problems with mass and volume are explicit parts of the Common Core State Math Standards beginning in third grade, so their underlying conceptual foundations should be well established in science lessons beforehand.

Any number of activities is appropriate even for very young children to help students explore mass and volume with hands-on exploration. A prekindergarten or kindergarten class might, for example, experiment with pouring a set volume of water into containers of different sizes. Even if the experiment gets messy and the containers overflow, students can gain an appreciation for what happens when the volume of the water exceeds the volume of the container.

In most of the early childhood grades (pre-K – second grade), activities involving the measurement of mass are generally combined with activities involving the measurement of weight. Mass and weight activities are associated because the concept of mass independent of gravity is hard for younger children to understand.

These activities usually center around the use of a balance scale or digital scale. Young students might first develop a hypothesis of which item they think might weigh more and then test this hypothesis. Any and all classroom and natural objects can be studied in this way, and older students can be encouraged to record their data into tables for further analysis.

Matter can be found in three states: solid, liquid, and gas. **Solids** have a firm shape that can be measured in length, width, and height. A brick is an example of a solid. **Liquids** flow easily, or move in a smooth way. They take the shape of any container they are poured into. Water is an example of a liquid. **Gases** are neither liquid nor solid. They spread out when warmed and contract when cooled.

One timeless experiment for students of any age is filling three balloons with a solid (ice perhaps), a liquid (usually water), and a gas (usually air or helium). Students can then record their observations of the three balloons. Which is heaviest? Which is the lightest, and which is the most sturdy, easiest to roll/move, and so on?

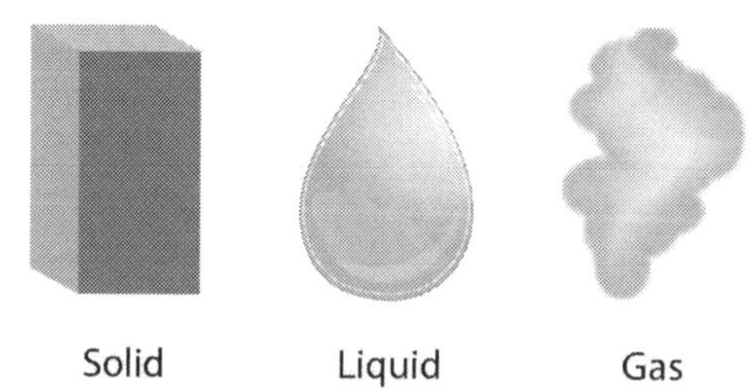


**Figure 6.2. States of Matter**

Students might also learn by having the different states of matter reinforced as they learn other scientific concepts. The water cycle, for example, gives students an opportunity to understand how water moves through these three states and how it is unique in that it is the only compound in which all three states of matter occur naturally.

**Temperature** is the measurement of how much energy is contained in the particles in matter. High energy materials have a higher temperature, and low energy materials have a lower temperature. Temperature is measured using a thermometer and can be described in units of Fahrenheit or Celsius.

During calendar and weather lessons for pre-K and kindergarten students, the concept of temperature as it pertains to weather should gradually be built. Young students can also experiment by describing certain objects or foods as hot, warm, cool, and cold; safety should be maintained, of course. Older elementary students in the first, second, and third grades might begin to use a thermometer to take various measurements: a glass of ice water, perhaps, or a cup of warm tea.

Substances will change states of matter when their temperature reaches a certain point, which is unique for every substance. Water, for example, will freeze to form ice at 32°F (0°C) and will boil to form water vapor at 212°F (100°C).

Generally, adding energy (making the material hotter) changes a substance to a higher energy state. Transitions from a higher to lower energy state release energy, making the material colder. Each of these changes has a specific name:

- solid to liquid: melting
- liquid to solid: freezing
- liquid to gas: evaporation
- gas to liquid: condensation
- solid to gas: sublimation
- gas to solid: deposition

These changes of substances can be observed by students in a variety of ways. Different items can be placed in the sun to observe melting and evaporation by measuring and drawing a line on a cup of water each day. Even sublimation can be observed (slowly) if ice is left in the freezer for a great length of time or if a teacher purchases a block of dry ice for a demonstration.

HELPFUL HINT

In both physical and chemical changes, matter is always conserved, meaning it can never be created or destroyed.

Matter can undergo two primary types of changes. An object is still fundamentally the same object after a **physical change**. For example, a pencil is still a pencil after it is broken into two pieces. Other examples of physical changes include melting butter and crushing a can.

On the other hand, an object or material is fundamentally different after a **chemical change**. Baking is a chemical change that converts flour, butter, milk, and sugar into a cake. One interesting activity with chemical changes is having students mix up several versions of the same cake recipe leaving out key ingredi-

QUICK REVIEW

What other safe, controlled, and developmentally appropriate activities involving chemical changes can you think of to use with early childhood students?

ents (such as oil, egg, baking powder, or flour) in each version. They can then make observations about the different cakes after they are baked (with scaffolding by the teacher). This will help students see how the chemical changes that happen during baking impact the final product.

SAMPLE QUESTIONS

4) **A first-grade student notices that there is dew on the grass in the morning but not in the afternoon after the sun has come out. What two phenomena is the student noticing?**

A. deposition and sublimation

B. melting and evaporation

C. condensation and evaporation

D. freezing and evaporation

5) **Which of the following states of matter adopt the shape AND size of the container they are placed in?**

A. liquids

B. solids

C. liquids and gases

D. gases

## Energy

**Energy** is the capacity of an object to do work—to cause some sort of movement or change. Basic concepts of energy can be related to light, heat, electricity, and magnetism.

**Light** is the form of energy that makes it possible for the eye to see. Colors are the result of objects interacting with light. When light hits an object, it can be **absorbed**—or soaked in. Some objects are **transparent**, meaning that they let all light pass though. Others are **translucent**, meaning they only let some light through. **Opaque** objects let no light pass through.

Light can also be **reflected**. When light is reflected, it bounces off an object or surface. This property of light can be demonstrated by shining a flashlight on a mirror. Light can also be broken into its spectral colors (red, orange, yellow, green, blue, indigo, and violet) by using a prism, or a material that **refracts** or bends light.

HELPFUL HINT

The order of the colors in the spectrum of visible light can be remembered using the mnemonic **ROY G. BIV:** red, orange, yellow, green, blue, indigo, violet.

There are numerous experiments and explorations that can be undertaken with light, from building a simple kaleidoscope with a paper towel tube to leaving "secret messages" that can only be decoded with black

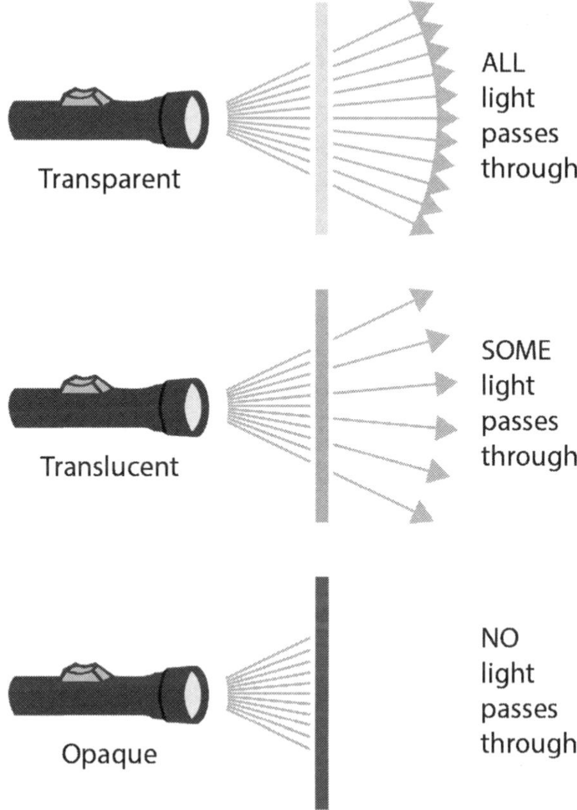

Figure 6.3. Transparent, Translucent, and Opaque Materials

lights. Students often really enjoy seeing the full spectrum of visible, and sometimes invisible, light. The Next Generation Science Standards include strands for investigating sunlight in kindergarten, and both sunlight and other types of light in first grade. These elements should be integrated into the curriculum in these grades as much as possible.

Another form of energy is **heat**. Heat is the transfer or flow of energy due to the difference in temperature between two objects. Heat energy is the result of the movement of atoms or molecules and can be transferred from one object to another through **conduction**. This occurs when heat energy is transferred between particles of different temperatures. For example, if you place a warm object and a cold one together, heat will pass from the warm object to the cold one through conduction. Conduction will continue until both objects achieve the same temperature.

**Electricity** is the movement of negatively charged electrons through matter. The electrical energy available through a wall outlet or stored in batteries is used to do work when it powers devices like light bulbs, televisions, and phones. Many experiments with electricity—conducted at very low voltages, often with holiday lights and 9-volt batteries—can take place in second- and third-grade classrooms with heavy scaffolding from the teacher to ensure student safety.

Figure 6.4. Reflection

**Magnetism** is a force that is closely related to electricity. It arises from the specific alignment of electrons in a material. The magnetic force can attract (pull) or repel (push) objects that contain a magnetic material, like iron, inside them. A magnet has two ends, called poles, where the magnets are the strongest. The **north**

**pole** of one magnet attracts (pulls) the **south pole** of a second magnet, but the like poles repel each other.

Students of all ages love magnets, and unlike some other hands-on science activities, allowing students to experiment freely with magnets is generally quite safe. Giving individual or groups of students a variety of objects to test as being either magnetic or non-magnetic is an appropriate activity for learners in kindergarten and beyond. The activity can be expanded in the elementary grades to include the recording of the magnetic properties (or lack thereof) of different objects in a table, chart, or graph.

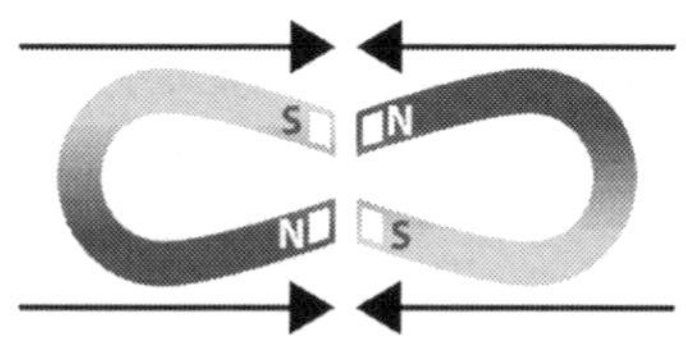


Opposite poles attract

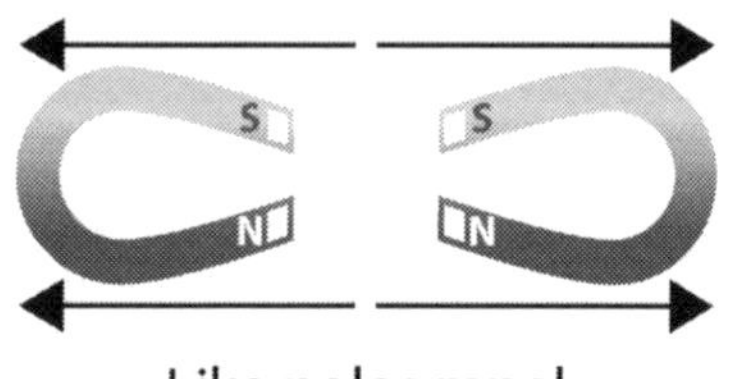


Like poles repel

**Figure 6.5. Magnets**

## SAMPLE QUESTIONS

6) **A first-grade teacher sets up a table with various materials, such as clear plastic, colored plastic, white paper, transparency film, cardboard, and flashlights. She encourages her students to make a hypothesis about what will happen when each material is placed in the beam of light from the flashlight. What topic is the teacher most likely going to introduce with the experiment?**

A. conduction

B. refraction

C. translucency

D. spectral light

7) **A second-grade teacher puts three spoons in her morning cup of very hot coffee: one plastic, one metal, and one wooden. She then invites students to come up and carefully feel the end of each spoon. What concept is the teacher introducing to the students?**

A. She is teaching them about heat-conductive materials.

B. She is teaching them to properly use laboratory equipment.

C. She is teaching them about electrical conductors and insulators.

D. She is encouraging students to make and test a hypothesis.

## Motion

Physics, or the science of motion, can be simplified for young students, but it should be taught starting in kindergarten when students begin to explore motion and the speed and position of an object. Students might experiment, for example, with pushing matchbox cars down an incline. They might notice that the steeper the incline, the higher the speed of the car as it races down the track.

**Speed** is the measurement of how fast something moves relative to a certain point. It is often measured in miles per hour in the United States, though a common measure in many scientific labs is meters per second. **Velocity** is different from speed in that it is the rate of change in an object's position, accounting for both speed and direction.

The Next Generation Science Standards call for explicit instruction of **force**, or the push or pull on an object, in kindergarten. By experimenting with various objects, students can see that the harder one pushes or pulls, the further the object in question will travel. Students can also see force in action with magnets and springs.

By third grade, students should be predicting a pattern of motion based on force and other factors, such as **gravity**—the force that attracts everything toward Earth's center or another body having mass—and **friction**, the resistance in motion when objects rub against each other. Friction causes moving objects to slow down as kinetic (or moving) energy changes to heat energy. Students can test this simply by going outside on a cold day and rubbing their hands together. The friction will create heat and make one's hands somewhat warmer.

Students can also experiment with force and friction with the use of wheeled cars or other toy vehicles. Students might hypothesize, for example, which type of surface (carpet, grass, dirt, concrete, tile, etc.) will make the car go the fastest and then test their hypothesis through experimentation. Students can further make and test predictions about gravity by dropping objects of different sizes and weight from a given point and timing how long they take to fall.

## SAMPLE QUESTIONS

8) **How is velocity different from speed?**

   A. Velocity applies only to objects in motion.
   B. Speed accounts for an object's direction.
   C. Velocity applies only to objects in an environment free of gravity.
   D. Velocity accounts for both speed and direction.

9) **A kindergarten student scoots around the classroom carpet on his knees and then notices red marks on his knee caps. What caused this?**

   A. high velocity
   B. rapid acceleration
   C. friction
   D. gravity

# Earth and Space Science

Earth and space science explores the relationships among the ocean, land, and atmosphere of our planet, as well as the properties of celestial objects and how they affect Earth. It includes understanding the movements and cycles that occur on Earth and in space: weather, seasons, daylight, water, carbon, tectonic plates, and more. It also includes studying the physical and chemical makeup of our planet and others.

## The Solar System

A **solar system** includes a **star** and all the matter that orbits that star, including asteroids, comets, meteoroids, planets, and their moons. Stars are giant balls of extremely hot gas made up of hydrogen and helium, held together by gravity. The core of a star produces energy. Some of that energy is released as light, which makes the star glow.

An **asteroid** is a small, rocky, planet-like body that circles the sun. The size of an asteroid can range from about three feet to more than five hundred miles across. A **comet** is a chunk of dust and ice that orbits the sun. There are billions of comets in our solar system. Most comets never pass close to Earth.

**Meteoroids** are very small, rocky bodies in our solar system; they range in size from a speck to several feet across. Meteoroids travel through space and occasionally enter Earth's atmosphere, where they become known as **meteors**—or shooting stars. If they do not burn up, the piece that ends up on Earth's surface is known as a **meteorite**.

A **moon** is a natural satellite that revolves around a planet. Planets vary in the number of moons they have. Moons do not give off their own light but reflect light from the sun, making them appear to shine.

HELPFUL HINT

The phrase ***M**y* ***V**ery* ***E**ducated* ***M**other* ***J**ust* ***S**erved* ***U**s* ***N**oodles* can help students remember the order of the planets: Mercury, Venus, Earth, Mars, Jupiter, Saturn, Uranus, Neptune.

**Planets** are an important part of the solar system, too. Planets are large, natural objects that orbit—or circle around—stars. Eight planets orbit our sun. From closest to the sun to farthest, these planets are **Mercury**, **Venus**, **Earth**, **Mars**, **Jupiter**, **Saturn**, **Uranus**, and **Neptune**.

- Mercury is the smallest planet and is only a little bit larger than Earth's moon. Mercury rotates very slowly and has no moon.
- Venus is the sixth-largest planet in the solar system and has a dense, cloudy atmosphere. The clouds that cover Venus reflect light and make it the brightest planet as seen from Earth. It is also the closest planet to Earth and only a little smaller in size by comparison.
- Earth is the fifth-largest planet in our solar system. Life, as we know it, has only been found on Earth.

- Mars is the seventh-largest planet in our solar system. It is known as the *Red Planet* because its surface is rich in iron oxide—rust—and so it appears red from Earth.
- Jupiter is the largest planet in the solar system; it has sixteen moons and is more than 1,000 times larger than Earth.
- Saturn is the second-largest planet in our solar system, known for the icy rings that encircle it.
- Uranus is the third-largest planet in our solar system.
- Neptune is the fourth-largest planet in the solar system.

**Figure 6.6. The Solar System**

The Next Generation Science Standards include explicit strands regarding space in first grade, when students are asked to make observations and describe patterns of the sun, moon, and stars. However, a basic understanding and identification of Earth, the moon, and the sun can be introduced in prekindergarten, as can space exploration. Many art projects, such as having students create a moonscape model out of modeling clay, or drawing/coloring the planets, are both developmentally appropriate and a great way to integrate fine motor skills development with basic science concepts.

## SAMPLE QUESTION

**10) Which astronomical bodies generate their own light?**

A. stars

B. planets

C. comets

D. moons

## Seasons and Weather

Weather and seasons are an important part of any preschool or kindergarten classroom, and rightly so since they help students observe what is somewhat predictable in the natural world—seasons—and what is often hard to predict—weather. Various tools can help scientists make observations about weather. A **thermometer** measures the air temperature and is a great tool to help students as young as kindergarten track and record the temperature. More advanced tools, such as **barometers**, which measure air pressure and are often used to help predict rain, and **anemometers**, which measure wind speed, can be useful for older students to make and record observations. Younger students might observe wind speed and direction from a wind sock, or track the rain over a period of days or weeks with a rain gauge.

Earth makes one complete **orbit** around the sun every 365 days, and this is called a year. A **day** is a twenty-four-hour period—the time elapsed for the earth to rotate once on its axis such that the sun appears at the same place in the sky the next day. Some people living near the equator have close to twelve hours of light and twelve hours of darkness each day.

**Seasons** happen because of the tilt of Earth's axis toward and away from the sun. Because the earth's axis tilts at 23.5 degrees, most of the planet's inhabitants experience varying amounts of light and darkness dependent upon the time of year. During the summer, the northern half of the earth is tilted toward the sun, making daytime longer. During winter, the northern half of the earth is tilted away from the sun, making nights longer. The opposite happens in the southern half, so when it is summer in the Northern Hemisphere, it is winter in the Southern Hemisphere.

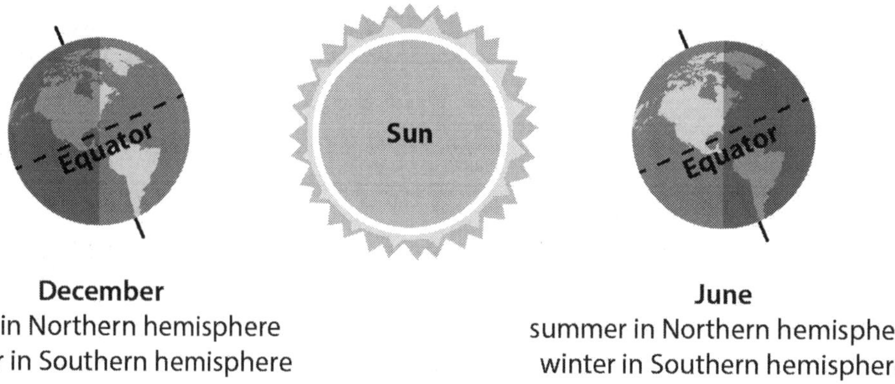


**Figure 6.7. Seasons**

Explicit instruction in seasons generally begins in preschool, and students will appreciate the seasons with thematic units on holidays and celebrations within these seasons. Bulletin boards, classroom decorations, and class- or school-wide celebrations (fall/spring carnivals, etc.) are all useful to help students recognize and look forward to certain seasons. Older students can begin to appreciate that seasons are relative and that not all places on Earth experience the same season at the same time.

Weather, particularly sunlight, should be emphasized in kindergarten. Beginning in first grade, students should make observations about different amounts of daylight at various times of the year. In second and third grade, observations and patterns about the weather, seasons, and sunlight can be expanded to include the way that these patterns impact all life on Earth.

A variety of tools and hands-on activities can be used to help students explore the weather and seasons. Simple observation and recording activities are appropriate for all age groups, with teacher scaffolding as necessary. These activities often work well when integrated with math activities, such as recording data in a table and recognizing patterns over time. Even prekindergarten students can participate in these types of activities with the aid of pictures.

Young students should also develop vocabulary to describe weather. This can be reinforced by asking students, for example, whether it is colder today than it was yesterday, or having them tell you whether the day is hot or *very* hot. These are good questions to help get very young students talking about the weather. Older students might benefit from hands-on activities, such as experimenting with a globe and a flashlight to better understand Earth's tilt, and even creating models showing the orbits of the earth, the sun, and the moon.

### QUICK REVIEW

How could you incorporate math skills, like data collection and organization, into lessons on weather and seasons for each grade level?

## SAMPLE QUESTIONS

**11) Ms. Bess, a third-grade teacher, points to the United States and South Africa on the globe and asks her class the following question: "Our longest day is June twenty-first, and our longest night is December twenty-first. What is the longest day and night in South Africa?" What is the correct response?**

A. The longest day and night are the same in South Africa as in the United States.

B. The longest day in South Africa is September twenty-second, and the longest night is March twenty-first.

C. South Africa has twelve hours of light and twelve hours of darkness each day.

D. The longest night in South Africa is June twenty-first, and the longest day is December twenty-first.

**12) A prekindergarten instructor wants to begin teaching her students about weather. What is the best activity for this age group?**

A. building a model of the earth, the sun, and the moon and relating it to the seasons

B. taking the class outside to make observations about the weather, such as hot, cold, windy, etc.

C. explaining seasonal variations in the Northern and Southern Hemispheres with orbital diagrams

D. having students fill in a compare-and-contrast chart showing the climate of different regions of the US

## Properties of Earth's Materials

Earth is made up of minerals, rocks, soil, and water. **Minerals** are naturally occurring substances formed in the earth that are not animals or plants. Examples of minerals are elements such as gold, silver, and iron, and combinations of elements, such as salt. **Rocks** are solid masses made up of minerals. Rocks form much of the earth's **outer crust**—the thinnest layer of the earth's surface—including cliffs and mountains.

**Fossils** can also make up some of the earth's surface. Fossils are impressions or remains left by plants or animals that lived a long time ago. They might be imprints of footprints, shells, or nests—known as trace fossils or body fossils—or the preserved remains of organisms themselves. Fossils are formed by replacing original organic material with minerals. This allows them to be preserved from decay.

HELPFUL HINT

Luster describes how light reflects off the surface of a mineral. Terms to describe luster include *dull*, *metallic*, *pearly*, and *waxy*.

**Soil** is formed slowly as rock breaks down into tiny pieces near the earth's surface and combines with organic matter. Soils have properties of texture and color and the capacity to hold water and grow plants. Soil provides a home for many animals, such as insects, spiders, and worms as well as bacteria and other living things. Soil affects the atmosphere by releasing gases, such as carbon dioxide, into the air. It is important because it cycles nutrients including carbon and nitrogen. Soil also helps filter and clean the water.

**Water** is a tasteless, odorless, and nearly colorless liquid. Many substances dissolve in water, so water in nature is rarely pure. Earth's water is always changing states from vapor to liquid to ice and back again. This **water cycle** affects Earth's materials. The water cycle describes the existence and movement of water on, in, and above the earth. These are the parts of the water cycle:

- precipitation: Water falls to the earth as rain, snow, sleet, or hail.
- evaporation: Water changes from liquid to gas as it is heated by the sun.

- condensation: Water vapor changes from a gas to a liquid and forms water droplets as it cools.
- runoff: Water drains from a high point of land and flows into an existing body of water.
- accumulation: Water collects on the earth's surface creating oceans, streams, and lakes.
- transportation: Water is absorbed by a plant, carried through to the leaves, and then turned into vapor and released into the atmosphere. Water can cause the earth's surface to break down through weathering and erosion, which create cliffs, canyons, and other rock formations.

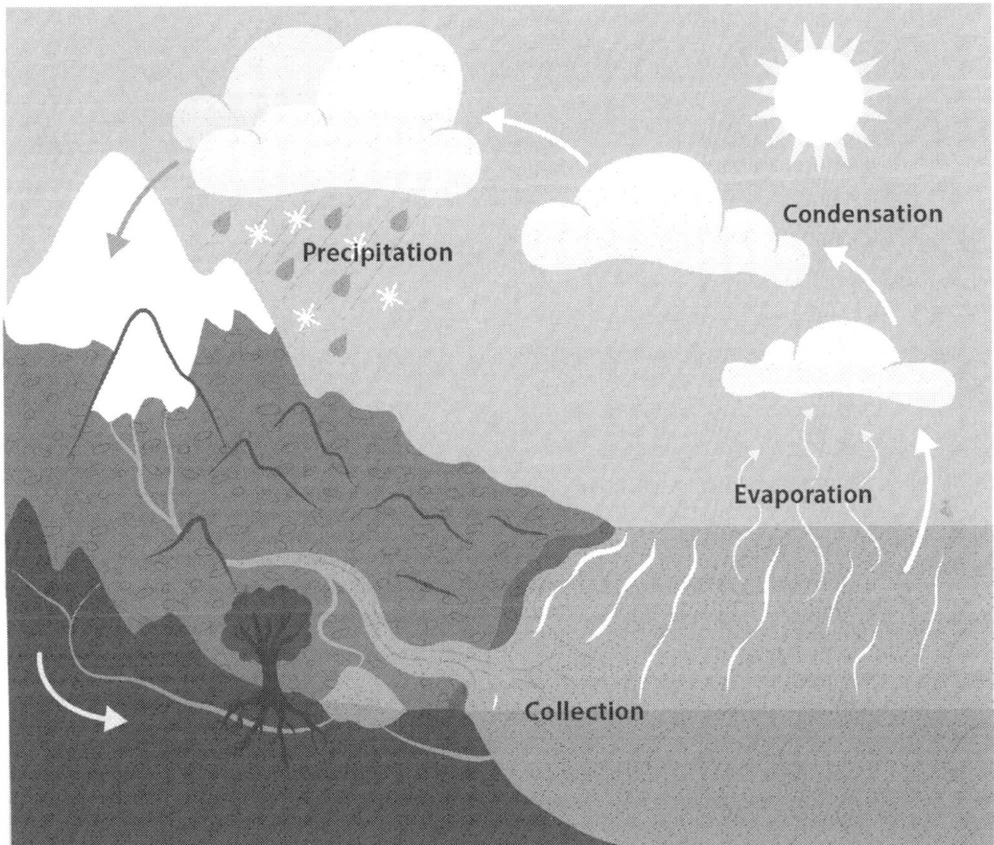


Figure 6.8. The Water Cycle

Changes in the earth's surface can happen quickly or slowly, and students should begin to make this distinction in second grade. Slow processes include:

- weathering: Wind, water, and ice cause large rocks to break up into smaller rocks.
- erosion: Rock and soil are carried from one place to another. Human actions, such as deforestation and construction, can accelerate erosion.
- deposition: Layers of sediment are deposited on one another, building up land mass. Deposition can lead to many different formations

depending upon where it occurs. Ocean sandbars and river deltas are both the products of deposition, which happens after erosion.

Other changes in the earth's surfaces happen very suddenly. These include:

- earthquakes: Earthquakes are the release of energy when two blocks of the earth slide past one another. They are most likely to occur along boundaries of tectonic plates—large pieces of the earth's crust and mantle that fit together like a puzzle over the earth's surface.
- volcanoes: These are eruptions caused when magma within the earth reaches its surface. Volcanoes also occur along plate boundaries.
- landslides/mudslides: These are large amounts of earth and rock that move down a slope. These occur most frequently in coastal and mountain areas, but they have been recorded in all fifty states.

> HELPFUL HINT
>
> **Weathering** is the process of breaking large rocks into smaller rocks over time. **Erosion** is the movement of weathered rock and soil from one place to another. Both are caused by wind, ice, water, and gravity.

At all levels, students should see the earth as a naturally changing environment, though human interactions with the planet can also cause changes. This might happen as the result of human-generated pollution that impacts the water cycle or rapid deforestation that leads to erosion. Students must be encouraged to be responsible stewards of both the earth's resources as well as the materials of the earth itself.

## SAMPLE QUESTIONS

**13) Which of the following changes the earth's surface slowly?**

A. volcanoes
B. earthquakes
C. wildfires
D. weathering

**14) Mrs. Hart teaches second grade in Houston, Texas. One of her students asks her the following question: "Why don't we have any earthquakes here?" What is her best response?**

A. "The climate here is too humid, so we do not have earthquakes."
B. "Unlike some other places, our city is not located near a plate boundary, so we do not usually get earthquakes."
C. "Because of erosion caused by tropical storms in the Gulf of Mexico, we are unlikely to experience earthquakes."
D. "We do not have earthquakes because we are at such a low elevation."

# Life Science

Life science focuses on biology—the study of life and living organisms—and on the changes that all living things undergo. It covers topics including characteristics of organisms, such as what plants and animals need to survive; life cycles, the different stages of the lives of plants and animals; and ecosystems, how living things interact with each other and their environment.

## Characteristics of Organisms

An **organism** is an individual living thing, such as a plant, an animal, or a bacterium. Organisms have five characteristics that nonliving things do not have:

- Organisms are made up of cells.
- Organisms collect and use energy.
- Organisms grow and develop.
- Organisms can reproduce.
- Organisms respond to changes in their environment.

A **cell** is the smallest unit of organization in a living thing. A cell contains a nucleus and is surrounded by a membrane. The cell contains the organism's DNA and can make copies of itself. Some organisms are made up of more than one cell. These organisms' cells have specific roles. For example, hair cells function to grow and repair hair, and that is their only job. A group of similar cells can form a **tissue**. Tissues make up **organs**, such as lungs, which perform specific duties. An **organ system** is a group of organs that work together for one or more purposes, such as the respiratory or digestive system.

> DID YOU KNOW?
>
> Having students study science through hands-on activities is a highly recommended strategy. Some districts recommend up to 80 percent of all science instructional time in kindergarten and first grade be spent in classroom and outdoor investigations; up to 60 percent is recommended for the second and third grades.

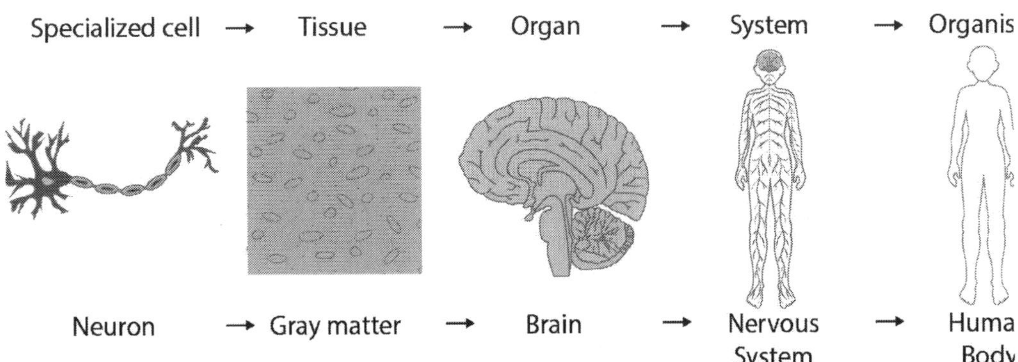


Figure 6.9. The Biological Hierarchy

Organisms collect and use energy. Cells, however, cannot survive by themselves. They need **nutrition** to grow, maintain balance, repair themselves, reproduce, move, and defend themselves. Nutrition is the act or process of taking in nutrients in order to grow and survive. Living organisms can either make their own food or depend on others to make food for them. Plants produce their own food through the process of photosynthesis. Other organisms eat plants to get energy.

The third characteristic of organisms is that they grow and develop. Living organisms begin life as a single cell. **Growth** is the increase in size and mass of an organism. For example, immature plants and animals are very similar to, but not exactly like, their parents.

Another characteristic of organisms is that they reproduce. **Reproduction** is the process by which new organisms are developed. Living things do not need to reproduce in order to survive; they need to reproduce to ensure that their species does not become extinct. Though it is not imperative, most organisms will go to great lengths to ensure they are able to reproduce.

The last characteristic of an organism is that it responds to changes in its environment. For example, if people hear a loud noise and wake up, the scare might make their hearts beat faster, and they might breathe faster. When this happens, the heart pumps more blood to the brain, which makes the people become fully alert. This response helps the people stay safe in a threatening or dangerous situation. Also, organisms can respond to their environment through **movement**. For example, geese temporarily move from the north to the south in winter because of their **sensitivity** to the cold. Sometimes the movement becomes permanent if the organism's habitat has changed such that its survival is no longer possible in its current location.

Even beginning in kindergarten, students should begin thinking about what different plants and animals (including humans) need to survive and how they can change the environment to meet their needs. This can be illustrated by a gopher digging a hole in which to live or a human digging a well from which to obtain water. In first grade, students should begin thinking about how the behaviors and structure of organisms help them survive and thrive. For example, fish have gills to enable them to breathe underwater, and mother bears aggressively protect their young to ensure survival. In second grade, students should start considering broader interactions among organisms, such as animals spreading plant seeds from one location to another. By third grade, students should be considering a broad range of environmental conditions that help organisms survive and how some organisms thrive while others do not, even though they are in the same environment.

SAMPLE QUESTION

15) **A third-grade teacher wants to illustrate that the same environment can be perfect for one organism but harmful to another. Which example might she use?**

A. fish and coral living in an ocean environment

B. camels and cactuses living in a desert environment

C. humans and pigeons living in a city environment

D. humans and deer living in a city environment

## LIFE CYCLES

A life cycle is a series of **stages**—or steps—in the process of growth and development during the life of all living things. **Development** is the steps along the way of an organism's transformation from a single cell to its mature form. Plants and animals **reproduce**; **parents**—a mother and father—produce young, or **offspring**. Offspring are the children or young of a particular human, animal, or plant. Life cycles are not the same across all living things, but they do all start with **birth** and end in **death**.

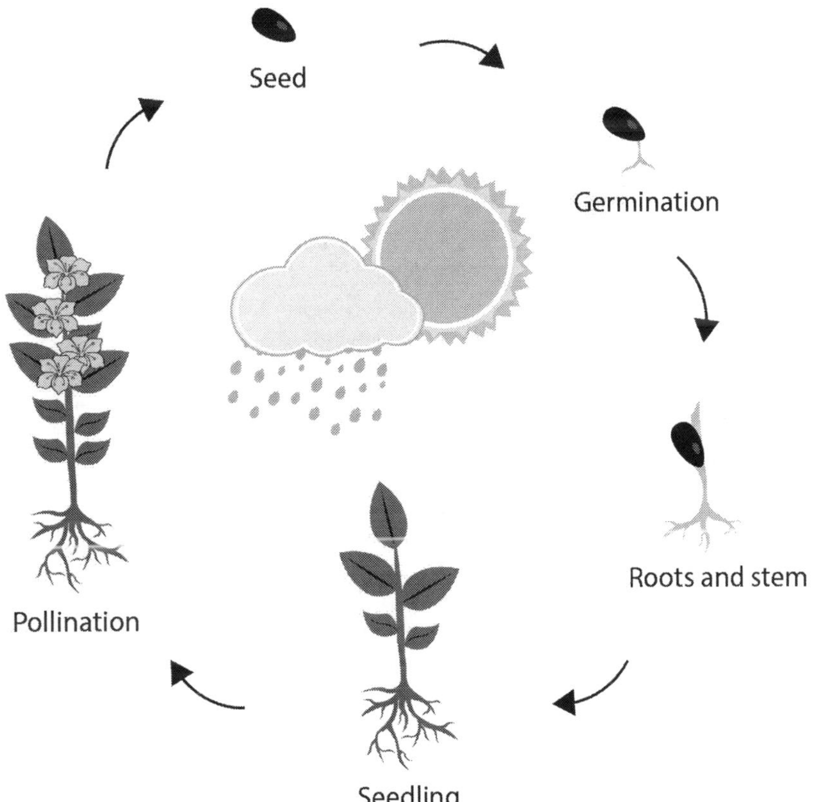


**Figure 6.10. The Plant Life Cycle**

The reproduction of many plants—the flowering plants—results in a **seed**, from which the offspring plant grows into a new plant. A seed starts to grow and sprout when the conditions of the soil are just right, including the temperature and the amount of water available. When the seed **germinates**, or starts to grow, a **seedling** begins to appear. A seedling is a young tree or plant grown from a seed. The seedling continues to grow and eventually becomes an adult plant, a process called **maturation**. Once the plant becomes mature, it starts to make flowers. Flowers contain the reproductive organs of the plant, allowing seeds to be created. The flowering plant life cycle then begins again.

Investigating how plants use their structures to survive is a first-grade objective per the Next Generation Science Standards. Experiments with plants pertaining to water and sunlight are recommended for second grade. Of course, various activities that allow even younger students to observe plant growth and development, such as school gardens or simple classroom plants, are appropriate at all ages.

HELPFUL HINT

Use the acronym ***LAWN*** to remember what plants need: **L**ight, **A**ir, **W**ater, **N**utrients.

Some animals develop through a process called **metamorphosis**—a series of physical changes—to become an adult. For example, a butterfly starts off as an **egg** and then **hatches** as a **larva**. Larvae—known as *caterpillars* in the case of butterflies—are very different from their parents. At the

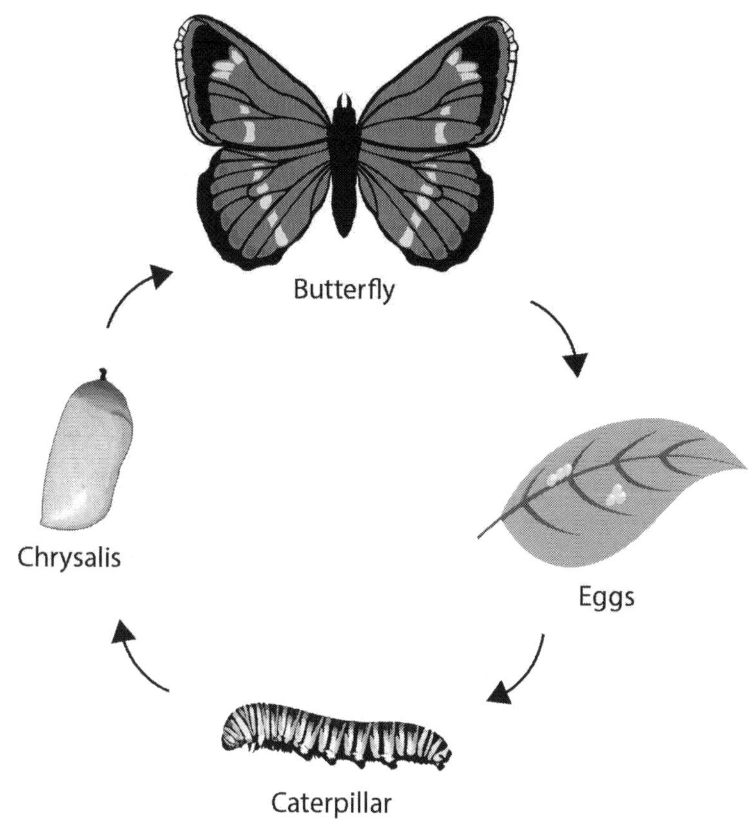


**Figure 6.11. The Butterfly Life Cycle**

end of the larval stage, a butterfly becomes a **pupa**, surrounded by a hard **chrysalis**, or cocoon. This is the middle stage of the butterfly's development. Pupae do not move or eat. Once the butterfly is fully developed into its adult form, the case around the pupa cracks open. The butterfly emerges to search for food and for other butterflies to mate with, and the cycle begins again.

Teaching basics about life cycles is a fabulous way for even preschool students to become interested in nature. Students can be encouraged to look for (but not touch!) eggs, cocoons, or buds in the natural environment. Students of all ages can also become highly engaged in the life cycle of the plant through class or school-wide projects, such as a garden. Gardens provide a unique opportunity to integrate a health and wellness curriculum into a science curriculum as students try different healthy, organically grown foods straight from the school garden. Health and wellness are also a key part of teaching about the human life cycle. Research has proven that healthy habits encouraged by teachers as early as the preschool years are often likely to be carried on throughout much of a student's life.

In addition to the life cycle of specific organisms, older students—namely those in second and third grade—should begin to understand the impacts that environmental changes may have on animal and plant species. Some organisms can withstand these changes while others cannot. Those that cannot will either relocate to a new environment or die out entirely.

> QUICK REVIEW
>
> What other ways can health and wellness be integrated into early childhood science instruction?

Extinction of a species can be likened to the end of its life cycle. While there is some debate as to the appropriateness of discussing upsetting themes, such as the decimation of habitats at the hands of humans, most research suggests that if conservation efforts are to be effectively carried out among future generations, they must be taught in the early childhood years. The key is to present information to students in a way that will first encourage their interest and appreciation for the natural world; this interest will then extend to a desire to protect it.

## SAMPLE QUESTIONS

**16) A third-grade teacher using the Next Generation Science Standards sees this strand: "Develop models to describe that organisms have unique and diverse life cycles, but all have in common birth, growth, reproduction, and death." What would be an appropriate activity to address this standard?**

A. creating a diagram of the life cycle of a star

B. creating an infographic of a mosquito and frog life cycle and comparing the two

C. planting a lima bean seed in a plastic bag with a wet paper towel and observing its growth

D. watching a video on asexual reproduction in bacteria

**17) Which of the following occurs during germination?**

A. The plant becomes mature.

B. The plant makes flowers.

C. The plant makes and releases seeds.

D. The seed begins to sprout.

## Ecosystems

An **ecosystem** is a large community of living organisms and the physical environment they live in. All living things need energy to grow, move, and reproduce; that energy comes from food. The feeding relationship between organisms in an ecosystem is described in a **food web**, which shows how each organism gets nutrients and energy. Each individual strand in the web is called a **food chain**. The food chain starts with plants. Green plants make their own food through a process called **photosynthesis**, during which they use sunlight to change water and carbon dioxide into food. Plants are generally referred to as **producers**, while those organisms that eat them are called **consumers**.

CONSIDER THIS

Ask students what would happen if all the decomposers disappeared from an ecosystem.

A food chain might start with grass, which rabbits eat. Rabbits are **herbivores**—animals that feed only on plants. The rabbit is **prey**—an animal that is hunted and eaten by another animal, such as a snake. Snakes are **predators**—animals that hunt and eat other animals for food. The snake eats the rabbit, and later, a **carnivore**—an animal that eats mainly meat, such as a hawk—eats the snake. Other animals, like some humans and bears, are **omnivores**, meaning they eat both plants and meat.

After the remains of dead animals are left behind by predators, decomposers—like **fungi** and bacteria— play an important role. Fungi are organisms that appear similar to plants but cannot make their own food using sunlight. Fungi consume plants, animals, and other living matter. Examples of fungi include mushrooms, yeasts, and mold. Fungi help **decompose** dead plants and animals. When fungi eat dead plants and animals, they release nutrients and minerals back into the soil; these will then be used by plants.

HELPFUL HINT

**Biotic** components are alive: they can move, grow, reproduce, eat, and drink. **Abiotic** elements are not alive.

Diverse ecosystems exist throughout the planet and have different varieties of plants and animals. Even in kindergarten, students can begin a simple study of this concept by matching animals with their habitats or natural environments. Deer and bears, for example, might live in a forest habitat whereas killer whales and jellyfish live in an ocean environment. Beginning in first grade, students should be considering how plants and animals use their own bodily structures to respond to their habitat in order to survive and grow.

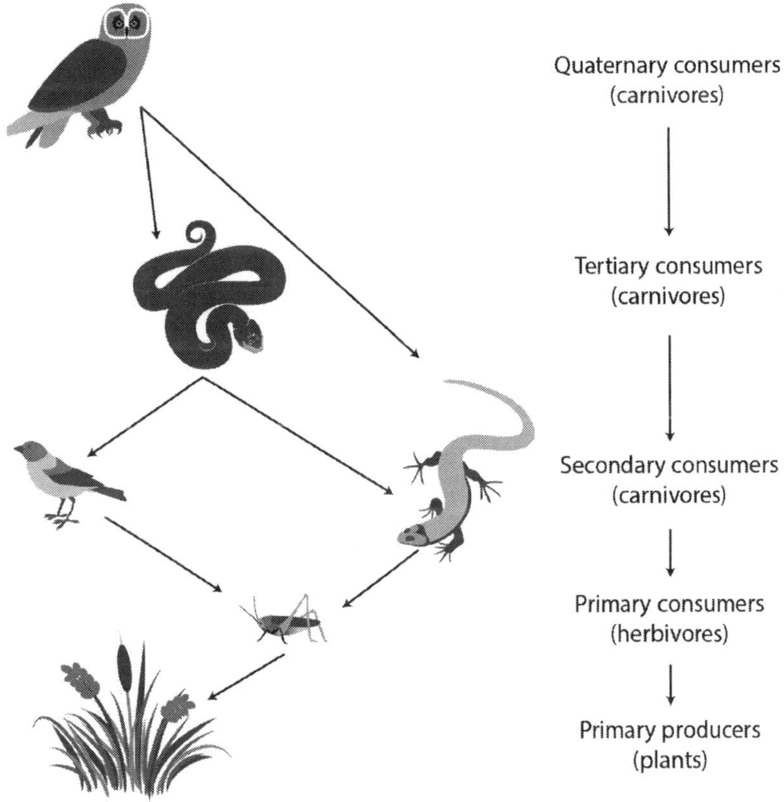


Figure 6.12. The Food Chain

## SAMPLE QUESTIONS

**18) Which of the following is an example of an herbivore?**

A. green algae

B. dolphin

C. cow

D. bird

**19) A second-grade class is conducting an experiment to test the following hypothesis: fungi will grow more quickly when exposed to sunlight. How might the class best set up the experiment?**

A. observe the height of mushrooms both in open fields and in forest habitats

B. leave one petri dish in the refrigerator and keep one on the counter

C. compare fungi growth on a hamburger bun to that on a piece of wheat bread

D. leave one piece of bread on the windowsill in sunlight and leave another in a dark place

# Engineering, Technology, and Applications of Science

Engineering, technology, and applications of science are closely connected and influence each other. Scientists use technology and engineering to facilitate their research and find solutions to problems. When engineers need to create something, such as a new type of car, they depend on the **design process** to lead them. The design process is the process by which new technologies are created. It is very similar to scientific investigation. Both build on evidence and reason and follow a logical sequence of steps to solve problems and find answers. The steps include:

- identify the problem
- brainstorm
- design
- build (redesign, test, evaluate, repeat)
- share a solution

Students should be participating in simple engineering projects starting in prekindergarten. This may begin with very simple tasks, such as building a tall tower out of blocks that will not fall. It can then progress, in kindergarten, to testing two different designs to see which one works better. In first and second grade, students should begin to analyze the data from these tests. In third grade, students can begin proposing their own solutions and designs to solve real-world problems.

For example, a teacher might give the class a real-life scenario such as the following: A family owns a cabin that floods each year when heavy summer rains come. This year, they want to protect their cabin from the water. The flood waters are expected to be about one inch.

The teacher can distribute a scaled model house and a variety of supplies to each student. The students will then have to brainstorm ideas for how to engineer the cabin to withstand the flood waters. Next, they may draw a design or write out their plans. Then, they will augment their model cabin with the flood-withstanding features and test it, perhaps by placing it in a tub with one inch of water. At this point, they can evaluate how much their model cabin flooded and what modifications they should make. They then redesign and test again. Once a design is successful, they can share it with others.

> QUICK REVIEW
>
> How can students be encouraged to conserve resources and reduce waste in schools?

Students should also be exposed to technology, even as early as prekindergarten. While various schools and programs may have different expectations regarding the use of computers, they will all most likely encourage students to be proficient in simple computer operations during the early childhood years. Many elements of computer science have been adapted to accommodate young learners. Students as young as kindergarten age can learn basic drag-and-drop programming, and older students can learn a variety of computer languages with sufficient instruction and practice.

As much as possible, students should not see science in a vacuum. Instead, they should be given multiple opportunities to apply scientific principles throughout the school day. Ideas for this include having students make hypotheses and conduct simple tests throughout the day, allowing them to make astute observations about their environment. Teachers should also encourage students to learn about different careers that involve the application of scientific principles and how these professionals study and improve the world around us.

QUICK REVIEW

How is technology integrated into your state's science standards?

## SAMPLE QUESTION

**20) A kindergarten teacher wants to make sure her students are proficient with basic computer technology by the end of the year. What is one objective that is reasonable for them to meet?**

A. using Java and Python

B. recording video on a tablet

C. turning on a computer

D. learning to type

# Answer Key

1) **A.** **Correct.** This activity will help students understand that plants begin as seeds and then change and grow over their life cycle.

   B. Incorrect. This activity is not necessarily about living organisms specifically.

   C. Incorrect. This activity, as described, will not aid in student understanding. If the teacher was pointing out along the way that the animals "grow fangs" or "shed feathers" as they mature, then this would be an appropriate activity.

   D. Incorrect. The vegetables aren't changing to meet their own needs; humans are meeting their own needs by harvesting the vegetables.

2) A. Incorrect. Although the hypothesis should be written clearly, that is not what makes it a good hypothesis.

   B. Incorrect. The hypothesis is not a question; it must be written as a statement.

   **C.** **Correct.** The hypothesis must be testable.

   D. Incorrect. The hypothesis does not need to describe the experiment. The hypothesis is a prediction about what will happen during the experiment.

3) **A.** **Correct.** Using words is a great way to combine overall vocabulary development as well as new science vocabulary that students will need an understanding of for explicit science instruction.

   B. Incorrect. Making observations does not relate to reading.

   C. Incorrect. Asking open-ended questions is very important but does not relate directly to integration into a reading curriculum.

   D. Incorrect. This activity pertains to reading and somewhat to science, but by second grade, most students should be reading on their own.

4) A. Incorrect. Deposition describes when a substance is transformed from a gas to a solid; sublimation describes a substance's transformation from a solid to a gas. No solids are involved here.

   B. Incorrect. Since dew is not a solid that is transformed into a liquid, this is not the correct answer.

   **C.** **Correct.** Dew is water vapor in the air that condenses as liquid on the ground. It then evaporates back into gas as the day heats up.

   D. Incorrect. Dew is not a liquid that has been transformed into a solid.

5) A. Incorrect. Liquids cannot change their size. They take the shape of their container, but their volume remains the same.

B. Incorrect. Solids cannot change their shape and size for a container, but they do expand and contract with temperature. Solids have a size and a shape of their own.

C. Incorrect. Liquids cannot change their size, but gases can.

**D.** **Correct.** Gases adopt the shape and size of the container in which they are placed.

**6)** A. Incorrect. Conduction refers to the process by which heat or electricity moves from one object to another.

B. Incorrect. While some refraction might happen during this experiment, the various objects indicate the teacher is likely focusing more on how light passes though objects.

**C.** **Correct.** The teacher is likely helping students grasp that some objects are translucent, and others transparent or opaque.

D. Incorrect. The experiment does not involve breaking light into its spectral colors.

**7)** **A.** **Correct.** The spoons will feel warm to varying degrees based on how heat conductive they are.

B. Incorrect. This is not necessarily laboratory equipment, just everyday items.

C. Incorrect. While the different spoon materials also have varying degrees of electrical conduction/insulation, this experiment is about heat conduction, not electrical conduction.

D. Incorrect. The teacher did not ask her students to form a hypothesis first.

**8)** A. Incorrect. Both speed and velocity apply to objects in motion.

B. Incorrect. Speed does not account for an object's direction.

C. Incorrect. Velocity applies to all objects in motion.

**D.** **Correct.** Unlike speed, velocity also accounts for an object's direction.

**9)** A. Incorrect. Velocity without contact with another object would not cause the rug burns.

B. Incorrect. Acceleration without contact with another object would not cause the rug burns.

**C.** **Correct.** Friction is the force of two objects (the knees and the carpet) rubbing against each other to produce heat (a rug burn).

D. Incorrect. While gravity keeps the student on the rug, it does not directly cause the red marks.

**10)** **A.** **Correct.** Stars—including the sun, which is a star—generate their own light. Planets, comets, and moons all reflect light from the sun.

B. Incorrect. Planets are large, natural objects that orbit stars; they do not generate their own light.

C. Incorrect. Comets are chunks of ice or dust that orbit the sun and do not generate their own light.

D. Incorrect. Moons revolve around a planet and do not give off their own light; instead, they reflect light from the sun, which makes them appear to shine.

**11)** A. Incorrect. In the Southern Hemisphere, the longest days and nights are reversed.

B. Incorrect. In most locations, these two dates generally have an approximately equal number of light and dark hours.

C. Incorrect. Places near the equator have this, but South Africa is in the Southern Hemisphere, not near the equator.

**D.** **Correct.** Because it is in the Southern Hemisphere, the longest day and night are reversed in South Africa.

**12)** A. Incorrect. This activity is not developmentally appropriate for a prekindergarten class and is not about weather.

**B.** **Correct.** This is an appropriate activity to help students begin to use weather-related vocabulary.

C. Incorrect. This is not developmentally appropriate for a prekindergarten class.

D. Incorrect. A compare-and-contrast chart is not developmentally appropriate for a prekindergarten class, and this one is more about overall climate than weather.

**13)** A. Incorrect. Volcanoes are eruptions that result in sudden changes to the earth's surface.

B. Incorrect. Earthquakes can happen suddenly and therefore change the earth's surface within moments, not slowly.

C. Incorrect. Wildfires result in sudden changes to the earth's surface.

**D.** **Correct.** Weathering changes the earth's surface slowly; the other processes change the earth's surface quickly.

**14)** A. Incorrect. Earthquakes are not related to humidity.

**B.** **Correct.** Earthquakes occur most frequently along boundaries between tectonic plates.

C. Incorrect. Earthquakes are not related to erosion.

D. Incorrect. Earthquakes are not related to elevation.

**15)** A. Incorrect. Fish and coral will both thrive in an ocean environment.

B. Incorrect. A desert environment is suitable for both of these organisms.

C. Incorrect. Living in a city environment can work well for both humans and pigeons.

**D.** **Correct.** Deer would not be able to find the vegetation they need to eat in order to survive and might be hit by cars in an urban environment. On the other hand, humans do just fine in an urban environment. The other choices describe organisms that are well-suited to their environments.

**16)** A. Incorrect. A star is not a living organism, though it does have a life cycle of sorts.

**B.** **Correct.** Working with an infographic will help students see that both a mosquito and a frog are born, grow, reproduce, and then die. It is also developmentally appropriate for third-grade students.

C. Incorrect. Planting and studying a lima bean will help students observe a plant life cycle, but it will not allow them to compare it to another life cycle.

D. Incorrect. This video might have some relevance, but it is not drawing a direct comparison to another life cycle.

**17)** A. Incorrect. Maturation is when the plant becomes mature.

B. Incorrect. A plant makes flowers after the maturation phase.

C. Incorrect. After the plant flowers, it makes seeds.

**D.** **Correct.** Germination is the phase of the plant's life cycle when the seed begins to sprout.

**18)** A. Incorrect. Algae are plants that make their own food; they do not eat plants.

B. Incorrect. Dolphins are carnivores that eat meat.

**C.** **Correct.** Cows eat only plants, so they are herbivores.

D. Incorrect. Birds eat both plants and other animals, so they are omnivores.

**19)** A. Incorrect. This is not the best choice since there may be other factors aside from exposure to sunlight that will impact the growth of the mushrooms.

B. Incorrect. This experiment introduces another variable—cold. An experiment should only change the one variable it is designed to test.

C. Incorrect. This experiment would determine which type of bread grows fungi the most quickly, not the effect of sunlight on fungi growth.

**D.** **Correct.** This would change only one variable and would allow the hypothesis to be tested by exposing one piece of bread to sunlight and not the other.

**20)** A. Incorrect. These computer languages are not developmentally appropriate for a kindergarten student.

**B.** **Correct.** This is an appropriate objective for kindergarten students. It might also aid students in recording observations.

C. Incorrect. This is too simple for an end-of-year goal for kindergarteners.

D. Incorrect. Most kindergarteners will not have the fine motor skills for this skill yet.

# Practice Test

## Subarea I: Knowledge of Child Development

Read the question, and then choose the most correct answer.

**1**

**A teacher wants to write effective learning objectives. The theorist she would most likely reference is**

A. Jean Piaget and his stages of cognitive development.

B. Jerome Bruner and his modes of representation.

C. Lev Vygotsky and his zone of proximal development (ZPD).

D. Benjamin Bloom and Bloom's taxonomy.

**2**

**First-grade students would be said to have typical language development if they are able to**

A. manage their own feelings.

B. recognize and read sight words at an increasing rate.

C. recognize only uppercase letters.

D. understand the difference between right and wrong.

**3**

**An example of typical moral development of a second grader would be**

A. offering to lend a pencil to another student who lost theirs.

B. continuously stealing other students' pencils.

C. telling the rest of the class to take another student's pencils.

D. breaking another student's pencil on purpose.

**4**

**Mia, a preschooler, is playing in the blocks center when another child comes and takes one of her blocks away. Mia would be said to have TYPICAL social-emotional development if she responds with which of the following behaviors?**

A. throwing the rest of the blocks across the room

B. crying uncontrollably and inconsolable

C. hitting the other child

D. telling the other they can play blocks together

**5**

**Sierra is a third grader in Ms. Walker's class. Her dad is a single father with two jobs, and she has three other siblings. The best method to schedule a conference with him is to**

A. offer a variety of times, dates, and locations.

B. not schedule one because he is too busy.

C. offer times on the weekend.

D. only offer times in the evening.

**6**

**When conducting a home visit, it is important for the educator to**

A. go alone.

B. go with his or her spouse.

C. go with another teacher or administrator.

D. go with a friend.

**7**

**Mr. Libman's kindergarten class is working on a project to keep the school playground clean by volunteering to pick up the trash every day and making sure all the toys are put away at the end of the day. This project is building his students'**

A. self-regulatory skills.

B. fine motor skills.

C. prosocial skills.

D. self-concept.

**8**

**Diana is a student in Ms. Harrison's third-grade class. She has a temperature of 102°F and has been vomiting. When Ms. Harrison calls home, Diana's mother tells her they just moved to the area, cannot afford health insurance, and do not have a family doctor. Ms. Harrison might provide Diana's family with information regarding**

A. fever-reducing medication.

B. how to apply for CHIP or Medicaid.

C. local pediatricians.

D. the flu shot.

**9**

**When a preschool child demonstrates thinking that is nonlogical, egocentric, and nonreversible, he is in what stage of Piaget's theory?**

A. pre-operational stage

B. sensorimotor stage

C. concrete operational stage

D. formal operational stage

**10**

**Which curriculum model embraces the idea of scaffolding through hands-on experiences with people and their environment?**

A. emergent curriculum

B. Creative Curriculum

C. Reggio Emilia approach

D. High Scope

**11**

**Which component of a learning objective describes how children's performance on a task will be evaluated?**

A. performance

B. behavior

C. conditions

D. criteria

**12**

**An example of a long-term planning goal for a class of kindergartners might be to**

A. incorporate strategies, such as providing consistent positive reinforcement, to develop children's self-esteem to encourage ongoing success.

B. provide children with daily opportunities to collaborate with one another to complete simple word puzzles.

C. provide children with varying learning center activities to practice recognizing words that begin with the letter sound *M*.

D. incorporate opportunities for children to practice problem-solving skills by allowing them to choose character roles during a reenactment of "The Three Little Pigs."

**13**

**Which list includes the critical components of a lesson plan?**

A. materials, procedures for instruction, activities for guided practice, and assessment

B. objectives, materials, procedures for instruction, activities for guided practice, accommodations and modifications, and assessment

C. objectives, procedures for instruction, activities for guided practice, accommodations and modifications, and assessment

D. objectives, activities for guided practice, and assessment

**14**

**Mr. Walsh, a kindergarten teacher, is implementing a science activity in which her students will match pictures of animals to pictures of their correct habitat. According to Bloom's taxonomy, in which level of learning will Mr. Walsh's activity fall?**

A. remember

B. understand

C. apply

D. analyze

**15**

**When choosing manipulatives for a kindergarten class, a teacher should choose those that**

A. focus on only one skill at a time.

B. only one child can work on at a time.

C. support language development in English.

D. support learning through problem-solving.

16

**Social play is described as**

A. running, jumping, and climbing.

B. playing with objects such as dolls, blocks, cars, and manipulatives.

C. children playing alongside each other with little or no interaction.

D. children sharing ideas and toys and communicating with each other.

17

**An effective strategy in transitioning preschool children from one activity to the next would be**

A. to ring a bell to gain children's attention, explain that it's time to clean up their current activity, and sing a clean-up song.

B. to go around to each activity and tell children it's time to clean up and ask them to sing the clean-up song.

C. to simply tell children it's time to clean up without gaining their attention first.

D. to ring a bell to gain children's attention but not give further instructions; they should know what to do.

18

**Mrs. Caldwell, a kindergarten teacher, incorporates several opportunities throughout the day to acknowledge positive behavior by giving high fives, praise and encouragement, and working on activities or games with children. Which child-guidance strategy is Mrs. Caldwell using?**

A. building relationships

B. teaching character development

C. incorporating positive interactions

D. teaching problem-solving strategies

19

**Which of the following would be a developmentally appropriate measurement activity for kindergarteners?**

A. measuring the length of their shoes using paper clips

B. measuring the distance from their home to school in miles

C. measuring the length of the classroom using feet

D. measuring the length of the playground using yards

20

**A second-grade teacher notices that one of her students has lost interest in reading or speaking in her home language. To encourage her, she asks for the student's "help" to read a short blurb in a newspaper in the student's home language. Why is the teacher most likely doing this?**

A. She wants to assess the student's oral fluency in her home language.

B. She wants to encourage the student to read more informational texts.

C. She wants to encourage the student to maintain her biliteracy.

D. She wants the student to practice prosody and rate in her home language.

21

**Mr. Hart, a third-grade teacher, has asked his students to write a short narrative about something interesting that happened to them during the week. What accommodation could he make for an English language learner to enable her to best participate in this activity?**

A. He could ask the student to write only two sentences instead of the full narrative.

B. He could have the student dictate the narrative into an audio recorder.

C. He could give the student a graphic organizer to organize her thoughts first before she writes.

D. He could allow the student to use an English picture dictionary or an electronic translating device.

22

**A second-grade teacher notices that many of her ELL students are more likely to practice oral reading when someone sits next to them and helps them with challenging vocabulary. Which instructional strategy might benefit these students?**

A. assistive technology

B. assignment modifications

C. peer tutoring

D. progress monitoring

23

**In most cases, what would be the least restrictive environment for the education of a student with a sensory disability?**

A. a self-contained special education classroom

B. a special school for those with sensory disabilities

C. the same classroom with students without disabilities

D. a home school environment

**24**

**What is an example of an assignment modification during silent reading time that a first-grade reading teacher could make for an academically gifted student?**

A. The teacher could have the student read from books at a higher Lexile level.

B. The teacher could have the student work on extra math or social studies instead.

C. The teacher could have the student track how many books he or she can read in one month.

D. The teacher could ask the student for more input on what would keep her engaged in the class.

**25**

**A non-verbal kindergartner with autism spectrum disorder has trouble with classroom communications. Which type of augmented communication device would be most helpful?**

A. a picture board

B. a laptop computer

C. an audio recorder

D. a text-to-speech application

**26**

**Mr. Weeks has made an initial request for an evaluation for a kindergartener in his class whom he suspects may have a disability. After the initial request for evaluation, the evaluation must be completed within what time period?**

A. There is no time frame.

B. one week

C. sixty days

D. the same school year

**27**

**A new child will begin in Mrs. Rodriguez's preschool classroom next week. As a first step in building a relationship with the family, Mrs. Rodriguez could**

A. make a phone call to the family to introduce herself and ask about their goals for their child.

B. speak to the family on the child's first day and ask what the child is looking forward to about the school year.

C. send a welcome email.

D. invite them to be Facebook friends.

28

**Ms. Waters would like to evaluate kindergarten students on their writing skills at the beginning of the year so she can plan for instruction. Which of the following methods should she use?**

A. ask the students to write sentences about what they did over summer break

B. read a story to the students and ask them to write what happened at the beginning, middle, and end of the story

C. ask the students to draw pictures of the characters from the story *The Three Little Pigs*

D. ask the students to write a story about themselves using pictures and words, and then have them tell her their story

29

**Mr. Hollingsworth is conferencing with a mother of one of his first-grade students and explains to her that the student is not meeting the state standard on subtraction. The mother argues that her child can successfully do subtraction at home and demands he change the grade. What is the most ethical way for Mr. Hollingsworth to handle this situation?**

A. change the grade at the mother's request, but do not tell anyone

B. provide the mother with documentation of assessments and observations explaining why the student is struggling

C. end the meeting and avoid future communication; there is no reasoning with this mother

D. tell her he cannot change the grade because it is against policy and if she would like to speak with the principal, he can arrange that

30

**Ms. Martinez referred one of her kindergarten students for a speech evaluation. However, the student did not meet the requirements to be eligible for an IEP. The student is still struggling with expressive speech when asked academic questions. Which of the following is the appropriate next step Ms. Martinez might try?**

A. do not provide interventions because the student did not qualify for special education services

B. when asking the student questions, allow for additional wait time for an answer

C. transfer the student to another class

D. ask the school speech pathologist to come deliver services anyway

31

**All of the statements are true of Developmentally Appropriate Practice (DAP) EXCEPT**

A. DAP provides a framework for best practice.

B. DAP guarantees all children in the same age group receive the same instruction.

C. DAP is based on research in child development and learning and educational effectiveness.

D. DAP ensures teachers modify lessons and activities to meet the needs of each child.

# Subarea II: Knowledge of Children's Literature and the Writing Process

Read the question, and then choose the most correct answer.

**32**

**Which skill is being developed during an activity for first graders in which they identify the sounds that consonant digraphs *ch*, *sh*, and *th* make?**

A. print awareness
B. phonics
C. phonological awareness
D. word recognition

**33**

**Which of the following is a characteristic of a print-rich classroom?**

A. a daily read-aloud time
B. many labeled objects
C. lots of pencils, pens, and markers
D. a library stocked with picture books

**34**

**Mrs. Cortez is quietly reading a book to Henry, a three-year-old student who did not fall asleep during nap time. As she reads, Mrs. Cortez points to each word on the page. Which of the following is the teacher trying to accomplish?**

A. reinforce Henry's print awareness
B. keep a steady pace and rhythm as she reads
C. lull Henry to sleep
D. focus Henry's attention toward reading the words along with her

**35**

**Mrs. Perez is teaching her first-grade class about meter in poetry. Which of the following activities would be most appropriate to help her students understand this concept?**

A. independently label each line of the poem with an *A*, *B*, *C*, or so on to indicate the rhyming pattern
B. read in a different voice for each character in the poem
C. copy each line of the poem multiple times until they pick up its meter
D. clap to the beat of a poem that she reads aloud

36

**Mr. Smith's second-grade class is going to read a story aloud. He wants to emphasize that the narrator has a different point of view from the other characters. Which of the following should he do to emphasize this point?**

A. read the entire story himself and point out when the narrator is speaking

B. have students read in a different voice when reading/speaking as the narrator versus when reading/speaking as the characters

C. have students label the text for each line that is spoken by the narrator

D. have students read very slowly when reading the narrator's lines so they can really appreciate the narrator's points

37

**Which of the following is an activity that will help students develop their procedural knowledge of writing?**

A. handwriting practice

B. drawing or scribbling to communicate an idea

C. writing a letter to a friend to tell about a vacation experience

D. reading a story aloud

38

**Mrs. Jett notices that her third-grade student Jo often leaves out the articles *a*, *an*, and *the* from her writing. A conference with Jo's parents recently revealed that this could be because her native language does not use articles. Which of the following revision strategies might be helpful for Jo?**

A. reading her work aloud

B. pairing her with another English language learner for peer review

C. having her memorize a list of prepositions

D. pairing her with a native English speaking partner for peer review

39

**A teacher has decided to create a class-wide digital literary sampler to show parents the hard work his class has done over the course of a unit on narrative writing. Which of the following phases in the authorship cycle is the teacher addressing?**

A. brainstorming

B. editing

C. drafting

D. publishing

**40**

**A teacher is working on a unit on forming the past tense of verbs with his second-grade class. Which of the following would be the most appropriate writing assignment to ensure sufficient practice with this skill?**

A. writing a paragraph that compares and contrasts cars and trucks

B. writing a paragraph about what they did over the winter break

C. writing a description of their living room

D. writing a persuasive paragraph about their favorite color

**41**

**Which of the following is a simile?**

A. He was taller than a building.

B. The engine panted and gasped.

C. The sun was like a glistening gem.

D. The house was a decaying corpse.

**42**

**Which of the following should be included in effective phonics instruction in a kindergarten classroom?**

A. a solid foundation of letter-sound correspondence

B. an emphasis on silent reading

C. identification of main ideas

D. early practice with chapter books

**43**

**Which of the following describes the role exposition plays in a story?**

A. It sets up the setting and characters.

B. It allows the climax to unfold.

C. It is the sequence of events leading up to the climax.

D. It ends the story.

**44**

**Which of the following is the highest point of the plot diagram?**

A. exposition

B. rising action

C. climax

D. resolution

**45**

**Mr. Hawks wants to give his kindergarten students a sight word assessment. Which of the following is the best way to conduct this assessment?**

A. direct the students to write the sight words from memory

B. ask students to read from a sight word list while he circles the words they know

C. have students sound out each sight word as he presents it to them

D. encourage students to clap out the beat as they repeat each word after him

**46**

**What is one advantage of repeated readings of children's literature in the classroom?**

A. Students will memorize the story and create alternate endings.

B. Teachers can expect students to make predictions about the story.

C. Students will focus more on the text and less on illustrations.

D. Students can better relate the story to their own lives.

**47**

**Characters in many early childhood storybooks are of what type?**

A. animals

B. adults

C. machines

D. imaginary friends

**48**

**A kindergarten teacher selects a book that rhymes to read to the class during circle time. After certain pages, she stops and asks students what words they can think of that rhyme with the last word read. What part of emergent literacy is the teacher addressing?**

A. comprehension of story events

B. letter-sound correspondence

C. print awareness

D. phonemic awareness

49

**In selecting a read-aloud book for an integrated unit on photosynthesis, which of the following is the most important for a kindergarten teacher to consider?**

A. presence of animal characters

B. complexity of science vocabulary

C. inclusion of a moral or lesson

D. dramatic climax and resolution

## Subarea III: Core Knowledge in the Content Areas

Read the question, and then choose the most correct answer.

**50**

**A second-grade class is learning about the properties of two-dimensional shapes. Which of the following activities would best reinforce the concept of perimeter?**

A. using playdough to make solid figures
B. working on a jigsaw puzzle
C. using toilet paper tubes to create a windsock
D. throwing a basketball through a hoop

**51**

**A preschool teacher is introducing his students to one-to-one correspondence. Which of the following activities should he use in his classroom?**

A. counting each toy as it is put away in a toy box
B. matching socks from a laundry basket
C. playing Go Fish to match cards with similar numbers
D. asking students to identify the color of a ball

**52**

**Miguel usually receives a $5 allowance each week and currently has $10 saved. If he does not receive his allowance the next week, he will have $10 when that week is over.**

**Which of the following properties is demonstrated by this scenario?**

A. identity property
B. commutative property
C. distributive property
D. associative property

**53**

**A second-grade teacher is teaching her student to count money. Which of the following skills should students have before starting the lesson?**

A. decomposing numbers
B. subitizing
C. division
D. skip counting

**54**

**Mrs. Collins asks her students to skip count by fives to 100. Which of the following basic skills is necessary for the students to complete the task?**

A. rote memorization of numeric words
B. writing numbers
C. matching patterns
D. sorting objects

**55**

**Which of the following concepts do students need to understand in order to answer the following question?**

What is the largest three-digit number you can make using the digits 3, 6, and 8?

A. rounding
B. place value
C. decomposing
D. subitizing

**56**

**Decomposing helps reinforce which of the following mathematical concepts?**

A. place value
B. cardinality
C. addition
D. skip counting

**57**

**A first-grade class is beginning a unit on basic addition. Which of the following should the teacher use to introduce the topic?**

A. a calculator
B. a number line
C. manipulatives
D. written equations

**58**

**Mr. Jones is teaching equivalent fractions. Which of the following skills could he use to show an application of this skill?**

A. reducing a very large fraction
B. finding the reciprocal of a fraction
C. drawing a visual fraction model
D. working with unit fractions

59

**When learning about improper fractions, students are asked to decompose the fraction $\frac{14}{3}$. Which of the following students has decomposed the fraction properly?**

A. Angel: $1\frac{4}{3}$

B. Dina: $\frac{3}{3} + \frac{3}{3} + \frac{3}{3} + \frac{3}{3} + \frac{2}{3} = 4\frac{2}{3}$

C. Roberto: $4\frac{1}{3}$

D. Danny: $\frac{3}{14}$

60

**Which of the following equations could a teacher use as an example of the commutative property of addition or multiplication?**

A. $5 + 3 = 4 + 4$

B. $5 + 3 = 3 + 5$

C. $5 \times 3 = 15 \times 1$

D. $5 + 3 = 3 \times 5$

61

**In order to demonstrate an application of the distributive property, Mr. Lopez presents the following problem and asks students to write an equation that solves the problem.**

At a party, six girls and nine boys order hotdogs for $2 each. How much money was spent for hot dogs?

**Which of the following students has written the correct equation?**

A. Julie: $2 \times 6 + 9 = \$21$

B. Samuel: $2 + 6 + 9 = \$17$

C. LaShawn: $2 \times (6 + 9) =$
$2 \times 6 + 2 \times 9 = \$30$

D. Omar: $2 \times 6 \times 9 = \$108$

62

**A teacher writes 65 + 35 = 35 + 65 on the board. Which of the following properties of addition is she demonstrating?**

A. distributive property of addition

B. commutative property of addition

C. identity property of addition

D. associative property of addition

63

**Emerson Elementary School has an on-campus store where students can purchase snacks. Which of the following activities involving the store would NOT be a good way to teach a second-grade class about money or the value of money?**

A. having students calculate the tax on certain items

B. explaining how price tags are used to show the cost of an item

C. encouraging them to find an item within a given budget

D. using play money to shop in the store

64

**Mrs. Lee is preparing to teach her students concepts related to time. Which of the following is NOT a reason she should begin her lesson with an analog clock rather than a digital clock?**

A. Analog clocks can be easily manipulated by students.

B. Analog clocks only show twelve hours.

C. Analog clocks have hands that constantly move.

D. Analog clocks can be used to demonstrate skip counting by fives.

65

**A third-grade class is divided into groups and asked to collect quantitative data for a class project. Each group submits its plan to the teacher. Which group will need to be redirected?**

A. group A: test scores of students in a class

B. group B: costs of different airline fares

C. group C: income of people in a company

D. group D: the favorite color of members in a family

66

**A second-grade teacher wants to have her students collect data and create a bar graph. Which of the following would be the best question for her to give her students?**

A. How does the temperature outside change during the day?

B. What percentage of students like different types of ice cream?

C. What is the relationship between a plant's age and height?

D. Which classroom has the largest number of students?

67

**Mr. Howard wants his first graders to work on the development of self-identity. Which activity would be most appropriate?**

A. having each student write down a nice thing about each member of the class and then sharing these affirmations

B. assigning students an essay to write on the roles of each of their family members

C. asking students what they want to be when they grow up and why

D. having students role-play resolving conflict through compromise

68

**Ms. Watts wants to prepare a unit on community helpers for her prekindergarten class. She wants to include a hands-on exploratory activity as part of this unit. Which activity would best meet her goal?**

A. inviting an attorney to speak to the class

B. reading a story about the role of the police in keeping the community safe

C. getting students to brainstorm different community helpers

D. allowing students to try on the protective equipment firefighters use

69

**Ms. Pi, the school's Mandarin teacher, wants to partner with the kindergarten classroom teacher to help students develop appreciation for Chinese culture outside of language. Which activity would be most appropriate?**

A. organizing a Chinese New Year celebration

B. having students create a poster about different dress and hairstyles in China

C. displaying an infographic comparing Taiwan, Hong Kong, and mainland China

D. showing a video on Mao Zedong

70

**Which of the following describes a relationship of economic interdependence?**

A. a subsistence farmer growing all of the food his family needs

B. a desert country importing food from the US while exporting oil there

C. a local shopkeeper selling basic goods to his community

D. a family in which the members make all of their own clothing

**71**

**What physical location has been determined to be the location of the prime meridian?**

A. Greenwich, United Kingdom
B. Moscow, Russia
C. New York City, United States
D. Juneau, United States

**72**

**Miss Greene is searching in her curriculum resources for a map to introduce her second-grade class to the idea of a legend. Which map would be the best resource for her to use?**

A. a political map of the United States showing each state in the same color
B. a topographical map showing different elevations
C. a map that uses corncob icons to denote the major corn-producing states in the United States
D. a map that includes latitude and longitude

**73**

**How are Supreme Court justices selected?**

A. through an election
B. nomination by the House with approval by the Senate
C. appointment by the president
D. nomination by the president with confirmation by the Senate

**74**

**Ms. Wilson knows that George, unlike the rest of her kindergarten students, did not attend any sort of preschool or prekindergarten program. Because of this, George has trouble adjusting to certain classroom routines during the first few weeks of school. Ms. Wilson assists George by giving him more verbal cues and help with transitions than she does with other students. What concept is Ms. Wilson promoting?**

A. equality
B. tolerance
C. natural consequences
D. equity

**75**

**A second-grade class has just read a story about a young girl whose family moved from Oklahoma City to Lagos, Nigeria. Which question might help spark appropriate discussion about recognition of and appreciation for cultural differences?**

A. Why did the family move to Lagos?

B. What is the population of Lagos?

C. Have you ever been to a big city?

D. How is Lagos different from Oklahoma?

**76**

**A second-grade teacher is trying to help her students learn how to use a compass rose. She gives each student a map of the United States with a compass rose. She asks students to follow a series of instructions. Which instruction might she include?**

A. Point to the state that is directly above Texas.

B. Point to the capital of Florida.

C. Point to the only state that is an island.

D. Point to the state that is directly to the west of Utah.

**77**

**Ms. Perez, a first-grade teacher, is working on map and globe skills with her class. To assess student knowledge of key concepts, she is calling students up one by one during independent work time to determine their level of proficiency with place identification. Which places would be most appropriate for Ms. Perez to ask students to identify on the large classroom maps?**

A. Canada, Mexico, and the Antarctic Ocean

B. the United States and their home state

C. the capital of their home state and major cities like Los Angeles, New York, and Chicago

D. the Great Lakes and the Mississippi River

**78**

**A second-grade teacher asks her class the following question: "What kind of houses would people living in forests most likely build?" What is she trying to help students understand?**

A. the relationship between conservation and resource depletion

B. economic interdependence

C. how people relate to their environment

D. the way the global economy and the environment impact each other

**79**

**Mr. Wise wants to impart to his third-grade class that they should stay in school until they graduate because high school graduates will earn much more and have more opportunity in society. What concept is Mr. Wise drawing upon?**

A. social condition

B. social systems

C. social institutions

D. shared experience

**80**

**A third-grade teacher wants to integrate a lesson on shared global culture with a lesson on using the internet to find information. Which activity would be most appropriate?**

A. asking students to research the culture of a country they know little about

B. researching the number of McDonald's restaurant locations that exist outside the United States

C. creating a simple website highlighting the major elements of American culture

D. looking for pictures of people in clothing different from that worn in the United States

**81**

**A first-grade class in San Antonio is on a field trip to a local theater. As the bus drives past the Alamo, the teacher points the building out. What is the teacher helping students to recognize?**

A. a landmark

B. the importance of directional terms

C. alternative housing types

D. the Native American heritage of the state

**82**

**Mrs. Markel's third-grade class reads an article about a community of people in a rain forest environment who are experiencing dramatic changes in their way of life because loggers are cutting down the trees in their home. What concept is Mrs. Markel imparting on her class?**

A. that economic development is never as important as maintaining biodiversity

B. that part of global citizenship is taking action

C. that humans are dependent on their environments

D. that there can always be compromise when different cultures interact

83

**A third-grade teacher notices that a student does not understand motion and force. Which of the following activities is best to help reteach the student the content?**

A. The teacher shows the student a video; the student writes down what he or she learned about motion and force.

B. The teacher meets with the student and re-explains each concept from the textbook.

C. Have another student who understands re-explain the concept using hands-on materials to demonstrate.

D. Have the student look up the definitions and write a report on the differences.

84

**Which of the following Earth science topics is developmentally appropriate for kindergartners?**

A. the four seasons

B. shifting continents and landforms

C. geological formation of different types of rocks

D. ozone depletion

85

**Which of the following science topics is developmentally appropriate for preschool students?**

A. density

B. DNA

C. plants and animals

D. magnets

86

**A first-grade teacher sets up a science center with an activity related to floating objects. The students have a bowl of salt water and a bowl of fresh water to put small objects in. Which of the following concepts is the teacher trying to help students better understand through the science center?**

A. the states of matter

B. the differences between freshwater and saltwater habitats

C. density

D. the scientific process

**87**

**Which of the following is the most appropriate activity for teaching prekindergarten students about states of matter?**

A. drawing a model of each state of matter

B. sorting objects or pictures into the different categories

C. writing what they learned about the states of matter

D. having students independently make a root beer float to see the states of matter

**88**

**Which of the following activities will be most effective in introducing first graders to the concept of the water cycle?**

A. teaching the students a song with motions about the water cycle

B. showing students a movie that explains the water cycle

C. asking students to copy the drawing of the water cycle that the teacher made

D. having the students write down the key vocabulary and definitions

**89**

**A first-grade teacher sets up a science center with an activity that has four candy canes and four glasses, each filled with a different liquid. The liquids are warm water, cold water, oil, and vinegar. The students are instructed to hypothesize which liquid they think will dissolve a candy cane the quickest and then test their predictions.**

**The teacher is trying to encourage student predictions on which of the following?**

A. physical properties

B. physical change

C. density

D. reactions

**90**

**A teacher in Los Angeles asks her first-grade class the following question: "Do you have more shorts and short-sleeved shirts at home or more coats and sweaters? Why?" These questions would most likely precede a discussion on**

A. the way climate impacts people.

B. different clothing choices among different cultures.

C. standards of modesty in dress that vary by culture.

D. the way in which one's social conditions impact him or her.

**91**

**A second-grade teacher is teaching her students about simple machines. Which of the following is the most hands-on, developmentally appropriate activity?**

A. The teacher puts students in groups and the students write a report on a simple machine.

B. The teacher reads a book and then hands out a sorting worksheet. The students must sort the machines into the correct category.

C. The teacher puts students in groups and they create a simple machine using materials provided; then they present their machine to the class.

D. The teacher puts students in groups and asks them to research the history of the automobile.

**92**

**A first-grade teacher sets up a science center with an activity that asks students to dissect owl pellets. Which of the following is the teacher trying to develop in students through the center?**

A. vocabulary

B. classification

C. hypothesis

D. observation

**93**

**A kindergarten teacher sets up a science center with many different types of buttons. The students must create categories and sort the buttons.**

**Which of the following skills is the teacher trying to develop in students through the center?**

A. The teacher wants the students to sort objects based on physical properties.

B. The teacher wants the students to sort objects based on chemical properties.

C. The teacher wants the students to use their counting skills.

D. The teacher wants the students to use their knowledge of basic shapes.

**94**

**Which of the following science topics is developmentally appropriate for kindergarteners?**

A. the parts of a plant

B. living and non-living

C. the digestive system of an owl

D. the human body systems

95

**A prekindergarten teacher is teaching her students about the four seasons. Which of the following is the most appropriate activity?**

A. The students do a sort. There are vocabulary words that relate to each season; they must put the words under the correct season.

B. The students write about their favorite season and why it is their favorite season.

C. The students have a piece of paper that is divided into four parts. Each square has a picture of a tree. The students draw what the tree looks like in each season.

D. The students are asked to describe how clothing varies across different cultures.

96

**A prekindergarten teacher is teaching her students about weather. Which of the following is the most appropriate activity?**

A. The teacher gives a spelling test of weather words; then the teacher and students talk about the words and their favorite weather.

B. The teacher takes the class outside to observe and brainstorm words that describe the day's weather.

C. The teacher gives the students a worksheet with weather words on it. The students must trace the words.

D. The teacher asks students to create a graph representing the weather patterns for each day of the month.

97

**As a quick assessment of lesson vocabulary, a second-grade teacher writes the following definition on the board:**

animals that only eat other animals

**The teacher then asks students to write on their whiteboard the vocabulary word related to the definition. Which of the following students is most correct?**

A. Kyle, who wrote *carnivores*

B. Sarah, who wrote *omnivores*

C. Jackson, who wrote *herbivores*

D. Hoda, who wrote *producers*

98

**A first-grade teacher is teaching her students about constellations. Which of the following is the most appropriate activity?**

A. The teacher reviews constellations. Then, the students write five facts about what they have learned from the lecture.

B. The teacher reviews constellations and the students use marshmallows and tooth picks to create various constellations, such as the Big Dipper.

C. The teacher puts students into groups; each group has pictures of constellations and facts. The students must match the constellation to the fact.

D. The teacher shows the students a video about constellations, then the students write two facts about what they learned.

99

**A second-grade teacher is teaching her students about landforms. Which of the following is the most appropriate activity?**

A. The students use their imagination to draw an island with a specific type of climate and vegetation.

B. The students use modeling clay to create an island. The students must include at least three different types of landforms on their island.

C. The students use books to read about landforms and write three facts that they learned.

D. The students listen to an interview with a geographer who explains the different types of landforms while showing pictures.

100

**A prekindergarten teacher is teaching her students about living and non-living things. Which of the following is the most appropriate activity?**

A. The students draw living and non-living things and label them.

B. The teacher asks the students to make two lists: one of ten living things and one of ten non-living things.

C. The teacher gives the students a cut and paste activity. The students must sort the words into the categories *living* or *non-living*.

D. The teacher has a center set up with a mat and toy objects representing both living and non-living things. The students separated them into categories.

# Subarea IV: Integration of Knowledge and Understanding

Use the information below to answer the question that follows.

1

**A third-grade teacher gives students the following assignment:**

- Write an autobiographical paragraph in the first person with at least eight sentences that has both an introductory sentence and a concluding sentence.
- Ensure that your paragraph uses time expressions ("first," "next," "then," "last," and so on) to help the reader follow the order of events.

Max was born in 2011 in Boston. First, he has three brother. Named Mark, Pat, and Ethan. He like ride bikes and eating pizza! His' favorite show is watching baseball on TV. Next, he will be an astronaut when he grows up. He also like swimming. Hopefully, he will get good grade this year. This is all about Max.

**Using your knowledge of the writing process and child development, prepare a response in which you:**

- Evaluate the student's work, listing strengths and errors.
- Explain how you would help the student correct one of the errors.

2

**A first-grade teacher is assessing social studies learning through an individual map skills/oral assessment as a benchmark assessment. Below are her notes from working with Jilian.**

| **Skill** | **Met Standard?** | **Notes** |
|---|---|---|
| Can point to the United States on the map/globe | Yes | Originally pointed to Russia but when realized the globe could spin, corrected herself. |
| Can point to Georgia on the map/globe | Yes | Pointed to Alabama and when asked to try again, pointed correctly to Georgia |
| Can put finger on Georgia and then point to a state that is north of Georgia | Yes | |
| Can put finger on Georgia and then point to a state that is west of Georgia | Yes | |
| Can locate the Atlantic and Pacific Oceans | No | Inverted Atlantic and Pacific Oceans |
| Identifies a picture of Benjamin Franklin and can name an accomplishment | Yes—identify<br>No—accomplishment | Said he invented the light bulb |
| Identifies a picture of Thomas Jefferson and can name an accomplishment | No—identify<br>No—accomplishment | Shrugged and would not guess even when prompted |

**Using your knowledge of social studies and child development, prepare a response in which you:**

- Evaluate the student's current proficiency level, listing strengths and opportunities.
- Explain how you would reteach ONE core concept to the student and assess mastery of this core concept.

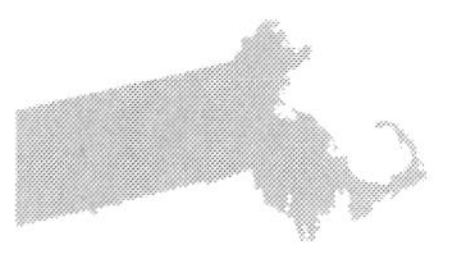

# Answer Key

## Subarea I

**1)**

A. Incorrect. Piaget discusses how children progress through the stages of cognitive development.

B. Incorrect. Bruner's modes of representation discuss how learners interpret the world.

C. Incorrect. Vygotsky's ZPD discusses what children can learn on their own and what they can learn from a more capable peer or an adult.

**D. Correct.** Bloom's taxonomy is a set of skills in order from simple to complex that build upon each other and are often used when developing learning objectives.

**2)**

A. Incorrect. Managing feelings describes typical social-emotional development.

**B. Correct.** Learning sight words is part of typical language progression for first graders.

C. Incorrect. Recognizing upper-case letters describes typical language development for a preschool child.

D. Incorrect. Understanding the difference between right and wrong is characteristic of typical moral development, not language development.

**3)**

**A. Correct.** This action shows empathy and consideration.

B. Incorrect. Theft shows atypical moral development.

C. Incorrect. This behavior shows atypical moral development.

D. Incorrect. This aggressive behavior indicates atypical moral development.

**4)**

**D. Correct.** Mia is able to manage her own feelings and positively interact with others; the other choices describe atypical social-emotional development.

**5)**

**A. Correct.** Because Sierra's dad is so busy, it is best to offer a variety of dates, times, and locations so that he is more likely to schedule a conference.

**6)**

A. Incorrect. It is not appropriate or safe to conduct a home visit alone.

B. Incorrect. Bringing a spouse to a home visit is unprofessional.

**C. Correct.** Going with another teacher or administrator will ensure that the information shared is kept confidential and the teacher is safe. It also ensures a witness for the visit.

D. Incorrect. Bringing a friend to a home visit is unprofessional.

**7)**

**C. Correct.** Mr. Libman's class is building prosocial skills by helping others in volunteering to clean up the playground and toys. Volunteering is a prosocial skill.

**8)**

A. Incorrect. This would not be appropriate to share with Diana's mother; the teacher is not a medical professional.

**B. Correct.** Since Diana's family cannot afford health insurance, sharing information about the community's free or income-based health clinics would be most appropriate.

C. Incorrect. Most local pediatricians have high fees for families without insurance.

D. Incorrect. Only a medical professional can determine what treatment Diana needs.

**9)**

**A. Correct.** The pre-operational stage is characterized by non-logical, egocentric, and non-reversible thinking.

B. Incorrect. The sensorimotor stage is characterized by intelligence through motor activities.

C. Incorrect. The concrete operational stage is characterized by logical and rational thinking when solving problems.

D. Incorrect. The formal operational stage occurs during adolescence through adulthood.

**10)**

A. Incorrect. The Montessori method embraces multiage groupings and children moving through the curriculum at their own pace.

B. Incorrect. Creative Curriculum embraces the idea of a balance between child-initiated and teacher-directed activities as well as small and large group learning.

C. Incorrect. Reggio Emilia embraces project-based learning in which children observe, explore, and work with others to solve real-life problems.

**D. Correct.** The High Scope approach embraces the idea of scaffolding through hands-on experiences.

**11)**

A. Incorrect. The performance describes what the children should be able to do as a result of the activity.

B. Incorrect. Behavior and performance are the same as concerns components of a learning objective.

C. Incorrect. The conditions describe how children will complete the task.

**D. Correct.** The criteria describe how children's performance will be evaluated.

**12)**

**A. Correct.** This is an example of a long-term planning goal since the strategies are ongoing over an extended time period. The rest are examples of short-term planning goals since they are strategies that can be implemented daily.

**13)**

A. Incorrect. The objective and accommodations and modifications have been omitted.

**B.** **Correct.** This list includes the critical components of a lesson plan.

C. Incorrect. The materials have been omitted.

D. Incorrect. The materials, procedures for instruction, and accommodations and modifications have been omitted.

**14)**

**A.** **Correct.** The action verb *match* falls into the remember level in which children identify and recall information.

**15)**

A. Incorrect. Materials should focus on more than one skill at a time.

B. Incorrect. Materials should facilitate cooperative learning.

C. Incorrect. Materials should support children's learning in English as well as their home language.

**D.** **Correct.** Materials should support learning through problem-solving.

**16)**

A. Incorrect. This describes physical play.

B. Incorrect. This describes object play.

C. Incorrect. This describes parallel play.

**D.** **Correct.** Social play is when children share materials, ideas, and communicate with others.

**17)**

**A.** **Correct.** Ringing a bell will gain students' attention so the teacher can explain what is happening next; singing the song keeps children interested and engaged.

B. Incorrect. This is an ineffective way to ask children to stop an activity and clean up. Since the teacher is going around to each activity, she hasn't gained everyone's attention; some children will finish cleaning up before others, leaving time for inappropriate behaviors.

C. Incorrect. If the teacher does not gain all of the children's attention, some may not hear and continue working while others are cleaning up.

D. Incorrect. After ringing the bell, the teacher should provide instructions on what children should do next to avoid confusion.

**18)**

A. Incorrect. Building relationships includes investing time and attention with the children to get to know their interests, backgrounds, and preferences.

B. Incorrect. Teaching character development would include teaching social rules and how children's behavior affects others.

**C.** **Correct.** By giving high fives, praise, and encouragement, Mrs. Caldwell is incorporating positive interactions into the daily routine.

D. Incorrect. Teaching problem-solving strategies is how children learn skills to navigate through problems.

**19)**

**A.** **Correct.** Measuring with non-standard units of measurement, such as paper clips, is developmentally appropriate for kindergarteners. The remaining answers are measurement activities that are not developmentally appropriate for this age group.

**20)**

A. Incorrect. Increasing fluency in the student's home language is not the teacher's main objective; her classroom curriculum likely centers around oral fluency in English.

B. Incorrect. The teacher could encourage this without the use of a text in the student's home language.

**C.** **Correct**. The teacher likely wants to encourage the student to continue to develop skills in reading and writing in both English and her home language.

D. Incorrect. Practicing prosody and rate in the home language is likely not a class objective; developing the student's prosody and rate is likely only an objective in English.

**21)**

A. Incorrect. This task is a modification of the assignment, not an accommodation. Further, this does not allow the student to better participate in the activity.

B. Incorrect. Dictation changes the assignment significantly from a writing assignment to an oral language assignment. It is more of a modification than an accommodation.

C. Incorrect. A graphic organizer might help the student organize her thoughts, but it does not directly address her limited English proficiency.

**D.** **Correct.** The dictionary or translating device would help the student write the narrative in English.

**22)**

A. Incorrect. Assistive technology, for all of its benefits, does not qualify as a "someone."

B. Incorrect. Modifying a reading assignment will not help these students with challenging vocabulary *as* they are reading.

**C.** **Correct**. In peer tutoring, a fluent peer can assist the ELL students with the challenging vocabulary.

D. Incorrect. While the teacher should certainly be engaged in progress monitoring, this in itself, will not encourage the ELL students to practice oral reading.

**23)**

A. Incorrect. A self-contained classroom separate from the rest of the school does not allow the student to be educated alongside the majority of his peers.

B. Incorrect. A special school also does not allow the student to be educated alongside the majority of his peers.

**C.** **Correct.** The least restrictive environment is the one that allows the student to be educated to the greatest possible extent alongside his or her peers without disabilities.

D. Incorrect. Home schooling does not allow any interaction with peers at all.

**24)**

**A.** **Correct.** Reading from books at a higher Lexile level is a simple modification to change the student's learning goal slightly by covering more complex texts.

B. Incorrect. Extra work in other subjects deviates too much from the overall goals of reading.

C. Incorrect. Tracking reading might help with engagement, but it does not address silent reading time directly.

D. Incorrect. A first-grade student likely does not have a good idea on her own of what will keep her engaged.

**25)**

**A. Correct.** A picture board is most developmentally appropriate for a kindergarten student. The student can point to the pictures on the board to communicate needs and desires.

B. Incorrect. A laptop computer does not, in itself, help the student communicate.

C. Incorrect. If the student is non-verbal, an audio recorder will not aid in communication.

D. Incorrect. Such an application might help a visually impaired student read, but it will not help a non-verbal student communicate.

**26)**

A. Incorrect. The evaluation cannot be completed at any time. By law it must be completed within sixty days of the initial request.

B. Incorrect. It may be completed within a week, but the law states there are a full sixty days to complete the evaluation.

**C. Correct.** The IDEA law states that it must be completed within sixty days of the initial request.

D. Incorrect. It will be completed during the same school year, but again, the regulation specifically states within sixty days of the initial request.

**27)**

**A. Correct.** Making a phone call to the family before they begin establishes a relationship and two-way communication, lets them know Mrs. Rodriguez cares, and gives her some information on the child from which she can plan some activities of interest for the child on their first day.

B. Incorrect. If Mrs. Rodriguez waits until the child's first day, she can establish a relationship, but reaching out early allows for an uninterrupted phone conversation in which she can gain valuable information and let the family know their child is important.

C. Incorrect. Sending an email can welcome the family, but is not the best method is establishing the relationship.

D. Incorrect. This is not the most effective way for beginning the relationship. It also may violate the school's guidelines on social media use.

**28)**

A. Incorrect. At the beginning of the year this would not be a developmentally appropriate activity, because most beginning kindergarteners are writing only letters or a few words.

B. Incorrect. At the beginning of the year this is not a developmentally appropriate activity.

C. Incorrect. This type of assessment would not be appropriate for judging writing skills.

**D. Correct.** Asking them to write a story with pictures and words is an appropriate activity for beginning kindergarteners. Asking the students to retell their story and taking notes will provide Ms. Waters with valuable information on their writing skills, and from there she can plan lessons and activities.

**29)**

A. Incorrect. This is not acting in the best interest of the child.

**B. Correct.** Mr. Hollingsworth is acting on the best interest of the child. He is providing the mother with adequate information on the assessments and including her in the student's education by providing activities that she can do at home to help her child succeed.

C. Incorrect. Mr. Hollingsworth is not including the mother in the decision-making process and working together to find a solution or communicating in a respectful way.

D. Incorrect. It is policy that he cannot change the grade, but Mr. Hollingsworth is not including the mother in a solution or explaining the assessment process to her.

**30)**

A. Incorrect. Even if a student does not qualify for special education services under IDEA, Ms. Martinez should still implement appropriate interventions to support the student's needs.

**B.** **Correct.** This would be an appropriate intervention to incorporate because it allows the student additional time to process the question and come up with an answer.

C. Incorrect. Transferring a student is an inappropriate support.

D. Incorrect. If speech services are not required in an IEP, the speech pathologist cannot deliver services. Ms. Martinez may consult with the speech pathologist but must implement her own interventions.

**31)**

**B.** **Correct.** This statement is false. DAP focuses on providing the most appropriate instruction for a child's development.

## Subarea II

**32)**

A. Incorrect. Print awareness is when children begin to recognize that oral language and written language are related.

**B.** **Correct.** Phonics is when children begin to correlate sounds with letters or groups of letters.

C. Incorrect. Phonological awareness is identifying and manipulating the sounds of spoken language.

D. Incorrect. Word recognition is the ability to recognize and read words effortlessly.

**33)**

A. Incorrect. Reading aloud is important but not necessarily characteristic of a print-rich classroom.

**B.** **Correct.** Labeling objects in the classroom such as a *door*, *whiteboard*, *cubby*, and so on will make a classroom rich in environmental print.

C. Incorrect. An abundance of writing utensils is important but not necessarily in direct relation to providing a print-rich classroom environment.

D. Incorrect. Picture books do not contain enough print to characterize a print-rich classroom.

**34)**

**A.** **Correct.** Understanding that words are what is read on a page is an important part of print awareness.

B. Incorrect. This would help Mrs. Cortez, not necessarily Henry, and this is likely not the primary reason for her pointing.

C. Incorrect. This would not lull him to sleep necessarily.

D. Incorrect. It is most unlikely that Henry is able to read the words.

**35)**

A. Incorrect. This activity would likely be too challenging for first graders to do independently.

B. Incorrect. Differentiating characters in this way would not help students recognize meter.

C. Incorrect. Copying lines of the poem would not necessarily help students recognize meter.

**D.** **Correct.** Clapping to the beat of the poem is a developmentally appropriate way to introduce this concept to first graders.

**36)**

A. Incorrect. This is not the best strategy and might bore the students.

**B.** **Correct.** This will help students understand that the narrator is telling the story from a different point of view.

C. Incorrect. This is not a read-aloud activity.

D. Incorrect. Read-alouds should always be designed to increase fluency through rate, accuracy, and prosody.

**37)**

**A.** **Correct.** Procedural knowledge involves how to write letters, words, and so on.

B. Incorrect. This is part of conceptual knowledge, or understanding the purpose of writing.

C. Incorrect. This is about generative knowledge, or being able to generate writing to accomplish a purpose.

D. Incorrect. This is a way to share or publish writing with others.

**38)**

A. Incorrect. This might not help Jo recognize her errors with missing articles since she is not a native English speaker.

B. Incorrect. This might not help her depending on the other student's proficiency with the use of articles.

C. Incorrect. This will not help her use articles appropriately.

**D.** **Correct.** This might aid Jo in finding the places she needs to insert articles.

**39)**

A. Incorrect. Brainstorming is the first phase in the authoring cycle when students generate ideas.

B. Incorrect. Editing involves revising work to make it more readable.

C. Incorrect. The students have already drafted the pieces.

**D.** **Correct.** Publishing student work involves sharing it with others.

**40)**

A. Incorrect. This paragraph would most logically be in the present tense.

**B.** **Correct.** This paragraph would most logically be written in the past tense and would provide practice with forming the past tense.

C. Incorrect. This paragraph would most logically be written in the present tense.

D. Incorrect. This paragraph would most logically be written in the present tense.

**41)**

A. Incorrect. This is a hyperbole, where something is greatly exaggerated.

B. Incorrect. This is personification, where a nonhuman object is given human qualities such as the ability to pant and gasp.

**C.** **Correct.** Similes make comparisons using the words *like* or *as*.

D. Incorrect. This is a metaphor, where two unlike things are compared without using *like* or *as*.

**42)**

**A.** **Correct.** Students need to draw on their knowledge bank of letter sounds to decode new words.

B. Incorrect. Most phonics instruction involves oral language since phonics connects written words to the sounds they make.

C. Incorrect. This is emphasized in reading comprehension, not phonics.

D. Incorrect. Phonics study is usually incremental and gradually advances to more complex words and texts.

**43)**

**A.** **Correct.** The exposition, or the beginning of the story, sets up the reader for what is to come by describing the setting and main characters.

B. Incorrect. The climax unfolds after the exposition.

C. Incorrect. This describes the rising action.

D. Incorrect. This describes the resolution.

**44)**

A. Incorrect. The exposition is the beginning of the diagram.

B. Incorrect. The rising action is the initial upward slope of the diagram.

**C.** **Correct.** The climax is the peak of the diagram.

D. Incorrect. The resolution is the end of the diagram.

**45)**

A. Incorrect. This activity is not developmentally appropriate for a kindergarten class and would not aid Mr. Hawks in knowing which sight words they can read from memory.

**B. Correct.** This activity will help Mr. Hawks identify which students know which words and what words they need to practice more.

C. Incorrect. Sight words should be said from memory, not through sounding out.

D. Incorrect. This activity will not tell Mr. Hawks which sight words the students know since they are repeating after him.

**46)**

A. Incorrect. While memorization might be an advantage, students will not necessarily and as a matter of course create alternate endings.

B. Incorrect. Teachers would not ask students to make predictions for a story they had heard multiple times.

C. Incorrect. Students will not necessarily focus more on the text; children are always very drawn to visual images.

**D. Correct.** Research shows that repeated readings help children delve more deeply into a story and relate it to their own lives.

**47)**

**A. Correct.** Animals are very often the central characters in early childhood storybooks.

B. Incorrect. Adults are sometimes characters, but animals are far more common.

C. Incorrect. Machines are sometimes characters (e.g., *The Little Engine That Could*), but animals are much more common.

D. Incorrect. While imaginary friends may serve as characters in some books, they are not as popular as animal characters.

**48)**

A. Incorrect. Comprehension is not addressed by asking students for rhyming words.

B. Incorrect. Students are not being asked to identify letter sounds.

C. Incorrect. Students are not being taught how the book is conveying information through print.

**D. Correct.** Books with rhymes can help students develop phonemic awareness, particularly as teachers ask students to come up with rhyming words.

**49)**

A. Incorrect. While animal characters are popular in children's books, this is not a crucial consideration for a unit on photosynthesis.

**B. Correct.** If the vocabulary is too complex for the class to understand, the book is unlikely to increase student interest and engagement.

C. Incorrect. A moral or lesson might be important in a unit on social learning, but this is not the most crucial consideration for a science unit.

D. Incorrect. While a climax and resolution might make the story exciting, these are not crucial to an integrated unit on photosynthesis.

# Subarea III

**50)**

**B.** **Correct.** The shape of the jigsaw puzzle pieces can be used to teach students about perimeter. The other choices focus on three-dimensional shapes.

**51)**

**A.** **Correct.** This activity teaches students to associate one object (a toy) to one number.

B. Incorrect. This activity relates to pattern matching.

C. Incorrect. This activity reinforces number matching.

D. Incorrect. This activity relates to learning colors, not mathematical concepts.

**52)**

**A.** **Correct.** Miguel started with $10 and did not receive his allowance: 10 + 0 = 10. This scenario describes the additive property of identity.

**53)**

A. Incorrect. Students do not need to know how to decompose numbers when counting money.

B. Incorrect. Subitizing—identifying the number of objects by sight—is not a skill needed to count money.

C. Incorrect. Student may need division to complete more complex calculations involving money, but they will not use it to count money.

**D.** **Correct.** Knowledge of skip counting will help children count the different denominations of money by their value (e.g., nickels are skip counted in fives).

**54)**

**A.** **Correct.** Skip counting involves rote memorization of numeric words in the proper order.

B. Incorrect. Writing of numbers is a follow-up activity.

C. Incorrect. Pattern matching involves categorizing objects in an environment.

D. Incorrect. Sorting objects is not a component of skip counting.

**55)**

A. Incorrect. Rounding does not involve finding the largest number.

**B.** **Correct.** An understanding of place value will lead students to write the number 863.

C. Incorrect. The problem does not present a number that can be decomposed.

D. Incorrect. Subitizing does not involve comparing numbers.

**56)**

**A.** **Correct.** Decomposing a number refers to breaking it down into its individual place values.

B. Incorrect. Cardinality refers to the number of items in a set.

C. Incorrect. Decomposing a number does not refer to addition.

D. Incorrect. Decomposing a number does involve skip counting.

**57)**

A. Incorrect. Calculators are used at a later stage with older children.

B. Incorrect. The number line can be used as an extension following basic introduction to addition.

C. **Correct.** Manipulatives are the best tools to teach children about basic addition.

D. Incorrect. Written equations are introduced after children have an understanding of addition.

**58)**

**A. Correct.** A large fraction can be simplified by finding an equivalent fraction.

**59)**

A. Incorrect. This is an incorrect way to interpret this fraction.

**B. Correct.** $\frac{14}{3}$ can be decomposed to four wholes and a fractional part of $\frac{2}{3}$.

C. Incorrect. This is an incorrect way to interpret this fraction.

D. Incorrect. This is the reciprocal of the original fraction.

**60)**

A. Incorrect. Although the expressions are equal, the addends are different.

**B. Correct.** The commutative property states that the order of the numbers in an addition or multiplication equation does not matter.

C. Incorrect. Although the expressions are equal, the factors are different.

D. Incorrect. The two expressions are not equal.

**61)**

A. Incorrect. Julie left out the needed parentheses.

B. Incorrect. Samuel added $2 rather than multiplying.

**C. Correct.** LaShawn's equation correctly applies the distributive property. The total number of children is contained within the parentheses. Since each hotdog costs $2, that total is multiplied by 2.

D. Incorrect. Omar multiplied 6 and 9, but he should have added them.

**62)**

**B. Correct.** The commutative property states that the order of the numbers in an equation does not matter.

**63)**

**A. Correct.** Calculating tax is an activity that is too advanced for second-grade students.

B. Incorrect. Explaining the way price tags list cost is a good way to teach children about money.

C. Incorrect. Encouraging children to find an item based on its cost shows them how prices are listed in real life.

D. Incorrect. Using play money is a fun activity to learn about money.

**64)**

A. Incorrect. This is true: the hands on analog clocks are much easier for students to manipulate than the buttons on a digital clock.

**B. Correct.** Unlike a digital clock, an analog clock can only be used to show twelve hours. This is not an advantage to using an analog clock.

C. Incorrect. This is true: the movement of the hands helps students understand the passage of time.

D. Incorrect. This is true: each number on an analog clock represents five minutes.

**65)**

**D. Correct.** Since color is a physical characteristic, it is a qualitative observation. The other choices are all numeric, or quantitative, qualities.

**66)**

A. Incorrect. Showing change over time is best done on a line plot.

B. Incorrect. Comparing percentages is done on a pie chart.

C. Incorrect. Showing the relationship between two continuous data sets is done on a line plot.

**D. Correct.** Comparing the number of items in different categories is done on a bar graph.

**67)**

A. Incorrect. This assignment would address self-concept.

B. Incorrect. Writing an essay on family members and their roles would not be developmentally appropriate for a first-grade class and would not address self-identity.

**C. Correct.** In discussing what they want to be when they grow up, students begin to think about how they fit into society and how they can contribute.

D. Incorrect. Role-playing conflict resolution would help students with developing social competence and developing interpersonal relationships.

**68)**

A. Incorrect. Listening to a guest speaker is not a hands-on or exploratory activity.

B. Incorrect. Reading a book about a community helper would be an appropriate activity for the unit, but it is not hands-on or exploratory.

C. Incorrect. Brainstorming and discussing community helpers is not hands-on or exploratory.

**D. Correct.** Handling protective equipment (under supervision) is an effective way for students to explore what it might be like to be a firefighter.

**69)**

**A. Correct.** Celebrating Chinese New Year is the most developmentally appropriate activity for a kindergarten class and will help them learn about holidays celebrated as part of Chinese culture.

B. Incorrect. Creating a poster is not developmentally appropriate for kindergarten students.

C. Incorrect. Displaying a geopolitical infographic is not developmentally appropriate for kindergarten students.

D. Incorrect. A video about Mao addresses history and politics more than culture, and it is most likely not appropriate for a kindergarten audience.

**70)**

A. Incorrect. A farmer growing his own food is independent.

**B. Correct.** Some desert countries cannot grow their own food because of the climate, so they must import food from elsewhere. Likewise, the United States does not have all the oil it needs, so it must import oil.

C. Incorrect. This is intradependence.

D. Incorrect. This family is independent (at least, in terms of clothing).

**71)**

**A. Correct.** The Royal Observatory in Greenwich has been designated as the location of the prime meridian, or 0°.

B. Incorrect. Moscow is at 38°E.

C. Incorrect. New York is at 74°W.

D. Incorrect. Juneau is at 134°W.

**72)**

A. Incorrect. A political map will not necessarily help students learn about a map's legend, particularly if the map does not use different colors.

B. Incorrect. A topographical map generally uses concentric rings versus symbols denoted by a legend. Additionally, this map will likely be too complicated for a second-grade class.

**C. Correct.** This map will include a legend explaining that the corncobs are symbols representing areas of corn production.

D. Incorrect. Most maps use latitude and longitude. This map is too general and is not directly related to a legend.

**73)**

**A. Correct.** This discussion is an appropriate way to help students understand that their warm climate impacts the type of clothing they need.

B. Incorrect. This question is not about clothing variance by culture, but by climate.

C. Incorrect. This question does not address how students relate climate to clothing.

D. Incorrect. While one's social condition might impact the ability to purchase clothing, this question is not designed to derive this response insomuch as it is about the type of clothing one needs in a warmer climate.

**74)**

A. Incorrect. Supreme Court justices are not elected.

B. Incorrect. Supreme Court justices are confirmed by the Senate but not nominated by the House.

C. Incorrect. Supreme Court justices must be confirmed by the Senate.

**D. Correct.** They are nominated by the president and confirmed by the Senate.

**75)**

A. Incorrect. This is a question about understanding plot, not necessarily recognizing cultural differences.

B. Incorrect. Lagos is indeed a very large city, but this is not something second graders would necessarily know. This is also related more to population density than to culture.

C. Incorrect. This question is not necessarily related to understanding cultural differences.

**D. Correct.** Asking students to consider the differences between the two locations in the story will encourage students to understand cultural differences among different places in general.

**76)**

A. Incorrect. By using words like "above," this instruction only addresses relative location, not the cardinal directions per the compass rose.

B. Incorrect. Locating a state capital is not necessarily related to the use of the compass rose.

C. Incorrect. Identifying an island is not necessarily related to the use of the compass rose.

**D. Correct.** Using a term like "west," one of the cardinal directions, helps students use the compass rose to identify locations on a map.

**77)**

A. Incorrect. This is more appropriate for second-grade students.

**B. Correct.** This would be a developmentally appropriate expectation for a first-grade student.

C. Incorrect. This is likely too advanced for a first-grade student.

D. Incorrect. This is also likely too advanced for first graders who are just learning map skills.

**78)**

A. Incorrect. The forest's resources are being used, not conserved. At the same time, it is not clear if resources are necessarily being depleted in any given forest.

B. Incorrect. The forest community is not necessarily obtaining goods from another community or country.

**C.** **Correct.** The students should understand that people use what is available in their environment. In this scenario, the people would use wood from trees to build houses.

D. Incorrect. This scenario does not address the global economy.

**79)**

**A.** **Correct.** One's social condition is his or her situation in society based on income, job, or level of education.

B. Incorrect. Social systems are relationships between individuals, groups, and institutions within society.

C. Incorrect. *Social institutions* is another term for *social systems*.

D. Incorrect. Shared experiences are experiences that people share with one another such as being in the same class at school.

**80)**

A. Incorrect. Studying one country's culture is not pertinent to a shared global culture.

**B.** **Correct.** This project will help students make the connection that McDonald's is a global brand and part of a shared global culture.

C. Incorrect. A website highlighting American culture does not focus on global culture.

D. Incorrect. This project highlights differences in culture around the world, not elements of shared culture.

**81)**

**A.** **Correct.** The Alamo is a famous landmark, or very recognizable symbol, associated with San Antonio.

B. Incorrect. Directional terms are not addressed in this scenario.

C. Incorrect. While the Alamo was once a mission that housed people, first-grade students likely would not make this association just by driving past it.

D. Incorrect. While the Alamo certainly played a role in Spanish colonialism and the Native American heritage of Texas, students would not be able to glean this simply by driving by it.

**82)**

A. Incorrect. This article is concerned not with biodiversity but with the changes one group of humans are experiencing.

B. Incorrect. Global citizenship requires taking action, but there is no reason to believe that Mrs. Markel is advocating for this just by reading the article.

**C.** **Correct.** The people in the rain forest environment are dependent on its resources for survival, so cutting down trees changes their lives dramatically.

D. Incorrect. It is not clear from this description that the article claims that compromise between cultures is possible.

**83)**

A. Incorrect. While the student might learn from the video, he or she is unable to physically manipulate materials. The student needs a hands-on experience to fully understand the content.

B. Incorrect. A one-on-one meeting between the teacher and the student would be a great way to help the student understand the content, but the teacher also needs to have the student use hands-on materials in order to reinforce the concept being taught.

**C.** **Correct.** Having another student teach a peer helps both of them understand the content better. The students have materials that they can manipulate to see and understand force and motion, and this enables hands-on learning.

D. Incorrect. The student will not understand motion and force by looking up definitions and writing a report. The student needs to manipulate objects to see and understand.

**84)**

**A.** **Correct.** The students would be able to understand the different seasons. The different seasons are basic and developmentally appropriate for kindergarteners.

B. Incorrect. Some study of the general ideas of globes and maps would be appropriate, but not the shifting of continents and landforms.

C. Incorrect. Studying rocks would be appropriate, but not how they are formed geologically.

D. Incorrect. Ozone depletion is far too advanced for a kindergarten class.

**85)**

A. Incorrect. Density is too advanced for preschool students.

B. Incorrect. DNA is also too advanced for preschool students.

**C.** **Correct.** The topic of plants and animals is basic and developmentally appropriate for preschool students; the other topics are too advanced.

D. Incorrect. Magnets might be explored, but they are not appropriate topically for preschool students who will not understand the science behind magnetism.

**86)**

A. Incorrect. Students might see the different states of matter, but that is not the purpose of the activity.

B. Incorrect. The students are not learning about habitats in this activity.

**C.** **Correct.** Students are seeing the ability of objects to float in fresh and salt water, which can be used to explain density. Objects will float more readily in the salt water because salt water is denser than tap water.

D. Incorrect. While the students are learning about experiments, this is not the main purpose of the activity.

**87)**

A. Incorrect. Drawing such models would be too advanced for three-year-old students.

**B.** **Correct.** Sorting objects or pictures into different categories is a great activity during which three-year-old students can apply their learning of the states of matter.

C. Incorrect. Writing about the states of matter would be too advanced for three-year-old students.

D. Incorrect. Making a root beer float is a fun activity; however, it is not the best activity for prekindergarten students to do independently.

**88)**

**A.** **Correct.** Teaching first graders a song or chant with motions about the water cycle is a great introduction. The students will be able to apply the song to a diagram at the end of the unit.

B. Incorrect. Showing a video is a great visual for the students; however, a song with movements is a better activity for first graders.

C. Incorrect. It would be ineffective for the students to copy down the drawing. The students should apply the knowledge that they learn about the water cycle and be able to make their own drawing at the end of the unit instead of drawing it at the introduction.

D. Incorrect. Having first-grade students write down definitions of vocabulary words is not developmentally appropriate. They need to know the words, but learning the words in a song is more developmentally appropriate.

**89)**

A. Incorrect. The students are incorporating what they know about physical properties, but that is not the main purpose of the activity. Physical properties are how something looks, feels, smells, tastes, or sounds.

B. Incorrect. The students are incorporating what they know about physical change, but that is not the main purpose of the activity. Physical change is when an object goes from one state to another, such as solid to liquid.

C. Incorrect. The experiment is not teaching the students about density, which describes how much an object weighs relating to its size.

**D.** **Correct.** The experiment is showing students how a liquid can dissolve an object. Some liquids create a reaction that makes the candy cane dissolve more quickly than others.

**90)**

A. Incorrect. Ms. Wilson is treating George differently, not identically, to the other students.

B. Incorrect. Ms. Wilson is not directly encouraging anyone to accept certain ideas or beliefs they do not agree with.

C. Incorrect. The example does not directly address consequences for George's actions.

**D.** **Correct.** Ms. Wilson is giving George what he needs to be successful, even if it is different from what she is giving other students.

**91)**

A. Incorrect. Writing a report would be a better activity for older students.

B. Incorrect. Reading a book is a good way for students to learn; however, a sorting worksheet is not the best option for second-grade students in this context.

**C.** **Correct.** Having the students create a simple machine is a great way to extend a student's understanding and is developmentally appropriate.

D. Incorrect. An automobile is a complex, not a simple, machine.

**92)**

A. Incorrect. The main focus of this activity is not to develop vocabulary since the students should have already learned the relevant vocabulary.

B. Incorrect. The students are not classifying objects.

C. Incorrect. The teacher never asked students to make a hypothesis prior to their dissection.

**D.** **Correct.** The students are making observations as they are dissecting the owl pellets and discovering what they contain.

**93)**

**A.** **Correct.** The students are using their senses to sort objects based on physical properties, which are how something looks, feels, smells, tastes, or sounds.

B. Incorrect. The students are not examining the chemical properties of the buttons.

C. Incorrect. The purpose of the activity is not to practice counting.

D. Incorrect. Since it is a science activity, the purpose of the activity is not to review shapes.

**94)**

A. Incorrect. The topic *parts of a plant* is a more appropriate activity for first graders.

**B. Correct.** Living and non-living is a great topic to teach kindergartners.

C. Incorrect. The digestive system of an owl is too advanced for kindergartners. This topic is not developmentally appropriate.

D. Incorrect. Kindergartners are not ready to learn about the human body systems. It is not a developmentally appropriate topic.

**95)**

A. Incorrect. This activity is not appropriate for prekindergarten students. The students are likely not able to read independently, and they will not be able to complete the activity.

B. Incorrect. This activity is not appropriate for prekindergarten students. The students are not able to write words or complete sentences at this time.

**C. Correct.** This is a great activity to help students understand the different weather and environmental conditions that are indicative of each season, such as leaves changing colors, snow, rain, etc.

D. Incorrect. This activity is more about culture than seasons.

**96)**

A. Incorrect. Since prekindergarten students are unable to read and spell words at this stage of development, this activity would not help them learn about weather.

**B. Correct.** Allowing students at this age to go outside and observe the day's weather and seek to describe it with "weather words" would be a good way to invest students in the study of this topic.

C. Incorrect. This would be a great way for pre-K and kindergarten students to practice their handwriting, but it is not the best way for them to learn about weather.

D. Incorrect. Having the students graph is a great way to incorporate math into science; however, it is not appropriate at this age level.

**97)**

**A. Correct.** Carnivores are animals that only eat other animals.

B. Incorrect. Omnivores are animals that both eat plants and animals.

C. Incorrect. Herbivores are animals that eat only plants.

D. Incorrect. Producers are organisms that make their own food.

**98)**

A. Incorrect. Lecture and recall are not developmentally appropriate for a first-grade class studying constellations.

**B. Correct.** Having the students build constellations is an appropriate activity for first graders.

C. Incorrect. This activity is too advanced for first-grade students. Most of the students are still learning to read and could have trouble matching pictures of constellations to facts.

D. Incorrect. Watching a video is a great way for students to see constellations, but it is not the best activity for first-grade students. This age group needs a lot of hands-on activities.

**99)**

A. Incorrect. Drawing is a great alternative to using modeling clay, but students would need to draw landforms, not climate and vegetation.

**B. Correct.** Using modeling clay is a great activity and is appropriate for second-grade students. They are having a hands-on experience and are able to use what they have learned and apply it to their island.

C. Incorrect. Reading and writing in this context is not an appropriate activity for this age group. The students need more engagement and hands-on experiences.

D. Incorrect. Second-grade students do not have the attention span to listen to a lecture. They need hands-on experiences.

**100)**

A. Incorrect. The students are unable to label at this stage in development.

B. Incorrect. Making lists would not be developmentally appropriate for prekindergarten students who likely cannot yet write words.

C. Incorrect. A cut-and-paste activity would be too difficult. Most students at this age are unable to read.

**D. Correct.** Categorizing objects is a great activity for this age group. The students will be engaged and able to sort the objects.

# Subarea IV

## Sample Response #1

The student has followed some of the assignment directions. He has written a paragraph of nine sentences (though one is actually a sentence fragment), and he includes a concluding sentence. He uses a variety of details about himself that aid in providing basic biographical information. He includes time expressions such as "first" and "next." However, "next" is not really an appropriate time expression to introduce a sentence about future hopes. His sentence structure is developing, and his paragraph contains only one sentence fragment along with eight solidly constructed sentences. The paragraph includes a few errors with singular and plural nouns ("three brother" vs. "three brothers" and "good grade" vs. "good grades"). He also has an apostrophe error with the possessive determiner "his," which does not need an apostrophe. Max has also written in the third person instead of the first person. Overall, however, Max has made a good effort at a first draft of a paragraph that can be easily revised to meet specifications.

I would focus on having Max rewrite his paragraph from the first-person point of view. I would have him first circle each time he uses third-person pronouns such as "he" and "his." I would then remind him that he needs to use the first-person pronoun "I" for the paragraph and change each of these instances. I would also direct him to change other words (for verb agreement). I will encourage him to read aloud to a partner or myself to check for subject-verb agreement and other errors after he revises these pronouns.

## Sample Response #2

Jilian is developing knowledge of first-grade social studies standards. She was able to self-correct once she realized she had made a mistake identifying Russia instead of the United States, a somewhat similarly shaped country. She has a solid grasp of using the cardinal directions to move north and west. While she initially pointed to Alabama, she clearly had a solid idea of the region in which Georgia is located. The inversion of the Atlantic and Pacific Oceans is somewhat common, and Jilian will hopefully meet this standard with more practice. Jilian does not seem to have retained as much historical knowledge as geographical knowledge, however. While she was able to identify a picture of Benjamin Franklin and knew he was an inventor, she was not able to say correctly what he had invented or any of his other accomplishments. She may be less confident in certain historical knowledge and facts, as evidenced by her unwillingness to take a guess when asked about Thomas Jefferson.

I would work to help Jilian grow more interested in historical topics and figures by providing lots of visual literacy and project-based activities. I would, perhaps, have Jilian make a collage featuring pictures she prints out about the lives of Thomas Jefferson and Benjamin Franklin. I might then display her work and other pictures relating to these two figures on a bulletin board in the classroom for reinforcement. I would then use informal assessment to reassess Jilian's understanding by asking her casually if she remembers the name of the person shown and what his accomplishments were.

Follow the link to take your second MTEL Early Childhood practice test:
**www.cirrustestprep.com/mtel-early-childhood-online-resources**

Made in the USA
Middletown, DE
27 May 2020

96040868R00152